Model Railroading Handbook

Model Railroading Handbook

Robert Schleicher

Chilton Book Company Radnor, Pennsylvania

Library of Congress Cataloging in Publication Data

Schleicher, Robert H
　　Model railroading handbook.

　　Includes index.
　　1. Railroads—Models.　I. Title
TF197.S34　　　　625.1'9　　　75-12688
ISBN 0-8019-6167-X
ISBN 0-8019-6168-8 pbk.

　　7890　43210

People are the one element that can make any hobby fun and I've been fortunate enough to have found two very close friends that have shared my efforts over the years. The late Bill Wright gave me the encouragement and advice needed to bridge that difficult transition from ready-built trains to kit-building; and more recently, Albert Hetzel has been a constant source of ideas and inspiration. Without these friends, model railroading would never have been my life-long hobby and this book would never have been written. Thank you both.

Contents

Layouts, Locomotives, and Rolling Stock

Welcome Aboard!

You can call this hobby 'playing with trains' if you please, but model railroading is no more a play toy than an oil painting or an outboard motorboat or a chess game. Some people like to call activities like ours "leisure time" pursuits. The adult hobby of model railroading certainly does fall into that leisure time category. However, I personally prefer to consider model railroading a three-dimensional art form that goes a giant step beyond an oil painting in providing both depth and life-like animation to the "picture."

I am one of a large number of modelers who mix a helping of nostalgia and history with miniature railroad modeling. There are an equal number of modelers who love today's modern diesels and slab-sided freight cars as much as I love the steam locomotives and tiny wooden freight cars of half a century ago.

Model railroading gives me a chance to create my own time machine and to set the dial at what I consider the most romantic period of railroading's history: the era around the turn-of-the-century when the automobile's effect on our country was not yet so drastic.

I also prefer the type of model railroad that is built on a continuous shelf around the walls of a room, rather than on an isolated table. With this type of setup, you can step right up to it and your peripheral vision will help bring you into the miniature scene. Switching operations provide more interest, to me, than simply running trains. The act of "spotting" a car at an industry and picking it up later when it has been loaded (with imagination, of course) gives a feeling of purpose since the trains are then made up of cars loaded with something going somewhere.

I've spent nearly 30 years developing my preferences in this versatile hobby and, during this time, I've met hundreds of other long-time model railroaders who derive just as much pleasure from their preferences. Above all else, model railroading is a very personal hobby with enough of a challenge and variety of skills to provide a satisfying hobby for just about anyone of any age.

My enthusiasm for the early steam period and for a scenic and operative layout is matched by other buffs who love today's diesels with an equal amount of enthusiasm, or by those who would rather just build cars or tracks or locomotives and by those who just like to run trains rather than build them. In fact, the majority of model railroaders are often content to dream about the layout they might build while they read and plan an occasional lapse into reality.

Empire builders and dreamers alike enjoy this hobby and a lot of us "old timers" have spent years as both armchair model railroaders and builders or operators. A personal, lifetime hobby for just about anyone is an apt description of model railroading.

I've been told that model railroading looks like far too serious a pastime to be called a hobby. The concept of a hobby is to enjoy oneself, and only the doer can be the judge as to whether or not he is having fun. Some model railroaders may set up miniature production lines to build twenty identical freight cars at a time; others may prepare and test complicated computer readout programs to establish timetables or to aid in the design of complex electrical circuitry for automated signal and train operation. I happen to enjoy researching full-size railroads to see if the equipment and operating techniques they used can be applied to my own models.

If you ever do get beyond the armchair

Fig. 1-1 Enjoy the nostalgia of the days when trains were powered by steam.

stage (which is where you are now that you're reading about the hobby) with enough enthusiasm to build a complete railroad, you'll find that the basic skills of an engineer, draftsman, carpenter, electrician, and artist, to say nothing of the skills of a master modelmaker, are all brought into play. As you progress, you'll find one or more of these aspects more appealing and more fun than the others and you'll probably spend more time in that one area. The hobby is versatile enough to allow you to specialize in whatever you find most enjoyable. For example, if you just want to run trains rather than take the time to build them, you can make a fine model railroad with snap-together tracks and ready-to-run locomotives and cars.

A large percentage of model railroaders are really collectors more than modelers—with accumulations of locomotives and rolling stock displayed on shelves because their model railroad layout (if they have one) is too small to accommodate more than a fraction of their collection. Still others are so enthralled by wiring and circuitry that they spend virtually all their time with the electrical aspects of the hobby. Some, whose interests exceed the amount of space they have available for a layout, join clubs where they can enjoy their specialty to the benefit of all.

ONE STEP AT A TIME

Model railroading, as a hobby, is like anything else in that you'll only get out of it what you put into it. If turning a television dial and sitting back is your idea of fun then you'll probably settle for a flat tabletop and a simple train set with snap-together track and ready-to-run equipment *and* you'll be bored to tears within a week or so and wonder why over 250,000 adults (and an equally great number of kids) consider this to be a lifetime hobby. It's all a matter of attitude.

There are thousands of active model railroaders who have assembled only a kit or two in their lifetimes but have spent endless evenings reading about the hobby and about real railroads; they may or may not get around to sketching the layout they may build someday. I've been in and out of that category myself over the years, and so have most modelers who have been in the hobby long enough. There's nothing wrong with being an armchair railroader and I'll be the last one to discourage you, but I hope to convince you to try your hand at assembling a few kits, building a few feet of test track, and operating some trains on a layout.

There's a wide scope of interests that this hobby satisfies and you may find some you aren't even aware of. A great many of today's model railroaders brought with them an interest from a previous hobby and you may do the same. For example, perhaps you've developed a model building skill from assembling stick model airplanes or an electronics aptitude from working on ham radio equipment or perhaps you're a practicing artist. The applications for all these avocations in model railroading should be obvious enough, but there may be some skills that the hobby can help you develop.

I'd like to encourage you to build one complete model railroad even if it's only on a 1' x 6' shelf or a 4' x 8' chunk of plywood. Build a few kits, lay a bit of track, wire a throttle, build a bit of scenery, operate some trains, and try some switching maneuvers. If you can't do all this at home, then join a model railroad club or a group of other modelers in your area and try some of these techniques on someone else's layout. A few conversations with your nearest model railroad dealer will unearth the locations of club and private layouts in your area, and it won't take much searching to find a group that you'll like—at least for a while.

There's a "normal" course of instruction in the hobby that most of us seem to fall into more-or-less naturally. As you read this book, you're already into the first stages of armchair model railroading and you'll find suggestions here for magazines and books that will provide more research material which may be of interest to you.

A train set of the type so popular at the Christmas season is often the next step but you won't get much of a feeling for the hobby from running trains around a loop on the living room rug. Train sets are a bargain *only* if you want the exact cars, locomotives, and track that are included, and you won't know enough about the hobby that soon. I'd suggest you postpone purchase of a complete train set and spend the money on a few kits and, perhaps, a locomotive that you really like.

Assembling a simple kit, like an Athearn HO scale box car kit, will give you some idea of the size and feeling of the parts involved and the satisfaction of having actually done it yourself. You can then progress to something like the slightly more complex plastic kits offered by MDC in HO scale; and if you like the kit assembly aspect of the hobby, you can go into the "craftsman" type kits like those offered by LaBelle, Central Valley, or Walthers. If car kit building fascinates you, your first locomotive might well be a simple diesel kit like Athearn's or a more complex steam locomotive kit like those sold by Tyco or English. There is a similar array of ready-built, simple, and craftsman kit items offered by various manufacturers for buildings, bridges, and trackwork as well as cars and locomotives.

You can apply your kit-building skills to all aspects of model railroading or, avoid kit building entirely and settle for ready-builts. Some modelers like the building aspect of the hobby so much that they eventually build most of their equipment from what is called "scratch"—plain wood or metal strips and sheets and wire with a few cast metal or plastic detail parts like doors, hinges, brake gears, trucks, and couplers. The ever-growing selection of kits, ready-builts, and scratch-building parts has opened up a whole new type of model building called *cross-kitting, customizing, or converting* (all similar names for the process of combining parts from two or more kits or ready-builts with, perhaps, a few extra detail parts to produce a unique car, locomotive, or structure).

You'll find examples of all four types of model building on most model railroad layouts: ready-builts, kits, cross-kits, and scratch-builts. Even the master model builders will buy an occasional ready-built car or locomotive if it is exactly what they want, even though most items on the layout have been built from scratch. Similarly, there are thousands of model railroad layouts where almost every item is a ready-built or a kit with just one or two cross-kits or scratch-built items.

This hobby is versatile enough to satisfy all interests and all skill levels with an ever-present challenge to develop and improve your modeling ability, *if* you find it fun to do so; or you may have just as much fun running or wiring ready-built trains or constructing elaborate and life-like scenery for ready-built trains.

THE AGE OF THE SPECIALIST

There is enough diversity in model railroading to allow you to specialize in the prototype that most appeals to you. With the exception of a few custom-made models and giant outdoor railroads, all model railroads are powered by electricity rather than by steam or diesel like some prototype. The electrical current, 12 to 14 volts of (direct current), is usually obtained with one of the commercial power packs that convert the standard 110-volt (alternating current) house wiring for use on a model railroad.

Your choice of model locomotives includes not just steam or diesel engines but specific models of prototypes that are rivet-for-rivet matches of the real thing. There are even kits and ready-built locomotives that duplicate full-size electric engines such as Pennsylvania's GG-1, city trolleys, and country interurban self-powered cars and engines.

The range of available locomotives extends from the earliest wood-burners of the 1860s right up to the latest Amtrac diesels with freight cars, passenger cars, and structures to match in both simple kits, craftsman kits, and ready-builts. The variety is so great that you can pick just about any prototype railroad for your miniature empire and match not only the equipment that the real railroad used but the period in history that most appeals to you.

The cost of your model railroad is going to depend on just how particular you are about the prototypes you pick for your models. A large percentage of modelers are content with a small switcher, a medium-size freight locomotive, a medium-size passenger locomotive, and, perhaps, a large-size freight locomotive. Steam or diesel switchers are available for around $10 in ready-built models or easily assembled kits, usually with highly detailed plastic superstructures and fittings.

If you must have one of the imported brass switchers of some particular prototype, the cost can skyrocket to over $100 for just that one locomotive plus $25 or more for a custom

Fig. 1-2   Railroad models and operations can be set, in your own "time machine," to include even the most modern Amtrak passenger train.

paint job if you can't or won't paint it yourself. If you're not so particular about the prototype, however, you can have an entire roster of four locomotives of the ready-built variety for about the same cost as that one "special" engine. Ready-to-run box cars sell for about $5, complete with trucks and accessory couplers like Kadee's; a craftsman kit can run four-times that; and a brass boxcar as much as $50.

A similar range of prices applies to passenger cars and structures. You can sometimes build a scratch-built model for the price of an inexpensive ready-to-run locomotive or car, but few modelers have the skill to make their own trucks and detail parts so the cost of even a "hand-made" model usually falls about halfway between a plastic ready-to-run and the expensive brass imports.

The one area where learning to do-it-yourself can really pay off is track systems. The better sectional track, like Lambert's in HO scale, and track that you build yourself by spiking the rails in individual ties with scale spikes doesn't cost much more than the cheapest train set track but is infinitely better.

The brass rail that is furnished as part of the least expensive sectional track oxidizes far faster than the nickle silver rail that the best sectional track and hand-spiked track features. The oxides act as insulation so the all-brass rails require constant cleaning to prevent stalled locomotives and erratic operation.

The do-it-yourself track-laying systems allow you to place switches closer together and to obtain a smoother flow of track more like the prototype. Either snap-together or hand-laid or flexible track sections will average about 50 cents a foot in HO or N scale and about double that for O scale. Remote-controlled switches will run about $5 to $10 a piece in any of the three popular scales, depending on the quality.

A single locomotive, a half-dozen cars, an oval of track to fit a 4' x 8' board, a pair of switches, and an inexpensive power pack can run as little as $70; but it could run ten times higher if you're particular about the prototypes for the locomotive and cars and decide to buy imported brass models or the most expensive craftsman kits.

If you have the skill to build everything from scratch, with just a minimum of detail parts, trucks, couplers, and the like, you can model any prototype you want on the 4' x 8' board for about $150 and have the best of everything, including a transistorized throttle and power pack. Most experienced model railroaders would compromise a bit here and there by buying a few ready-builts and a few kits so the cost would range somewhere between that $150 figure and about $200.

Model railroading is very much an "add-on" hobby so the cost of that 4' x 8' hypothetical layout would be spread over many weeks or months of fun-time construction. Locomotives, cars, track, structures, and scenery would be added in the weeks, months, and years to come. No one ever really *finishes* a model railroad; there's always something to add or replace or rebuild to make it more realistic or larger or more fun to operate. You may take a breather to enjoy operation or just plain admire the accomplishments to date, but there is always something else you can do when you're ready—that's what makes it a lifetime hobby.

HOW BIG?

The size of the space you have available for your model railroad layout is one of the main factors in determining the size of the models themselves. All the ready-to-run and kit items of rolling stock and locomotives are reduced, or scaled-down, replicas of some specific prototype. The amount of that scale reduction determines the "scale" of the model itself and everything, including the track, the buildings, and even the miniature people, is reduced to exactly that same proportion or scale.

Approximately 75 percent of the current number of model railroaders work with what is called *HO scale* wherein all the models are reduced to 1/87 the size of the real thing. The next most popular scale is *N scale* or 1/160 scale with about 20 percent of the model railroaders as active N scalers. Most of the remaining 5 percent of today's model railroaders work in O scale, usually to a reduction of 1/48. A small fraction of that remaining 5 percent prefers S scale with a reduction of 1/64 (the size of the now-defunct American Flyer train sets) and fewer still prefer *TT scale* (1/120 reduction). There are some definite advantages to each of the popular scales.

HO scale is the most popular scale for a

Fig. 1-3 An identical prototype, the Santa Fe's 4-8-4 steam locomotive, inspired these N, HO, and O scale miniatures.

very good reason: it's just the "right" size for most modelers. It's small enough to allow room for a complete layout, with curves broad enough to accommodate models of modern 80-foot passenger and freight cars and large enough to see the tiny details on the models with the naked eye. The selection of ready-to-run items, kits, and scratch-builder's parts is by far the greatest in HO scale; and the components are priced as inexpensively as any.

N scale has only been an active scale for about a decade or so, but it already has a following that is greater than many other scales. It takes the skill and eye and patience of a watchmaker (although you'd be surprised how many of *us* have that talent for a pastime) to build kits or scratch-built models in N scale and, consequently, there are very few kits in N scale. Most N scale equipment is of the ready-to-run variety.

O scale is at the opposite end of the size spectrum with models large enough to capture much of the giant bulk of real railroading. An O scale locomotive or freight car is truly large enough to sound more like the real thing as it rumbles and clatters over rail joints and switches.

S scale and TT scale are the "in between" sizes for those who can't quite find the space for O or HO scale models; a scarcity of kits and lack of ready-to-run items makes these two scales very popular with scratch-builders.

You can, of course, begin modeling in the scale that now seems most appropriate to your space and skill level and later trade or sell your equipment if you decide on another scale; a few hundred modelers do just that every year. Some dealers will accept trades or you may get the swap or price you want through a want ad in the classified sections of the monthly model railroad magazines.

Not all railroad prototypes were the same size. In the earliest days of the railroad boom, it was often less expensive to build the locomotives and rolling stock a bit smaller so track curves could be tighter. The spacing of the rails was reduced, proportionately, to the size of the equipment to something narrower than the standard rail gauge of 4 feet 8½ inches between the tops of the rails.

The most popular "narrow gauge" was 3 feet between the rails and that was the one chosen for most of the mountain railroads built in western Colorado (most notably, the Rio Grande) during the 1880s. Similar narrow gauge railroads appeared in the mountains on both coasts for inexpensive access to coal, gold and silver ores, and logs. The narrow gauge lasted until the Second World War when the paved road and the cost of transport by truck made the operation of such lines just too expensive. Most of these lines faced ever-diminishing revenues as the ores were depleted and as paved roads crept into the mountains during the first half of this century. With the exception of the White Pass & Yukon in Alaska, the only narrow gauge lines still operating serve mostly as tourist attractions. However, the narrow gauge remains a favorite prototype for a lot of model railroaders.

A model of the 2-foot gauge lines that ran in Maine and Massachusetts need only be about the size of an O scale model with the track gauge and all the equipment scaled to O scale's 1/48 proportion. It's one way for the people who prefer the visibility of O scale equipment to squeeze an O scale layout into an area that would normally be large enough only for HO. When the model is built to O scale with track gauged to 2-foot narrow gauge, the models are often referred to (erroneously) as On2 scale models; in fact, they are O scale models built to a scale 2-foot gauge.

Three-foot narrow gauge models are called HOn3 if built to HO scale (the rolling stock is about the same size as TT scale equipment), Sn3 if built to S scale's 1/64 proportion (these models are about the size of HO scale standard gauge items), or On3 if built to O scale proportions (On3 box cars are about the size of S scale standard gauge box cars). All the buildings and miniature people on, for example, an HOn3 layout are 1/87 life-size and so are the trains and track; but the prototype's trains and track were smaller and so they are on the model empire.

The major problem facing the prospective model empire builder is that of finding enough space for the layout itself. The absolute minimum table size for an O scale layout is about 8' x 16', for HO scale about 4' x 8', and for N scale about 2' x 4'. The minimum radius curves that most models can negotiate without looking like toys demand that much

Fig. 1-4   Albert Hetzel assembled this O scale trolley from individual pieces of "scale" lumber; the interior detail is just as fine.

space and, preferably, about twice that in the respective scales.

There are ways around the minimum radius problem and modeling in narrow gauge is just one of them. By limiting your models to duplicates of the prototypes of the earlier eras of railroading's history, you can take advantage of the fact that freight cars were only about 36-feet long (around the turn-of-the-century) with shorter locomotives that pulled shorter trains.

An HO scale layout with 18-inch radius curves looks reasonably realistic if none of the freight cars are over 36-feet long and if the model includes short, three or four car passenger trains of 60-foot cars. The minimum curve radius for an HO scale layout with today's 86-foot box cars and Piggyback cars and multiple-unit diesels should be at least 30-inches which means a table width of 6-feet or more to allow room for both rails and a bit

of roadbed on the outer edges. The largest narrow gauge freight cars were seldom more than 30-feet long even in the 1940s, so a far more modern HOn3 layout would look fine with 18-inch radius curves.

The third alternative to period modeling or narrow gauge, in solving the space problem for a layout, is trolley or interurban modeling. The term trolley, incidentally, usually applies only to those self-powered electric rail cars that traveled on the tight turns within the streets of cities and towns while the term interurban applied to the similar prototype self-powered electrics that were used in longer runs between cities or towns. Both trolleys and interurbans ran as one car "trains" as well as in multiple-units of two or three or more and, with both types of "traction" equipment, the freight units often pulled conventional freight cars into industrial sidings along the line. The incredibly tight

10

curves on the prototype traction lines reduce to a size small enough to allow a lot of action in a minimum space for a model railroader; a 4' x 8' layout is large enough for even an O scale traction layout.

There is little or no ready-to-run equipment, except for a few expensive brass imports, in HO, S, or O scale narrow gauge (there's none in N scale although European-prototype Z scale at 1/220 proportion works out to about Nn3); so most of the rolling stock will have to be assembled from craftsman kits but all the buildings and accessory items can be standard HO, S, or O scale kits.

Trolley and interurban models will have to be built from kits or scratch-built and the overhead wires should be at least simulated if not incorporated into the wiring system. Unless you have some model building experience, you're wise to stick to more conventional standard gauge N, HO, or O scale models for your first layout.

WHERE TO FIND HELP

It may seem that model railroading is the kind of hobby meant for the person who wants to hide-away in his shop alone for hours on end; but, in reality, it's a hobby like all others that's most enjoyable if the results of your efforts can be shared with others. I would suggest that you subscribe to both of the major model railroad magazines: *Model Railroader* (sample copy $1.00 from Kalmbach Publishing Co., 1027 No. 7th st., Milwaukee, WI 53233) and *Railroad Model Craftsman* (sample copy 75¢ from Carstens Publications, Inc., P.O. Box 700, Newton, NJ 07860).

There is surprisingly little duplication between the two magazines and a year's worth of issues will be enough for you to decide for yourself which one appeals most to your modeling needs. Both magazines feature monthly listings of model railroad shops so you can locate all those in your area as well as any you might want to visit on business trips or vacations. There are also numerous advertisements for the shops that specialize in mail order so you can obtain the kits or parts you may not be able to find in a nearby shop. Advertisements will keep you up to date on the newest items in the hobby and, almost incidentally, the editorial format will give you

ideas for modeling and operating your own layout.

The $5 annual membership fee for the National Model Railroad Association (P.O. Box 1328, Station C, Canton, OH 44708) includes a subscription to their monthly *Bulletin* with some excellent modeling ideas and, of most importance, access to their annual listing of members and clubs and the sets of "NMRA Standards" and "NMRA Reccommended Practices." The standards and practices will give you the data you'll need for building and installing bridges, for wiring, for trackwork, and for dozens of other practical and essential model railroad features.

You'll also be able to attend the regional NMRA conventions and their annual national convention where you can visit the classroom-like "clinics" that deal with all aspects of model railroading, and you'll be able to see hundreds of top-quality models that are entered in the model building contests. There are usually conducted tours around the best model railroad layouts in the area and, often, tours through some of the nearby prototype railroad facilities.

Visits to model railroad dealers in your area and a membership in the NMRA should unearth several clubs and private layouts within easy travel distance of your home—all chances to meet and make friends to share the hobby with you.

ABOUT THE BOOK

You should have some idea of how complex—and how simple—this hobby of model railroading can be. There are several dozen books that deal with the hobby in general and in some of the specific areas like electrical wiring, scenery, track planning, operation, scratch-building, trolleys and interurbans, and other subjects. There are also several hundred beautifully illustrated volumes on the full-size railroads. Obviously, all that data cannot be condensed into just one book.

What I have tried to do is to show what have been proven to be the best materials and techniques for the aspects of the hobby that are not available as kits or ready-builts. True-to-prototype track planning, operation, scenery, weathering, painting, and decal application, and other subjects that receive the most attention on these pages are things that you have to learn to do yourself with materials which you collect from various sources beyond the local hobby shop.

There are very few "bests" in this hobby. Paper towel scenery is a bit better than plaster-over-wire screen, but carved and molded Styrofoam has applications where weight is a problem. There are dozens of methods of building trees and your scenery will be more realistic if you use several of them for a natural variety.

It is *best*, however, to try to pattern your trackage as well as the switching and, perhaps, even some timetable operation after a real railroad. It's best to use artist's Matte Medium to lay ballast around your trackwork because the liquid has a bit of resiliency and because it flows well. Kadee's automatic couplers are another best for reliable and realistic coupling and uncoupling. No one has yet found a roadbed that will hold spikes and still provide a certain amount of sound-deadening as well as Homosote wallboard. Nickel silver rail, whether hand-spiked or pre-mounted on flexible plastic tie strips and pre-assembled switches, looks like steel and conducts electricity with far less oxidation than brass.

Every switch should have separate electrical contacts, whether part of an accessory under-the-table switch machine or a manually operated slide-type D.P.D.T. switch, to provide reliable electrical flow; and all wire connections should be soldered, again for electrical reliability. Transistorized throttles cost about twice as much as conventional rheostat throttles, but they allow you to operate your locomotives (even the always too-high-geared N scale engines) at speeds as slow and smooth as the prototype.

All these "bests" and most of the best choices of optional methods are discussed on these pages. If you find one aspect of the hobby you like enough to demand even more information, there is likely a special book on that subject available through your hobby dealer; but all the basics of this most enjoyable and lasting hobby are presented here. Have fun!

The six model railroad layouts in this chapter represent the whole spectrum of model railroading—from a mantlepiece-size layout to the modular layouts of the future to museum-size club efforts with examples of N, HOn3, HO, Lionel, and O scale modeling at its very best. None of the men who completed these miniature empires are experts in any sense of the word—yet, they had the interest and patience to proceed with the fulfillment of their dreams.

The techniques shown on these pages, applied to the kits and materials available to everyone, are all it takes for you to have a model railroad every bit as effective and enjoyable as those shown here. A careful study of the photographs, before and after you read about the techniques, will provide an endless array of ideas; enough, in fact, to fill another volume. Take a good look at the layouts now, before you find out what you can do if you try, and later look again to see where things like weathering methods, rock casting, decal-application, and countless other ideas have been used.

Some of the layouts, like Dan Wilson's shelf-size empire, were built in a matter of weeks; and others, like Irv Schultz' basement diorama, have been under construction for half a lifetime; and not one of these modelers considers their layout complete. It's inspiration enough for me and, I hope, for you to make this your hobby.

THE BETTER LATE THAN NEVER LINE

Dan Wilson's DL&D Short Lines should provide a quick stop to any excuses you might have about not being able to build an operating model railroad because you don't have the space. Dan's empire occupies a scant 1' x 6' area with enough operation to require a full half-hour just to move a three-car train from one end of the line to the other. Operation is switchback-style (see Fig. 2-2) from the three-track yard at the front right of the layout to the stub at the left, then under the bridge and up the hill to the stub at the first level, and back again to the left up a short hill and over the bridge to the two-track yard. Train lengths are limited to a tank-type switcher of the steam era or a short industrial diesel with two freight cars of less than 40-foot lengths

Inspiration

and a 24-foot, four-wheel caboose. The grades behind and over the bridge are a steep 9 percent but that's no problem with the short train lengths. The lack of a passing siding means that there is no way for a locomotive to run around the train to shove cars into sidings that branch-off (called "facing sidings") in the direction of the train's travel; so two locomotives are required to operate this tiny layout: one to couple onto the left end of the cars that are to be switched around the lower-level, three-track yard and a second "main line" locomotive to take the train up the hill and into the two-track yard.

We'll leave you to develop your own ideas on how the switching moves are accomplished; but remember that those two stubs in the lower left and upper right corners of the layout limit the train's length to three cars and a locomotive, and only one locomotive at a time can pull or push a train. The locomotive that is not being used is placed on one of the sidings and the switch is thrown to the main track to electrically isolate the "dead" engine while the second one does its work.

Dan patterened his layout after one that Chuck Yungkurth built and described in the

Fig. 2-1 The short sidings on Dan Wilson's shelf-size HO scale layout limit the train lengths to three cars and a locomotive.

April 1965, issue of *Model Railroader* magazine. Yungkurth later incorporated his shelf layout into a larger around-the-wall system and Dan Wilson plans to do the same.

The layout is assembled from 1' x 6' and 1' x 2' clear pine and ½-inch plywood to make it sturdy enough to be stored in a closet. The trackwork is the Peco brand from England with flexible track sections and pre-assembled switches. Hand-laid track would allow a bit closer switch spacing for a bit longer siding lengths and smoother curves

Fig. 2-2 The "Better Late than Never" railroad compresses a lot of real railroad operation into just 2' x 8'.

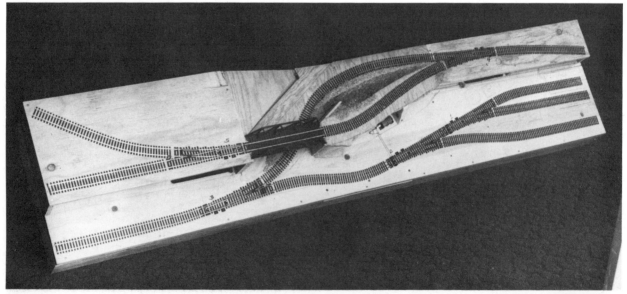

beneath the bridge. Four of the switches are actuated by remote control with Lambert brand switch machines mounted beneath the table. The fifth switch sits above the slide-out control panel so it was mounted on the tabletop and will be concealed by a removable retaining wall when the scenery is complete.

Dan intends to modify several kit buildings to fit the cramped spaces. The layout would be a natural for several "low-relief" structures (just the fronts and a hint of the sides) along the back side. Dan has converted several 40-foot box cars, tank cars, and hopper cars to 30-foot cars by cutting a section from the center of the plastic bodies and metal underframes and then gluing the ends back together to allow the use of rolling stock from the 1930-1940 era. The 1890-era freight cars with the wire truss rod underframes like Central Valley and MDC 34 and 36-foot cars would be excellent choices for rolling stock on this layout as well.

The action-paced DL&D Short Lines could be duplicated on a 6-inch wide windowsill in N scale or along a 12-foot bedroom or den wall in O scale. Remember, there's always room for a layout if you really want one, and few designs offer so much action in so little space.

MODULAR MODEL RAILROADING

The era of the lifetime model railroad may finally have arrived. Many model railroaders have built a small layout or even a large one only to find that they had to dismantle it when they moved to a new home. The modular concept allows a modeler to build a small layout, then another and another with each succeeding layout connected to the previous one with a few bolts and a strip of break-away scenery.

Each of the modules is large enough to incorporate plenty of scenery and switching action by itself; and when grouped together, a series of these modules constitutes a complete railroad in every way. One of the modules may, for example, be a yard and terminal facility; another a small town with industries; another a bit of country and mountain scenery; and yet another might include a small

Fig. 2-3   This 2' x 4' N scale "module" was joined to twenty-four others to create a portable N-TRAK empire.

branch line junction to a mining or logging railroad in either standard or narrow gauge.

The important point is that each of the modules becomes a segment of a model railroad that you can move with you throughout your lifetime. Building a model railroad around the walls of a room or a garage, one module or segment at a time, has the added appeal of the railroad truly going somewhere—and of being constructed much like the real ones, one step at a time.

As your skills improve with practice, each succeeding module will likely be better than your previous one. Keep in mind that the project of updating and redetailing the earlier work, *if* desired, only involves a small segment of your complete railroad; and it's the kind of work that you're far more likely to accomplish rather than attempting to rebuild a complete layout.

There are three possible ways to incorporate the modular concept into your own model railroad but all three *must* be done while the layout is still in the planning stages. First, you can build two or more individual modules of a size less than 3' x 8' (anything larger is just too much to handle when moving and 3' x 6' is even better). If you need a larger area for, say, a yard, you can bolt two or three of these 3' x 6' tables together to form a single, but still portable, take-apart module. The individual modules can then be joined, often to snake the track around the corners of the room, with connecting pieces that may or may not (depending on the available space in that "next" home) be moved with the modules. These connecting pieces can be considered "expendable" since they'll only constitute a small portion of the overall layout size.

The second alternate is the one I've incor-

Fig. 2-4   The N-TRAK "module" design standards allow portable model railroads from distant cities to operate as one layout.

Fig. 2-5 2' x 4' is enough space for a mine and branch line as well as a short section of main line in N scale.

porated in the complex "Colorado Midland" layout in the later chapters of this book. This layout was designed to "grow" one module at a time from a 5' x 16' single-level layout to a giant 18' 6-inch square, two-tier empire with dozens of options between the two extremes, including a 12½' x 16½' den-size layout with one or two tiers and a 9½' x 18½' one-level plan for a garage-size area. There are areas, on the narrower along-the-wall portions of the Colorado Midland plan, that can be built with a removable 1 to 2½-foot section to allow the layout to be expanded or contracted a bit to fit the space in the "next" house.

The third alternative for a lifetime modular layout is the "N-TRAK" concept pioneered by members of the N scale Belmont Shores Model Railroad Club; and it is, perhaps, the most practical, in terms of portability, with

some sacrifice in the variety of the track plan itself.

At least four different clubs, San Francisco Bay, Los Angeles, Chicago, and Vancouver areas, are building club-size model railroads, using the N TRAK modular concept. The basic idea is to provide track plan and benchwork standards for 2' x 4' and 2' x 8' modules so the ends of any modules, built anywhere in the country, will fit snugly against the ends of the next modules.

The various clubs also have designs for "end" modules where the tracks can be curved for an island or an around-the-wall layout assembled from multiples of individual modules. The whole concept sounds like somebody's pipe dream but it has been proven to work and work extremely well.

Over 25 separate modules, from four differ-

17

ent cities and dozens of builders, were assembled at the San Diego, California, NMRA national convention in 1974. The resulting layout was a giant 12' x 72' "island" with operation so smooth that 150-car N scale trains were operated for hours on end!

The three 2' x 4' modules here were part of that "portable" layout in San Diego; the oil refinery and logging modules were assembled and the scenery constructed by Ben Davis with logging structures by Karen Overgaard and the sand and water towers by Dana Zimmerli; the mountain mine module was made and assembled by Hal Riegger.

All structures on these three N TRAK modules are scratch-built. If you're interested in obtaining the standards for building your own N TRAK modules, you can contact James FitzGerald, P.O. Box 1368, Atascadero, CA 93422 for the latest specifications. Be sure to include a stamped, self-addressed return envelope if you do inquire.

The basic plan calls for a double-track main line along the forward edge of the module with a third track for access to industrial sidings and your own trackage along the back portion of the module; but the track spacing, lumber sizes, and other details must be an exact match if your module is to mate with the other N TRAK modules.

Similar plans are underway through the National Model Railroad Association for HO scale modules. There's really no reason why you can't build your own layout using the N TRAK concept but with the modules interchangeable only with your own to allow a personalized portable layout in any scale.

A LARGE LIONEL LAYOUT

A large percentage of today's model railroaders, myself included, were introduced to the hobby with a Lionel or Marx or American

Fig. 2-6   This type of realism can result when you lift a Lionel train set from the living room rug onto a permanent layout.

Flyer train set. Most of us tired of the toy-like appearance of these trains, particularly the three-rail Lionel and Marx tracks, and went on to other ready-built or kit models for our scale layouts.

There are, however, certain advantages to the three-rail trackage and the most notable is not having to worry about short circuits at switches and the simplified wiring with reversing loops or wyes. These "toy" trains are extremely reliable pieces of equipment with parts large enough to repair or service without the aid of tweezers and a magnifying glass.

If you're interested in operating trains, with the least possible amount of work, then I'd suggest you take a close look at the current line of Lionel "tinplate" O scale equipment and at what Burt Blanton and his grandson, G. Robert Freeman, have accomplished in the 20' x 40' attic of the Blanton home during the layout's 25-year existence.

Equipment like that used by Burt and his grandson falls under the classification of "semi-scale"—the track has rails (the outer two) spaced nearly the same as O scale two-rail track, but most of the cars and locomotives that Lionel and Marx offer are slightly undersize. Since each piece of equipment is scaled to match the rest, however, the effect is realistic enough. This type of modeling is usually referred to as "tinplate" O scale, a term dating back to the days when the models were stamped from tinplate stock rather than the plastic moldings that are used today.

Burt prefers trackwork a bit more realistic than Lionel's so he used the flexible 3-foot track sections with wooden ties sold by the GarGraves Trackage Company, R.D. No. 1, Box 255, North Rose, NY 14516. The latest GarGraves track has a blackened center rail to further enhance the realism as compared to Lionel track and it will mate with most Lionel track sections. Burt Blanton assembled his

Fig. 2-7   The running gear beneath this MKT steamer is a Marx toy but Burt Blanton rebuilt it into a credible miniature.

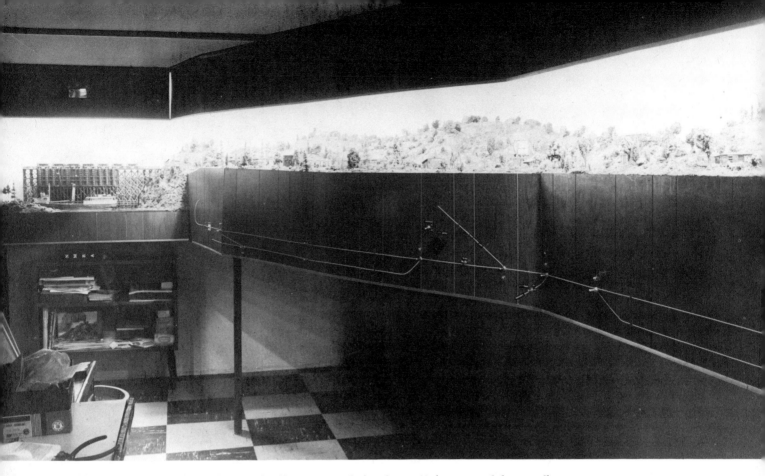

Fig. 2-8   Irv Schultz' HO scale shelf layout extends for almost 60-feet around three walls of his basement study.

own switches from steel rail to match the GarGraves flexible track, but the better Lionel switches are almost as realistic.

Burt Blanton is one of the most-traveled Americans around and nearly all of his travel has been by rail. He has ridden nearly half a million miles on passenger trains and many of his journeys are described in his book *400,000 Miles by Rail* (from Howell-North Books, Berkeley, CA 94710). With that kind of a background, he wasn't satisfied with the limited number of steam locomotives offered by Lionel or Marx so he has "converted" a dozen of them to match the MKT and Santa Fe prototypes that once operated near his Texas home.

He uses brass sheet and tin can stock (what else?) for the new locomotive cabs and tenders with wire, hand-filed metal fittings and few commercial castings for details. New paint and Champ or Walthers brand decals complete the conversions and, while not contest-quality models, they're all very credible examples of the steamers that used to operate in Texas.

20

Most of his rolling stock and structures are assembled from sheet wood and metal and other scratch pieces and are scaled to match his Lionel equipment rather than any particular prototype blueprints. The layout scenery is completely assembled with a combination of plaster over wire screening and real rocks for the best effect. The Blanton-Freeman Model Railroad is a superb example of how an average modeler can achieve the overall effect of realism even with toy equipment.

THE SAINT CLAIR NORTHERN

If I had to pick the six best model railroads in the country, Irv Schultz' HO scale layout would certainly be among them. Irv has won several contests with his scratch-built structures, and virtually all his rolling stock is lettered for some unusual prototype with special sets of rub-on dry transfer lettering which he sells (his catalog of lettering is available for 25¢ from 29319 Elmwood Court, Saint Clair Shores, MI 48081).

Fig. 2-9 Another view of Irv Schultz' layout.

Fig. 2-10 When a layout is placed near eye level, like Irv Schultz', the models are visible enough so you can almost feel the "life."

Fig. 2-11   A scratch-built gallows frame turntable rests on an Atlas brand ready-built mechanism in this clever conversion.

Fig. 2-12   Some industries are obvious sources of "revenue" on a model railroad. This scratch-built ore dock rests on resin "water."

Fig. 2-13 All the cars on Irv Schultz' layout are stock kits lettered with the dry transfers he sells.

The majority of the rolling stock, however, are simple craftsman kits; and the railroad's four locomotives are brass imports carefully painted and lettered by Irv. The track is code 100-size nickle silver rail spiked to TruScale's roadbed that incorporates the shape of the ballast, the ties, and tie plates to automatically space the rails in one milled wooden section of straight, curved, or switch stock.

The scenery is plaster over wire screening with a liberal coating of ground and colored foam rubber (available from the better-stocked model railroad shops) for surface texture. There's nothing about the layout, except those few structures and the relettered cars, that would make it difficult for any model railroader, even a newcomer, to duplicate.

The outstanding features of this layout are its simple track plan and the effect Irv Schultz has achieved in positioning the layout rather high above the floor with upper and lower valances to give the effect of a 48-foot, three-dimensional painting of a real railroad. The layout itself is basically a two-foot wide shelf that wraps about 8-feet around each end of a 35-foot basement room. The forward edges of the benchwork and valances angle out, at each end of the room, to give just enough space for a half-hidden reversing loop behind the sky blue backdrop.

There's a large ore dock at one terminal on one of the room's end walls and a small town on the other end to allow point-to-point operation like the prototype with switches to provide an optional loop-to-loop route for "main line" trains while a second train switches the various industrial sidings on the layout. There are nine separate stub-end sidings and three passing sidings with ten different industries and an interchange track, so there's plenty of places to switch and spot cars.

The effect of that shoulder-level and nearly endless diorama is uncanny. Remember how much better movies became when they switched to "VistaVision" or "Panavision"? Well, Irv's layout goes even further in filling the viewer's peripheral vision. When you step up to the edge of a layout like this, you soon find yourself completely a part of the scene and the realism is truly breath-taking; you have to keep reminding yourself that it's really only a 1/87 scale model!

The push buttons that control the track's switches are located on a schematic diagram of the track plan painted on the lower valance so the controls for each switch are very close to the switch itself. The throttle and reversing controls are mounted in a small, hand-held box with a tether cable of wires leading to the power pack and track. The tether cable is long enough to reach from the center location to the extremes of the layout, and it's mounted in a self-reeling drum to keep it from getting entangled in the operators' feet. This "walk-around" style control allows the "engineer" to follow right beside his train as it makes its way from one end of the layout to the other.

The relatively narrow shelf-style layout keeps the trains well within reach of the operators and close enough so they can watch the locomotive's drivers and side rods operate to further enhance the feeling of realism. If you can find the space, this around-the-wall style railroad should be your choice (even if only along one wall) for a plan rather than the more conventional island-style tabletop empires.

THE SLIM GAUGE GUILD

The essence of the prototype railroads that once operated in the Colorado Rockies was that of tiny trains struggling and twisting their way through giant mountains. It's easy enough to capture the tiny train aspect of that picture but few modelers even attempt to create anything as large as a full-size mountain, even in 1/87 scale.

A very dedicated group of model railroaders, all with a love of modeling only the Denver & Rio Grande, the Rio Grande Southern, and the Colorado & Southern prototype railroads that once ran through the mountains of Colorado, banded together to form the Slim Gauge Guild to capture the feeling of those railroads in an HOn3 layout. The club leased a 30' x 50' room above some stores in Pasadena, California; and within 3 years, they constructed about 800-square feet of their planned total of 1,600-square feet of mountains, ranging from waist level to the ceiling. There is, almost incidentally, nearly 900-feet of HOn3 trackage winding its way around and through those plaster mountains.

Photographs really don't capture the effect that the Slim Gauge Guild has achieved. As the viewer walks through the aisles, he has the feeling that he is strolling along a valley floor with the mountains soaring to the heavens (the ceiling) above him; and occasionally, a tiny replica of one of the Colorado narrow gauge trains will inch its way along the tracks. The club has arranged the trackage so it is seldom more than a few feet from the viewer. The trackage is routed along the walls and out onto peninsulas where the viewer can walk out and around and still stay within a few feet of the tracks.

The proximity of the models to the spectators and operators is a particularly good thing on this layout, since the modeling standards of the members are extremely high; and the closer you look at the locomotives, the cars, the scenery, and even the track, the more minute details you see. There are only a few layouts in the world that look as good from 10 feet as they do from 10 inches, but the Slim Gauge Guild's is one of them.

The layout is built entirely on open-grid types of benchwork to allow the scenery to flow in natural contours both above and below the actual track level. The yards and other areas of concentrated trackage are laid on 1/2-inch Homosote with a 1/2-inch plywood support. The "country" trackwork, however, is supported by an unusual method; acoustical plaster is cast in roadbed-wide bands with lath strips of wood as the molds. The lath is spaced apart every few inches with a spacer block and common electrical wire is laced through it to provide a reinforcing for the acoustical plaster. The method allows a smooth flow of ess bends and curves with a quiet support for the trackage, but it takes some practice to get it just right.

The track itself is all laid on individual wooden ties glued to the top of the acoustical plaster roadbed. Code 55 rail is then hand-spiked (with needle-nose pliers) in place. The switches are handmade in jigs with automobile choke cables to actuate them. Small micro-switches direct the electrical current to the diverging routes at each switch and they, too, are actuated by the same choke cables that move the switch's rails.

The basic shapes of the mountains are formed with paper towels soaked in plaster. The rock details are formed in latex molds taken from real rocks or chunks of coal. The plaster is poured into the flexible mold, and the mold and the still-soft plaster are pressed into place on the plaster mountains. This must be held for a few moments while the plaster sets. The latex molds are then peeled away and the rockwork is stained and painted. The rock rubble pictured here includes scraps of plaster and some real rock broken into tiny pieces and glued in place.

Most of the actual tracks are at eye level, but a small portion of the line dips down to 40 inches above the floor and the "Alpine" section rises to 82 1/2 inches. The bridges are all scratch-built from scale-size stripwood to match prototypes on the various Colorado narrow gauge railroads. Some of the scenery and trackwork and structures that appeared on the real railroads are modeled on the layout, including the famous Alpine Tunnel, Lizard Head Pass, the Georgetown loop, the Palisades, and the Black Canyon of the Gunnison; that's right, even the scenery is a duplicate of the prototype!

THE CITRUS EMPIRE

There are times when the modeling project at hand is so great that only a group of people, or a club, can ever hope to accomplish the goal. The Slim Gauge Guild is one example and the giant O scale layout of the Citrus Empire Model Railroad Club in Pomana, California, is another.

Every major city in America can boast of at least one club as large as this one, but the Citrus Empire is one of the best. The layout is immense, larger than a basketball court, and is housed beneath the concrete stadium at the Los Angeles County Fairgrounds. The club puts on a tremendous display of operation each September, but operation and construction go on year-round.

The club atmosphere gives each member a chance to do what suits him best; the wiring buffs and the operation and timetable enthusiasts and the track experts all have plenty of space and time to enjoy the segment of the hobby that most appeals to them.

The layout is large enough to accommodate all types of equipment, too, with mountains (including rarely modeled snowsheds) for logging and mining trains, a large freight yard and engine facility, and a passenger terminal. There's a city with a trolley line and, on the edge of the city, a circus and a circus

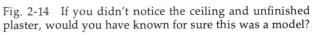
Fig. 2-14   If you didn't notice the ceiling and unfinished plaster, would you have known for sure this was a model?

Fig. 2-15 The narrow gauge trains on the Slim Gauge Guild's HOn3 layout are dwarfed by the mountains and so were the prototypes.

Fig. 2-16 Many of the scenes on the Slim Gauge Guild's layout are almost rock-for-rock duplicates of sites in Colorado.

train. The members' equipment ranges from 1860-era steamers to the most modern diesels, and most members bring their equipment to the operating sessions in special carrying cases so they can take it home again at the end of the evening.

The mere existence, and the successful year-after-year operation, of clubs like the Citrus Empire points up the fact that not every model railroader has his own model railroad. Some of the club members join because they don't have space for the kind of railroad they want; they consider anything less than a fifty-car train just playing with toys and a club is the only place with enough space. A surprisingly large percentage of the model railroad club members who want to go way beyond the armchair stage and do have both the time and the space for a model railroad, prefer not to build their own layouts. On a club layout, you can do just about anything you could do on your own and you can still build cars, locomotives, structures, and even bridges in the comfort of your home workshop.

Most clubs insist that the buildings and any

Fig. 2-17 Judge the size of this O scale empire by that Coke can near the roundhouse. The long shed on the mountain is a snowshed.

Fig. 2-18   Most of the trackage on the Citrus Empire Model Railroad Club's layout is
Tru-Scale's milled wood roadbed and tie unit.

bridges the members build for the club become the property of the club, but the
locomotives and rolling stock are always the
property of the individual members. There
are a lot of modelers who would rather just
model than do the carpentry, wiring, track-
laying, and maintenance that a layout requires. All members do have to share in the
construction and maintenance of the layout,
but there are usually enough people who
enjoy the benchwork, wiring, or track-laying,
which you might consider a chore, to leave
you the majority of your club time to do what
you like best.

Frankly, you'll be missing out on a major
portion of the fun if you don't build your own
home layout, no matter how small it may be.
But if you feel this is the only way you'll ever
get out of that armchair, then check with your
local hobby shop to find the club nearest your
home.

The Rolling Stock Workshop

With model railroading, like anything else, you can really learn only by doing; and the best place to start that "doing" is with a simple freight car kit and, if you wish, a short piece of track to display the car or to roll it back and forth to get the feel of things. There are enough ready-to-run pieces of rolling stock (freight cars, passenger cars, and maintenance of way equipment) so you can build and operate a complete model railroad without ever building a car kit; but it is supposed to be a model building hobby and the inexpensive freight car kits like Athearn's or MDC's or Train Miniature's in HO scale are good first-time trys for anyone. I'll leave the exact choice of type of freight car up to you.

If you're really curious as to how wide the choice is, I recommend you join the National Model Railroad Association and purchase their $10 NMRA Data-Pack book. The book illustrates and describes just about everything that the full/size railroads did right down to details like brake rigging, switch stands, and bridge supports—with tips on how to model such prototype features and, above all, why.

You'll discover that there are several vari-

eties of the common boxcar and you'll pick up some knowledge about the various types of passenger cars, steam, diesel, and electric locomotives.

The NMRA Data-Pack doesn't say much about how to build models, but it will answer just about any question you might have as to why there was a prototype for the models that are available. You may already have some favorite types of rolling stock; cabooses are perhaps the most popular with modelers because there were so many unusual types from tiny four-wheel "bobbers" to passenger cars that have been converted, with a cupola and interior changes, for use as combination crew cars, baggage cars, and coaches.

The era you've picked for your miniature empire can affect your choice of rolling stock too. You can always "excuse" a few cars from the 1880s as a "tourist" train on a modern railroad, but it's difficult to justify why an all-steel boxcar would appear on a model railroad that otherwise features 1880-era equipment. If the era doesn't matter much to you, then I'd suggest you do what most model railroaders do and "date" your railroad to the early 1950s when both diesel and steam power shared the rails with a few wooden cars from the early part of the century and the modern steel equipment.

If you want to have anything like a prototype-patterned model railroad (and not everybody does), then avoid the models of the newest 86-foot cube boxcars and Trailer Train Piggyback flat cars because these newer pieces of equipment only appeared on the real railroads long after steam power and wooden cars had vanished. The longer modern cars can present operating problems as well, since they require at least 24-inch radius curves (in HO scale) to operate properly.

The choice of freight cars, like the choice of passenger cars, locomotives, or structures, ranges from ready-built rolling stock from every era of real railroading to simple kits to craftsman kits. The simple kits require only a screwdriver and a hobby knife for assembly and most have everything painted except, perhaps, the metal underframe and a few detail parts. You can assemble most of them in less than an hour, including the time it takes to read the instructions. Most of these simple kits include trucks and couplers but, for reasons I'll explain in later chapters, I would

Fig. 3-1 This Kadee brand, N scale, ready-built boxcar has superb detail with working doors, nearly scale wheel flanges, and couplers.

suggest you replace the couplers with the Kadee automatic couplers. The craftsman kits seldom include trucks or couplers; be sure to buy those items when you buy the kit so you'll have all the parts it takes to complete the model.

The craftsman kits derive their "craftsman" (sometimes call craft-trains) title from the fact that they require a certain amount of cutting and fitting and painting for assembly and most must be lettered with dry transfers or decals which are supplied with the kit. Assembly time can vary considerably with the brand and the type of car but most require at least 6 hours and many demand 12 or more hours of enjoyable construction time. When you complete a craftsman kit, there is definitely a feeling of accomplishment that is lacking with the simpler kits which virtually

snap together with three or four assembly screws at most. There is nothing difficult about any of the craftsman kits, but they do require a careful study of the instruction sheets and test-fit of each and every piece to be sure that the work is progressing as planned.

TOOLS

The array of tools shown in Fig. 3-3 represents the maximum number of items you'd need to assemble any of the craftsman kits; and some of the items, like a motor tool and the Lambert rail cutters, are optional items that make things quicker and easier. You can buy the tools as you need them; most are available from any hobby dealer that stocks

Fig. 3-2   Simple kits, like this Athearn brand HO scale boxcar, can be completed in less than an hour.

the craftsman kits. Not all these tools will be needed for any one kit; the LaBelle HO scale Soo Line box car, for example, only required nine items from the complete workshop assortment. The tools in this assortment are enough to hand-spike track; to perform any locomotive maintenance, as well as most of the other chores; and to assemble locomotive kits and structures, as well as rolling stock.

The assortment includes: Lambert brand rail-cutting pliers; a Suydam model-size miter box; a heavy-duty razor knife; diagonal cutters; two-part epoxy glue; an eye dropper; liquid cement for plastics; white glue; Goodyear brand Pliobond; Aron Alpha (or it's equivalent) cyanoacrylate cement; a small vise; a set of number drill bits from 61 through 80 plus numbers 42, 50, 51, and 55

drills; a 2-56 threading tap and a 0-80 tap; a pin vise (to hold the tiny drills and taps); a 12-inch steel ruler; tweezers; round, triangular, and half-round jewelers' files; needle-nose pliers; an X-Acto hobby knife with number 11 blades; a steel ruler calibrated in scale feet and inches; scissors; an X-Acto razor saw and handle; a small screwdriver; a jewelers' screwdriver; toothpicks; single-edge razor blades; and an NMRA standards gauge (usually only available for HO scale). If necessary, spend the extra money to buy the very best cutters, files, drills and pliers; tools are a life-long investment. If you buy the best, this total array should cost well under $100.

There are some major tool investments that you should consider for your model railroad,

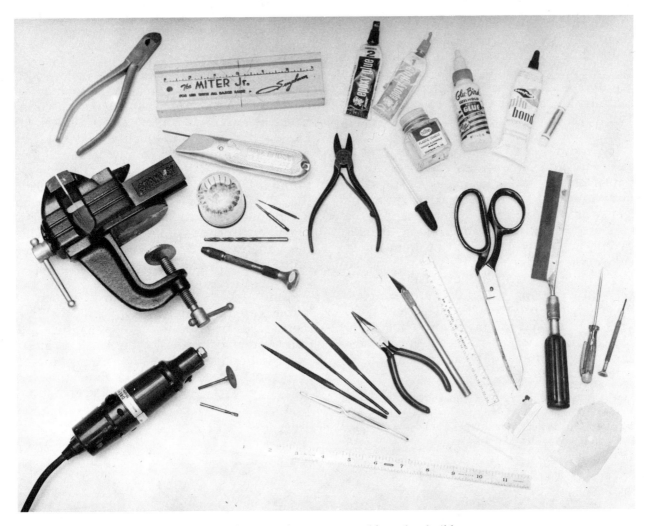

Fig. 3-3   These tools comprise the complete assortment you would need to build even the most-complex craftsman kits.

but I would rank all of them behind a good transistorized throttle (two, if you're wise) and power pack. Plan to spend at least $80 for the combination power pack and transistor throttle and at least $60 for the additional throttle. I've found that the less expensive units really don't offer enough performance features to make them anything like the "bargains" they should be.

If you already have (or have budgeted for) all the hand tools and a transistor throttle (the transistorized throttle is purely for controlling your trains at realistically smooth and slow speeds) then your next major item should be a quality airbrush with an air compressor. An artists' supply store can help you decide on an airbrush (Binks, Paasche, Badger, and Wren are the most popular), but you can expect to

pay about $40 plus another $50 or more for a suitable air compressor. You'll see the airbrush in use in later chapters; basically, it's a miniature version of the spray guns used to paint automobiles. If you were wise enough to buy an air compressor with an adjustable air pressure feature, the airbrush can be used to spray dots as small as the periods on these pages or to spray a pattern that is large enough to cover a boxcar in one pass. You can duplicate just about any paint or weathering effect seen on these pages with a brush or with aerosol cans but the airbrush makes it much easier because you can control the air pressure, the spray pattern, and, of course, the color and thinner mix of the paint itself.

I'd rank a motor tool, like Dremel's, next in any list of major tool purchases. These high-speed grinders are available in kits, selling for about $40, that include sanding, grinding, and milling bits. They save countless hours of filing, sawing, or sanding with hand tools. If you opt for one of the $20 Variac-type speed controls, you can even use the motor tool for drilling holes, ranging from the size of a hair to about ⅛ inch.

There are some other major tool investments for you to consider, such as Kadee's stapler-like rail spiker, a circular saw, a saber saw, and an assortment of carpenter's tools—but they will only be necessary if you build a complete layout and you may be able to rent or borrow most of them. Remember, none of these expensive tools are really necessary (except, perhaps, that transistor throttle) for your modeling work; you can complete any modeling project with just a few hand tools. I've ranked the major investments so you can plan future purchases to include the most essential items in what I consider their order of usefulness.

BUILDING A BOXCAR

This LaBelle boxcar kit is typical of the vast majority of craftsman kits. This particular kit is HO scale but LaBelle makes the same kit in O scale. There are dozens of other kits from firms like Central Valley, Ambroid, Silver Streak, Northeastern, Quality Craft, Walthers, Scotia Scale Models, Suncoast, and other models from LaBelle in every scale from N through O and for most eras from the 1890s (like this LaBelle kit) to the most modern cars (from Quality Craft, Ambroid, and others). Their construction differs only in detail with the variations necessary to match whatever prototype car the kit was designed to duplicate.

Some of the other craftsman kits such as Ulrich's are completely metal, some combine metal sides or ends with wood bodies and others are mostly plastic pieces. The metal and plastic kits have nearly as many pieces and, most often, some extra time must be

Fig. 3-4   This LaBelle brand HO scale boxcar is typical of many craftsman kits; trucks and couplers must be added.

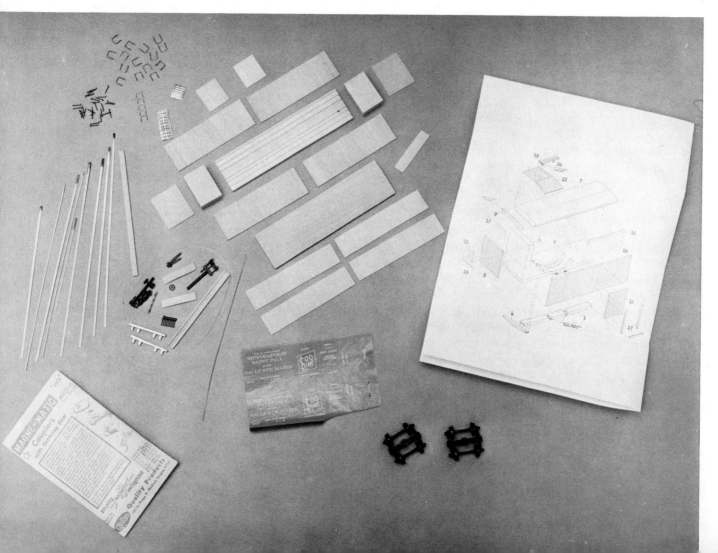

spent filing away traces of the molds from the edges of the parts. Some of the kits have pre-painted and lettered sides and some require that the modeler apply the lettering with dry transfers (again, like this LaBelle kit) or decals after it is assembled and painted.

The techniques you learn on one kit can usually be applied to most other kits; if you're adept enough at the process, you can even scratch-build your own equipment by cutting strip wood to size and detailing the model with wire grab irons and detail castings like those in the kits. Most of the wood shapes and detail parts you find in these kits are available as individual pieces for modelers who want to scratch-build their own equipment to match a prototype not offered in kit form. The monthly model railroad magazines and several books have plans for hundreds of pieces of rolling stock that aren't available as either kits or ready-built items.

The first step, in assembling any kit, is to read the instructions so you have some idea of how the pieces are supposed to fit. There are basically only two mistakes you can make in building one of these kits: (1) cutting the wrong size piece of wood so it doesn't fit where it belongs and (2) cutting or filing a part so it is the wrong size or so it won't fit.

If you take the time, before cutting or gluing anything, to identify each piece and learn where and when it is supposed to be used, the kit should fit together perfectly. The major pitfall, with any wood kit, is a mistaken feeling that more glue will make a stronger model; use the least amount of glue possible and, to be sure, apply the glue with a toothpick rather than directly from the tube or bottle. Watch for any glue that may dribble out of the seams and wipe any excess away immediately. A careful study of the instructions should tell you what tools may be required to complete the kit, so you should have them on hand when you reach that stage of the assembly.

I prefer white glue for assembling any wood models but for others I use the tube-type cements like Ambroid. White glue takes a bit longer to dry but it seems to penetrate the wood grain a bit better for a stronger joint. The cyanoacrylate cements (Eastman's 910 was one of the first) are expensive but a tiny drop is all that's required. This type of cement dries almost instantly and will adhere

Fig. 3-5   Use white glue for any wood-to-wood joints with rubber bands as clamps to hold the larger pieces while it dries.

just about anything to anything (including your fingers)—it's the best cement for assembling kits with many metal parts. The *only* cement you should consider for plastic-to-plastic joints is a liquid type such as Testors Liquid Cement for Plastics or the Plastruct brand. Tube-type plastic cements have dissolved filler material that almost guarantees a sloppy joint. The plastics surfaces must mate perfectly in order for the liquid cement to do it's job of dissolving the touching faces, but the parts should be filed and trimmed to fit that well in any case.

Goodyear's Pliobond is an excellent cement for attaching metal parts to wood or for some small metal-to-metal applications, but don't use it on plastics because it will warp and soften the surface in a most unpredictable way. Epoxy cements are best for attaching metal parts to other metal parts, particularly where the joint must be extremely strong. If you can find it, 3M's Sprayment adhesive is excellent for laminating large areas like two pieces of wood or cardboard. The Sprayment is simply sprayed over the two surfaces that will be joined and the two are then pressed together.

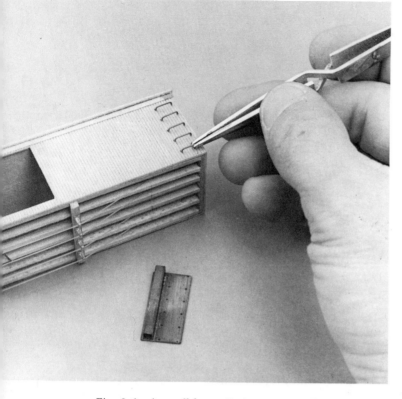

Fig. 3-6   A small brass jig is easy to make; it helps to position the holes for the individual wire grab irons.

Fig. 3-7   Kadee's coupler-height gauge should be used to ensure that the couplers on all cars and locomotives will mate.

There are a few occasions where you might want to build your own assembly jigs to make your work easier and more precise. I've found that a metal drilling jig is the tool I most frequently use in my shop whenever I'm constructing rolling stock. The jig was made from a piece of 0.020-inch thick brass and a piece of 1/8-inch square brass tubing soldered together. The square tube aligns the jig with the end of the car and the holes in the jig provide positive and evenly spaced locations for drilling the tiny holes for grab irons.

Two or three such jigs, with holes spaced to match the prototype you're modeling, are usually enough to match the needed spacing in any kit. The holes are just one number-size larger than the drill size needed to fit the grab irons.

A Kadee coupler-height jig is another essential item with which you can adjust the height of the couplers to match all your other equipment. If the coupler is too low, washers are placed between the trucks and the bolsters to raise the entire car or, if you prefer, the underbody can be notched to inset the coupler and coupler pocket. If the coupler is too high, then the bolster must be trimmed or a few plastic shims installed between the coupler and the car body. It's far better to make such adjustments before the car is painted and lettered.

Check to see that the kit provides some means of attaching the trucks to the car (many do not) and purchase the necessary bolsters or wood screws when you buy the trucks, couplers, and paint. Swivel the trucks from side-to-side to see that they don't interfere with the underbody details when the car moves through tight turns.

PAINTING AND LETTERING

Most of the craftsman kits can be painted with a brush but be sure you use a model railroad paint such as Floquil, Scale-Coat, or Polly S; most conventional paints dry so thick that they obscure much of the tiny detail. There is more information in a later chapter on painting and applying "wet" decals.

This particular (LaBelle boxcar) kit, however, can be completed (and was) by simply brush-painting and then rubbing on the dry

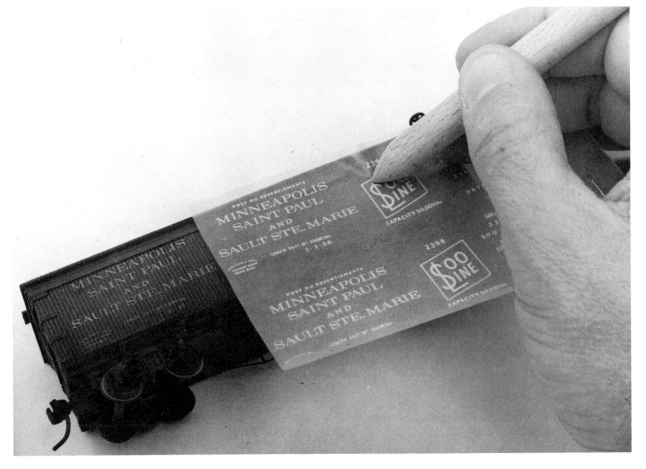

Fig. 3-8   An artist's wooden burnishing stick is the tool to use to apply run-on dry transfer lettering.

transfer letters and numbers supplied with the kit. The dry transfer process isn't quite as simple as it sounds. I'd suggest you try to obtain some samples of dry transfer lettering from an art or drafting supply store and experiment on a piece of wood painted with the same paint you've used on the model.

The two tricks in dry transfer lettering are to use just enough pressure and to be sure the lettering is exactly where you want it—you cannot move it once it's on! You can use a ball-point pen or a lead pencil with a dull point, but you'll probably get better results if you spend a quarter for one of the commercial artist's burnishing tools. The kit instructions should show you where the lettering is supposed to be placed. Chances are, you'll discover that the sheet has to be moved around

quite a bit to get each group of letters and numbers in the proper position.

Place the sheet exactly where you want the letters and hold the sheet in position with pressure on some part that does not have any lettering on it. Rub over the dry transfer in one back-and-forth direction until you have rubbed over the entire dry transfer. You can tell which parts you've burnished because the lettering will fade a bit when it has adhered to the model's surface. If you apply too much pressure with the burnishing tool, you'll actually burnish the lettering to the transparent paper backing rather than to the car side; if you apply too little pressure, the lettering won't transfer at all. When all the lettering is complete, you should spray the car with a very light coat of clear paint such as Testor's

Fig. 3-9   There is no decal film to hide with dry transfer lettering, but it takes practice to
apply the transfers properly.

Dull-Cote; but, again, test whatever you use on a sample of dry transfer and paint to be sure it doesn't attack or dissolve either the paint or the dry transfer. If you ruin the dry transfer, you may be able to purchase another set from the kit manufacturer and, then again, you may not. However, most hobby dealers do carry decals and some dry transfers, so you could letter the car with another railroad name and number set if you can't find an exact match for the markings in the kit.

You'll learn the tricks of a lot of trades through this hobby: the talents of an engineer in designing and building the layout; of a stage director in operating those trains; of a master craftsman in building the actual models; and now, you'll learn to function, for at least a moment, as an artist.

One of an artist's primary talents is an ability to really see what is there. The best oil painters don't paint the subject, they paint the shadow and the light that makes up our vision of the subject. You'll have to bring that kind of vision into play when your layout is ready for scenery.

For now, practice the art by really looking at the next train you see. You'll discover that very few of the cars are really the same color; even those that belong to the same prototype railroad and should be the same shade of, say, boxcar red carry subtle coloring differences. The differences in color aren't the result of poor paint but the effects of Mother Nature's gentle (or firm) touch.

There's usually only two or three cars in a hundred that still have a fresh-from-the-shops paint look; all the rest show varying degrees of exposure to natural elements. The sun bleaches the colors; dust and mud kicked-up from the roadbed discolor the cars; rain washes and mixes the dust and settles it in around the rivets and seams and provokes a blotch of rust here and there. The paint may be peeling in spots or the railroad may have repainted just the numbers so the yard and switching crews could identify it.

Some cars show definite signs of their cargo with streaks of biege grain dust or light grey concrete or black fuel oil dribbles. Cars that spend most of their lives near a coal mining area will have a blackish hue while those that "live" on the desert will be bleached and coated with tan dust and still others, from the regions heavy with iron ore deposits, will have a red/brown cast from the local soil. Any model, whether a ready-built plastic kit or a scratch-built contest-winner, will look more realistic if it is weathered to some degree.

There are two basic methods for producing weathered effects on model railroad equipment: to literally *paint* the "weather" on with washes of about nine parts clear paint and one part color or to dust it on with powdered artists' chalks. You can achieve almost the same variety of effects with either medium,

Weathering Artistry

particularly if you have an airbrush so you can dust thinned paint or by blending the pastel chalk dust with a water-wet paintbrush. If you study a hundred different prototype freight cars, you'll find about ninty-nine different types of weathering. We can only suggest a few of those here to help give you the feeling of the two types of weathering techniques for models.

Your best "tool" for reproducing the variations of the prototype's weathering is a camera and some color film. Photographs are an invaluable aid for this type of work because as you weather the model you can keep referring to the photos to be certain you get the colors and shading similar to those in real life. Notice such seemingly minor things as the way dust collects under the eaves and around the trucks, how the color of rust can vary from a dull brown to almost orange, and how the lettering varies from almost new to barely legible. Notice, too, that every car really is different and be particularly careful to apply a slightly different weathering touch to each of your models.

The model's decal or dry transfer lettering should be protected with a light spray of flat,

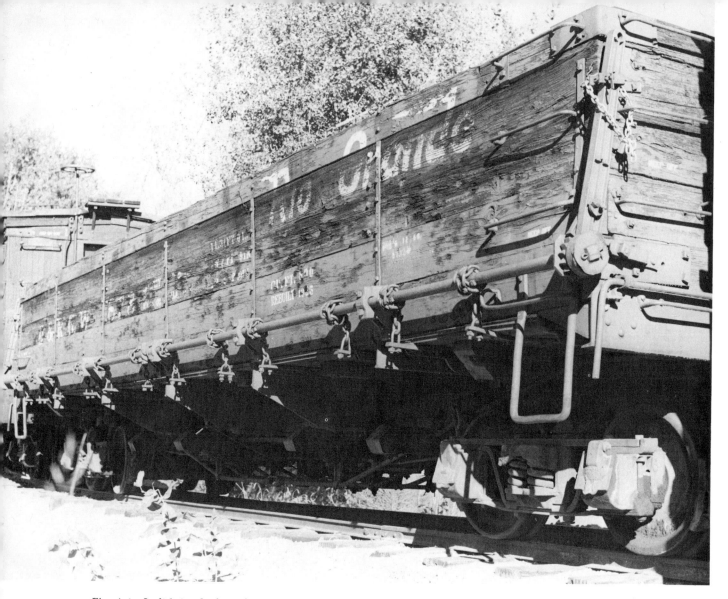

Fig. 4-1　It didn't take long for wooden rolling stock to show the effects of the weather on this narrow gauge gondola.

clear enamel like Testor's Dullcote or artist's fixative. Practice spraying on some scrap surface until you master the technique of dusting the clear on so it is almost dry when it touches the model; usually, you must hold the spray can about 2 feet away from the model and make short, quick passes with the spray pattern over the model. Even unpainted models should receive the clear coat if you're going to weather them with pastel chalk dust. Let the clear coating dry overnight.

There are dozens of choices of colors and brands of chalks but the best I've found is the Nupastel brand; it should be available in individual square sticks at any good art supply shop. There are far more color choices than you'll ever need and nearly all of them are

useful; a simple assortment of dark grey (better than black), burnt sienna (a reddish brown) burnt umber (a dark brown), ochre (a brownish yellow), and light grey will do for a start. These colors can be mixed to provide just about any shade you'd desire. Rub the Nupastel stick on a piece of fine sandpaper or scrape it with a knife to reduce a small portion of it to powder; do the same with each color you intend to use for any particular weathering project. The dust can then be brushed onto the car (or locomotive or structure—it even adds realism to scale model people) to produce the desired degree of "dirt."

It's best to practice on a painted scrap first to get the feeling of the Nupastel's dust. You'll find that you can vary the amount of coloring by adding more and more to the brush to the point where you can almost obscure the lettering on the car's side. Remember to apply the dust in a vertical direction so the color patterns and shades will look like they were washed down the car by rain water flowing off the roof.

Once you've mastered the technique of dry-brushing with the Nupastels, you can experiment with them wet. Add just a touch of water to the brush and you'll find that the Nupastel powder almost dissolves. With careful strokes and just a touch of powder, you can barely shade the entire side of a car so it has that very subtle look of sun-bleaching. Thicker mixes of water and the colored dust can be used for rust spots and grease stains

and even dust-soaked oil drippings on a tank car's domes.

The trucks and lower edges of any car should receive the most amount of weathering and should show the most signs of rust (if any, and there usually is some). The light grey can be used to "bleach out" a darker car or to simulate the calcium deposits left streaked on the boilers of older steam locomotives.

You'll find that you can control the flow of the wetted Nupastel powder well enough to produce hairline streaks of rust or oil dribbles or even to simulate a few individual weathered boards on the sides of a wooden car. Use at least three different brush sizes: a number 000, a number 1, and a ½-inch size, so you

Fig. 4-2 Powder Nupastel brand chalks on fine sandpaper, and brush them on models to simulate weather stains and dirt.

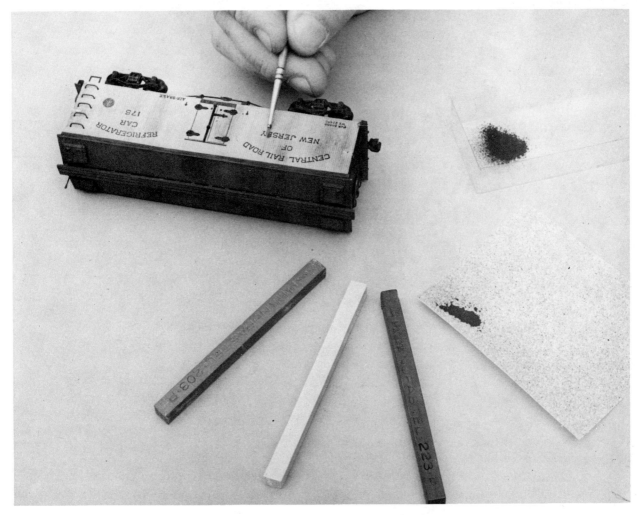

Fig. 4-3　A well-thinned wash of acrylic paint or model railroad paint is used here to apply streaks of grime.

Fig. 4-4 Standard railroad colors can be dabbed onto cars to simulate oil spills and a variety of rust stains.

can vary the dust patterns with both dry and wetted Nupastels.

Weathering with paint is a bit more difficult than weathering with Nupastels because you have to be careful to use just enough paint and thinner so that you don't dissolve the model's paint and lettering. There's usually only time for a few quick brush strokes before the paint will begin to soften and blend with the weathering coats. If you're trying for a badly weathered effect, where even the lettering has begun to oxidize and run down the car side, this is fine but it takes a deft touch to achieve a moderate amount of weathering.

A mixture of one part Floquil (or Polly S acrylic) RR-13 Grimy Black, two parts F-72 burnt umber, and seven parts clear will provide a start for a typical blackish-grey soot color. Notice how the half of the Santa Fe boxcar that was protected from rain runoff by the door slide is clean and the rest of that side is dirty (see Fig. 4-3); an example copied directly from a prototype freight car. Floquil's

Grimy Black color can be used directly from the bottle to simulate the oil dribbles on the top of a tank car that transports fuel or lubricating oil (see Fig. 4-4). Floquil's orange-colored Rust and their Roof Brown can be used alone or mixed together to provide most of the variations you'll observe in real rust stains. That same mixture can be used to weather all the rails on your trackwork as well as any other bare iron or steel items that appear around the layout.

The airbrush (Fig. 4-5) is one of the best tools for applying a weathering or aging effect, particularly when you want the effect to be very subtle. Any of the quality airbrushes can be adjusted to give a barely perceptible flow of paint. The paint can be thinned with about nine parts thinner; and since the paint will be almost dry by the time it reaches the car side, there's no chance for the thinner to dissolve the model's decals or paint. The air compressor should have an adjustable air pressure regulator so you can turn the pressure up to about 32 pounds per square inch

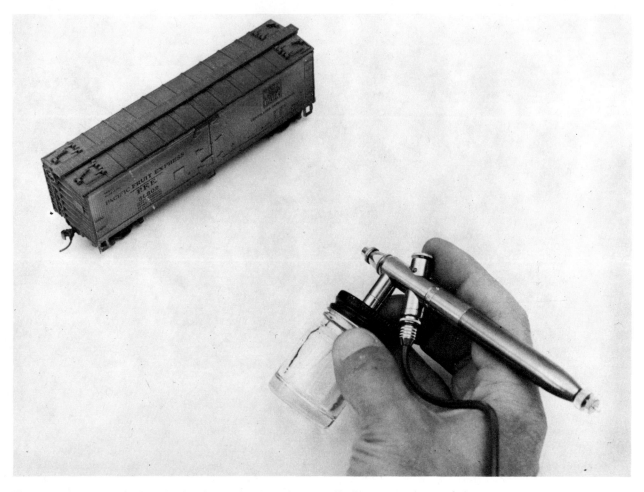

Fig. 4-5   An artist's airbrush like this Badge brand unit will allow you to control the
paint spray and colors.

for this type of "dry brushing." The thin haze
of dark brown "diesel soot" on this reefer car
(see Fig. 4-5) required about ten passes with a
very fine mist from the Badger airbrush to get
even this dark a tone. The degree of weathering on this particular car is about
average—most cars have a bit less shading
and a few have very much more.

You can practice the airbrush weathering
technique (or either of the other techniques)
on a single car or two but it's best to weather
half a dozen cars or so at a time to be sure that
you're getting a different effect on each one.

There's no reason why the hand-brushed and
airbrushed weathering techniques cannot be
used on the same car to provide a few hand-
painted streaks, dots of rust or oil, and then
an overall patina of light dust from an airbrush. It's virtually impossible to capture this
dust effect with an aerosol can, by the way,
because the paint comes out of the can in
droplets that are far too large; but you can
approximate the effect by using the water and
Nupastel technique with a bare trace of the
colored dust.

Passenger transport is one element of real railroading that you can eliminate from your miniature empire and still keep it true-to-prototype. Today, nostalgia buffs are saddened by the fact that the glamorous rolling hotels of yesteryear are such a small part of the railroad scene; but even in the heyday of passenger travel (the 1920s), there were still a number of railroads that hauled nothing but freight. Amtrac has taken over the passenger traffic from all but a few of today's railroads and the rainbow hues of the various railroad's streamliners have vanished along with the varnished wood and gold filagree and kerosene lamps of previous eras.

On the other hand, there are a number of model railroaders whose major interest is passenger cars and passenger train operation and who have only enough freight equipment to give some credence to the fact that it exists. The model manufacturers are well aware of this interest in passenger equipment and they have responded to it with an array of equipment nearly as great as the assortment of freight cars.

The modeler has a choice of both plastic and brass ready-to-run passenger cars, simple plastic kits, and dozens of craftsman kits which are exact replicas of prototypes from the various railroading eras. You'll find a choice of 1860-era open platform cars; 1890-era open platform cars, the first cars (still wood) with enclosed vestibules on each end; the "heavyweight" steel passenger cars of the 1920s; and the most modern streamliners in HO scale. Most of the list is also offered in N scale and O scale.

The N scale equipment is all of the ready-to-run variety and most of the O scale cars (and a few in S and TT scales) are the craftsman types. The variety of HO scale streamliners includes ready-to-run cars painted to match most of the full-size streamliners of the 1950s. The decal makers like Champion, Walthers, and Micro-Scale offer striping and lettering decals for dozens of other full-size railroads' streamliners. Some of the ready-to-run cars have interior detailing and lighting, and Walthers has interior detail kits and lighting sets for just about any type of car from any era.

Passenger train operation can present some problems, however, if you aren't wary enough to design your layout to accommo-

Passenger Cars

date the extra-long cars. Around the turn of the century, 80-foot passenger cars appeared on the full-size railroads and most equipment made after that time averaged 80-feet in length. These longer cars require larger radius curves than the conventional 40 to 50-foot freight cars; and there must be enough clearance between any double tracks, around tunnel portals, and near lineside buildings so that the cars' overhang on curves has adequate operating clearance. The long overhang at the coupler end and the touching diaphragms (the accordian-pleated devices that shield the passenger walkways between two connecting cars) can cause the cars to derail when they enter curves in the track. When coupled in trains of two or more cars, 80-foot passenger cars can operate on curves as sharp as 24-inch radius in HO scale (about 15-inch radius in N scale and 42-inch in O scale) if the diaphragms just touch so they can move to an offset position in a curve without binding *and* if the couplers are mounted to the trucks rather than to the ends of the car bodies in the conventional manner.

Talgo, or truck-mounted, trucks and couplers are common even on freight cars in the

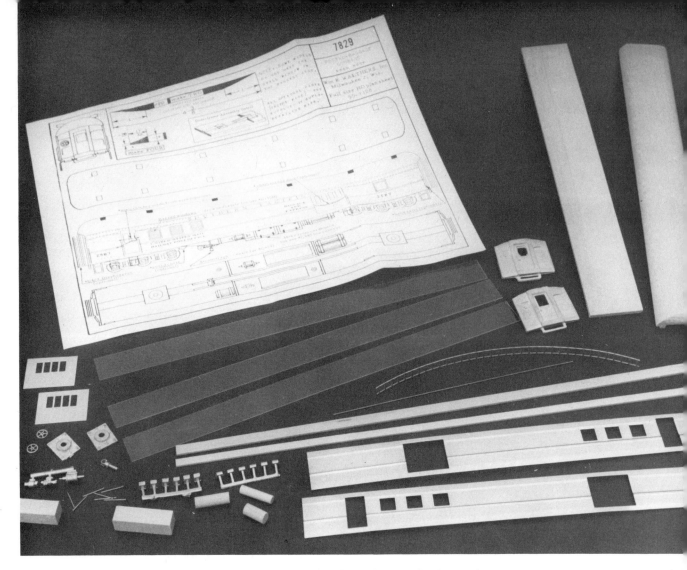

Fig. 5-1 Some of the craftsman kits include both wood and metal parts like this Walthers brand heavyweight postal car.

inexpensive plastic train sets; and most of the ready-to-run HO and N scale models of 80-foot prototype passenger cars have Talgo-style trucks with the couplers mounted to the trucks. Kadee makes an adaptor kit to either mount their couplers to Talgo-type trucks or adapt conventional trucks to the Talgo style for HO and N scale modelers; a similar adaptor could be fabricated from plastic sheet stock for the larger scales.

There is a third way around the extra-long passenger car problem and that is simply to use shorter cars. A few of the full-size passenger cars were shorter than the normal 80-foot but most of them were just coaches, baggage cars, or postal cars. Some of the models that are available have been shortened so that all the cars in the train, including the normally longer Pullmans, diners, and observation cars, are only about 72-feet long.

The Athearn streamlined and heavyweight steel cars and the Tyco streamlined cars are "shorties" in HO scale and the Rapido streamliners and the ConCor and Bachmann heavyweights in N scale are all shorter than most prototype passenger equipment. Walthers makes a number of craftsman kits in HO and O scale that can also be adapted to the shorter length. Most of the open platform passenger cars of the 1890s and earlier were 60-footers with a few 72-foot cars on the main line railroads.

The shorter length of both passenger and freight cars is one of the things that makes modeling old-timers so attractive to many model railroaders. There are exceptions to most rules and there were, in fact, many passenger cars that were no longer than an average freight car. These short passenger cars were mostly either head-end cars or cars that were used only on small branchline railroads. The most famous of these tiny passenger cars are the baggage-coach combine and coach that the Sierra Railway (see Fig. 5-2) used in the foothills of the Sierra Nevada Mountains of California. These two little cars have appeared in dozens of motion pictures and television shows, including the "Petticoat Junction" series. MDC has some similar models in HO scale plastic kits with additional varieties of the same length car, so the modeler who favors old-time equipment can make up an entire train. There are a number of brands of HO, TT, S, and O scale craftsman kits of open-platform passenger cars that could easily be shortened to match the Sierra's 36-foot prototypes.

The concept of cross-kitting (also called kit-bashing or converting or even customizing) can be applied to any model railroad kit or ready-to-run locomotive, freight car, passenger car, or structure to produce a model that is unique to your railroad alone. The model may be a free-lance design adapted from available kit parts or it may be an exact duplicate of some prototype for which there is no exact kit.

If, for example, you find that the N and HO scale ready-built models of prototype 80-foot cars are too long for the curves on your layout, it's relatively easy to remove some of the car's length from the center and then to glue the remaining ends back together. If you use a razor saw and work carefully so the cuts are perfectly straight and square in all three dimensions, the glue joint will be almost invisible. A bit of automobile metal-base body filler can be used to hide whatever remains of the seam and a jewelers' file and number 600 sandpaper can be used to smooth and match the rest of the sides and roof.

This same body-sawing process can be used to lengthen cars, but two body pieces will be needed. A single cut is made through each

Fig. 5-2   Most of the plastic kits have pre-painted and lettered sides. The modeler must apply these detail parts.

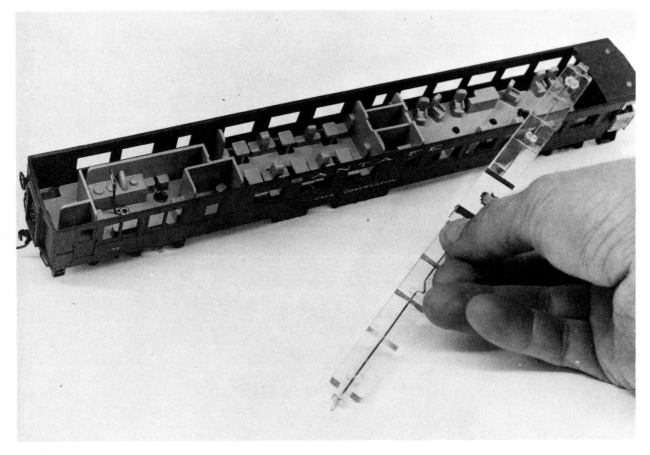

Fig. 5-3 The deluxe series of AHM brand ready-built passenger cars have interior details and lights.

body but the cut is offset so that the two longer halves can be glued together to produce a car the exact length you desire. Athearn's too-short heavyweight and streamlined cars can be lengthened to true-to-prototype length in this manner, or you may want to combine two of the MDC 36-foot car bodies to build a more typical 60-foot open platform car.

The books on full-size passenger trains, especially Arthur Dubin's excellent *Some Classic Trains* and the companion volume *More Classic Trains* (from Kalmbach Publishers, Milwaukee, WI 53233) have hundreds of photos and floor plans of passenger cars of all eras; most of them can be modeled by splicing pieces of plastic passenger car bodies together in N and HO scales. These same books can provide all the information you need to completely detail the interior of just about any passenger car model.

Passenger cars can serve yet another pur-

pose on your model railroad—as work cars—just as they do on the prototype. Much of a modern railroad's work equipment is made up of older heavyweight, as well as some streamlined passenger cars that have been renumbered and repainted in the railroad's color scheme. Some of these cars, like diners and Pullman sleeping cars, are used for the original purposes, but others have been gutted and rebuilt with parts, racks, and machine shops and even with hospital equipment. Many railroads use the strong underframes from the heavyweight passenger cars of the 1920s for flat cars and gondolas by "chopping off" the body just below the window line. If you're modeling a modern era, some of your work equipment should be modified passenger cars to supplement the rebuilt boxcars that make up the balance of the various wrecking and maintenance of way trains on the prototype.

Fig. 5-4 John Buchner won second place in the NMRA's national modeling contest with his scratch-built HO scale coach.

Fig. 5-5 Modern railroads have relegated most of their passenger equipment to work trains, with new paint and numbers.

Locomotives

The motive power for your model railroad is going to be the major single model investment you'll make and, for that reason alone, it should be a wise one. There is seldom any correlation between cost and performance; the locomotives with multi-hundred dollar price tags are often the best-looking but cost is not necessarily the determining factor for performance.

There are a large number of armchair model railroaders who qualify only as modelers in that they have purchased models; the locomotives they buy are immediately relegated to a glass showcase and seldom, if ever, turn a wheel. The model railroad *collector* often concentrates his efforts and expenses in trying to obtain a complete collection of some particular type of imported brass locomotive. In some ways, these collectors are a boon to the guy who actually operates his locomotives because they have created enough of a demand for brass locomotives to make it worthwhile for the importers to produce literally hundreds of different prototypes as HO and O scale miniatures. These brass locomotives are virtually rivet-for-rivet replicas of a specific full-size locomotive right down to the

nail-head size builders' plates on the sides of the boiler (just below the stack) that give the name of the builder of the prototype.

A few years ago I would have said that brass locomotives were the best bargains in model railroading because you could buy one of these jewels for about twice the price of a ready-to-run with plastic boiler or a metal kit locomotive. Today, though, the prices of brass have been boosted by higher wages in the Orient and monetary exchange and inflation factors so that a brass locomotive can cost four-times or more the price of an equivalent-size ready-built or kit. The prices have reached the point where a lot of modelers are buying brass as an investment, just as they would jewelry, because they can see that the supply is dwindling each year and the demand is rising.

A few importers, notably NorthWest Short Line (with their Far East Distributors brand) have produced a few brass locomotives without most of the expensive lost-wax castings and wiring to bring the price down once again to about twice that of a ready-built or kit. But the ready-builts and kits often have more detail than these models, so the low-cost brass engine's appeal is mainly that they offer replicas of prototypes which aren't available anywhere else at twice the price. Today, the bargains in locomotive models are in the ready-to-run miniatures with plastic boilers and particularly the models of prototype diesel locomotives.

There's little or no chance that the cost of the better imported brass locomotives is going to go down in the coming years because a scarcity of labor to produce the models is the prime factor in their constant price increases. A popular 2-8-0 "consolidation" steam locomotive that sold, for example, for $40 just 5 years ago sells for $140 today and, if the rate continues, it will sell for close to $300 in another 5 years.

Most of the ready-to-run locomotives with their plastic boilers or superstructures and plastic tenders are produced in Europe and their prices have almost doubled in the last 5 years but that still pegs their prices at a fraction of a brass locomotive; an engine that is about the same size as that 2-8-0 sells for less than $40 and the price won't increase at nearly the same rate as the brass version. These ever-increasing costs, on imported

Fig. 6-1   With just a bit of weathering, this Life-Like brand Pacific could be as realistic
as PFM's AT&SF consolidation.

locomotives, are beginning to open up some markets for American manufacturers to produce kits once again.

Prior to the influx of brass ready-to-run locomotives in the late 1950's, most model railroaders built all their locomotives from American-made kits or operated one of the very few well-detailed ready-to-runs of the time. Some of the better locomotive kits of the 1950s, notably Tyco, MDC, and English (who markets the old Penn Line and Bowser brands) are still available today at prices just a few dollars above what they sold for two decades ago. Most of these HO scale kits have cast metal boilers, frames, tenders, and detail parts like the MDC 4-4-2 "Atlantic" discussed in the next chapter. Most of the piping details that are molded in the plastic boilers of the ready-to-run locomotives are missing from these kits but it only takes a few hours with a hand drill and some wire for the modeler to add piping details. The kits must be painted and lettered, but that's part of the fun of building any model, Several firms, like Cary, Kemtron, Cal-Scale, the Back Shop, and others, offer hundreds of highly detailed lost-wax process castings (many of them the same parts that are used on the brass imports)

so the modeler can apply as much detail to a locomotive kit (or even to a plastic ready-to-run model) as he feels is worthwhile.

There are photographs, and sometimes even scale plans, of virtually every prototype locomotive in the hundreds of books on prototype railroads; these books can be used as reference sources for adding to kits and ready-builts as much or more detail and realism as you'll find on any brass import, and at a fraction of the cost.

The prices on these HO scale locomotive kits range from $10 to $60, depending on the size of the model. An average-size kit will have a retail price of around $30. If you want to add as many of those lost-wax brass castings as you'd find on a similar brass import, the price of the parts alone could easily exceed $40; but your investment is still about half what it would be for a typical imported brass locomotive.

The plastic-bodied kits and ready-built models of diesel locomotives often have far more detail than many of the brass imports. The primary appeal of the imported brass deisel locomotive lies in the fact that there are dozens of prototypes that are available only as brass imports. It is possible to reproduce

Fig. 6-2 Murray Sincoff added several lost-wax brass detail castings and wire piping to super-detail this HO scale kit.

these models by cutting grills and vents and cabs from various plastic bodies, but few modelers are willing to go to that extent to obtain the exact miniature they want.

The diesel locomotives in the ready-to-run category are even greater bargains, as compared to brass imports, than steam locomotives. Prices on N, HO, and O scale diesel models (as simple kits like Athearn's or ready-builts) range from $7 to $30 with HO scale brass versions selling for at least three times that and the few O scale brass diesels at $200 or more. The HO scale diesel kits are so simple to assemble (a few screws and some snap-on hand-rails) that they hardly qualify as kits.

There are, however, some excellent cast metal and brass diesel locomotive kits in O scale from firms like All-Nation and Keystone Locomotive Works. A surprising number of these kits and ready-to-run diesel locomotives, particularly the Model Power and Athearn models with their flywheel drive systems, provide smooth performance and power that is as good as some of the brass diesels. There are only three or four models of the prototype locomotives that were powered

by electricity in the kit or ready-built ranges; so if you're an "electric" enthusiast, you'll have to pay the price of the imported brass locomotives as they become available.

Very few of the ready-to-run or kit locomotives that are models of steam prototypes perform as well as their imported brass equivalents. The less expensive models lack both the power and the slow speed performance of the better brass locomotives. There are several replacement motors, at an additional $10 to $30, that can be fitted to the kit and ready-built models to give them the power they lack. Very few model railroaders really need that much power, however, because their layouts just aren't large enough to pull 20 to 100-car trains. A transistorized throttle is often enough to allow less than 5 scale miles-an-hour speeds with the least expensive engines (a standard rheostat control gives about an average of 15 scale miles-an-hour control) so even that aspect of performance can be solved to most modelers' satisfaction without buying expensive brass motive power.

The ready-to-run steam and diesel locomotives that are imported from Europe often have wheel flanges, with contours to European modeling standards, that are so large that they hit the spikes and ties on scale model track. You won't have any problem if you use the brass railed plastic snap-together track sections furnished with most train sets. The rail on this type of track (in HO scale) is 0.100-inch high and is called "code 100." This size rail, however, is larger than any of the prototype railroad's rail (when reduced to 1/87 scale) except for some of the heaviest main line tracks.

Code 70 rail (0.070-inch high) is much closer to the average-size rail on American prototype railroads and most experienced modelers prefer the greater realism of the smaller rail. Only Lambert brand flexible track-and-tie sections and ready-laid switches have this size rail (if you specify it); the only other way to use code 70 rail is to spike your own track to wooden ties. Some older American-made cars and locomotives had oversize flanges too.

The newest American freight car trucks should have the wheel contour you're looking for and the contour is built into the side of the metal NMRA Standards Gauge—items that any model railroad dealer should have. Your dealer should have replacement wheel sets (two wheels and an axle) or complete trucks to correct any rolling stock with oversize flanges, but you'll have to reduce the sizes of the flanges on most locomotives yourself. AHM has offered complete sets of replacement wheels for their Y6b 2-8-8-2 articulated locomotive and for their USRA-prototype 0-6-0 switcher (with tender) with smaller flanges; but those sets are hard to find. You can file-down the flanges on your locomotives by connecting the 12-volt power leads from your power pack to the motor so the locomotive can revolve its own wheels. Hold a jewelers' file against the flange while the wheel turns to reduce the flange's size. Clean the file frequently and check the motor to be sure it isn't getting too hot from the overload. It's far better to remove the wheels (drivers) from the engine so they can be turned-down in a lathe, but that process requires both the lathe and a special jig to hold the drivers. Some of the large hobby dealers may be able to machine the flanges for you or they may have a customer who is willing to perform the work.

Traction equipment (trolleys and interurbans) fits into the locomotive category even

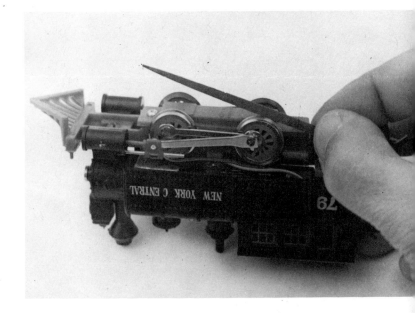

Fig. 6-3 The wheel flanges on many of the locomotives imported from Europe are too large for code 70 HO track.

though the majority of the equipment was self-powered and passenger-hauling. The prototype traction railroads often did provide freight service with self-powered freight cars and small electric switchers that pulled conventional freight cars. There are no inexpensive ready-to-run trolleys or interurbans patterned after American prototypes, but there are a few N and HO scale models of European trolleys.

There are, however, several dozen trolley and interurban car kits in HO, S, and O scales. Soho and Suydam have imported an array of brass ready-to-run equipment in HO scale and a few O scale models. Most of the trolley and interurban car kits from firms like Walthers, English, and LaBelle provide only the basic car body; the trucks, motor and drive train, power poles or pantographs, and couplers must be purchased as separate items. Walthers lists most of these items in their catalog and other, O scale, traction parts and kits are available from the Wagner Car Company, 59 Euclid, in Wyoming, OH 45215. Your dealer can order the Walthers, English, or LaBelle kits and parts; but Wagner is one of those firms (others can be found in monthly model railroad magazines) who sells only direct to the customer.

A surprisingly large percentage of trolley

Fig. 6-4   Trolley modeling allows the most operation in the least amount of space; some operate from overhead wires.

modelers build most of their cars from scratch and operate them with a mixture of kit and scratch-built freight cars. There are two excellent books on trolley and interurban modeling that describe everything from special track plans to how to build working overhead wire systems: *Traction Guidebook for Model Railroaders* (from Kalmbach Publishers, Milwaukee, WI 53233) and Paul and Steven Mallery's *Model Traction Handbook* (from Vane A. Jones Co., 6710 Hampton Dr., E., Indianapolis, IN 46226). There are dozens of books and booklets on the full-size trolley and interurban railroads to provide the data you need to duplicate any particular car.

There is something particularly satisfying about the work required to complete one of the many metal locomotive, rolling stock, or structure kits, especially if the prototype itself was made of metal. Most of these kits fall into the craftsman category because they require a considerable amount of filing and fitting and, usually, painting and lettering. The MDC-brand HO scale 4-4-2 atlantic locomotive kit is about average in terms of complexity, some of the the rolling stock kits from Ulrich are easier to assemble, and some of the O scale kits require more fitting and assembly.

The first step, in assembling one of these kits, is the same as for any kit: read the instructions twice to familiarize yourself with the way things are supposed to fit together and identify each and every one of the parts. Most of these metal kits can be assembled with the aid of a round, triangular, and flat trio of jewelers' files; a small screwdriver; and a jewelers' screwdriver. Some are so designed that the modeler must drill a few holes and, in some cases, tap a few of the holes to provide threads for assembly screws. A few of the O scale kits require the use of a soldering iron, but most have holes for attaching parts with round pegs and they can be attached with Pliobond, cyanoacrylate cement, or epoxy glue.

The actual construction should begin when you have sorted out each of the parts to see where it fits; the excess metal left when the parts were removed from the molds (called flash) must be filed flush with the part's surface. You need to know exactly which part fits where you can be certain you aren't filing away some of the aligning pegs or the surface details. Test-fit each of the parts with one another in a mock run-through of the assembly sequence to be sure that none of the molding flash interferes with the fit of the parts; file away any metal that prevents a perfect fit. You can carefully smooth any of the bearing areas where the motor shaft or axle will run, and polish the surfaces with some common automobile chrome polish. The areas where parts such as side rods and trucks will rub can also be polished. Be sure to smooth the holes where the screws will go; test-fit the screws to be sure everything aligns as it should. Some of the tight areas, like the spaces between the spokes on the driving wheel, can be cleaned with a sharp hobby knife.

VII
Assembling Metal Models

The most important step, in assembling a locomotive kit, is to be sure that the mechanism rolls freely and smoothly *before* the motor is installed. Try the frame with just the drivers installed to be sure they roll smoothly; then install one side rod; again, check for free-rolling before installing the other side rod; finally, check it with both side rods and both main rods (with the cylinders) in place. You may find that the far end holes in the side rods must be enlarged slightly, with a jewelers' round file, to prevent any side rod bind in the mechanism.

Next, install the motor and connect it to the partially assembled tender so you can test-run the mechanism without the superstructure. Very few kit manufacturers bother to include any extra rivets for the valve gear (the myriad of tiny rods around the rear of the cylinders that operates in front of the first two drivers); I'd suggest you purchase a few extra rivets of each size from your dealer when you buy the kit. Use two or three of the rivets to practice the technique of lightly hammering the rivet shank (with a hammer and small punch) to form a second head. Each of the tiny rods in the valve gear kit (not included in some of the

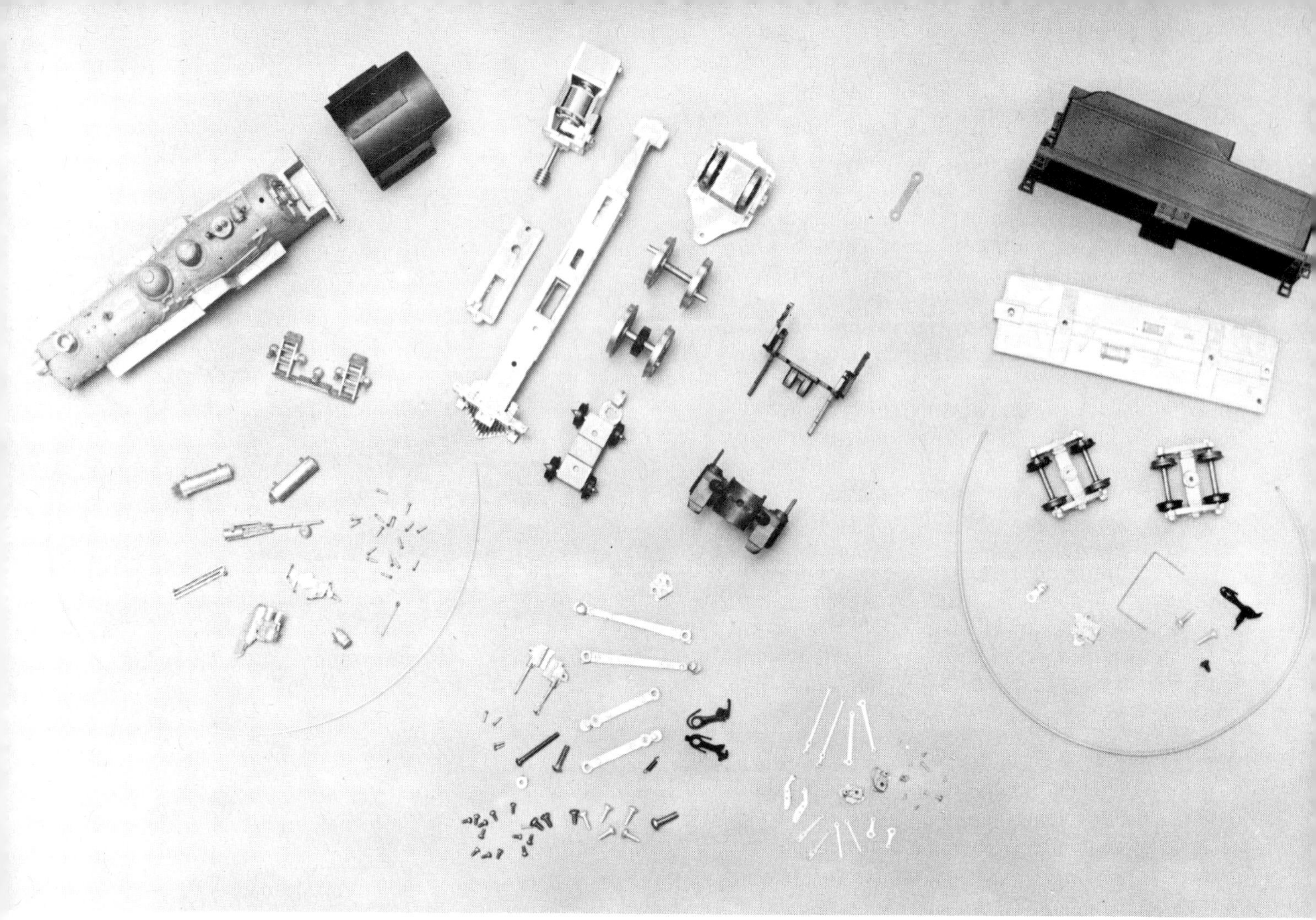

Fig. 7-1 Locomotive kits are becoming popular again as the prices of imported brass models continue to rise.

least expensive steam locomotive kits) must be riveted to the appropriate mating rod to complete the assembly of the valve gear, and the rivet must be punched (headed) just right to hold the rods together and still allow them to move without binding. When the valve gear is assembled and installed on the chassis, remove the motor temporarily and roll the chassis back and forth to be sure the valve gear isn't binding.

Next, the drivers will have to be removed from the frame so the frame can be painted. Paint behind the drivers but keep the paint away from the edges of the bearings and away from the areas where the pilot and trailing trucks will pivot. When the chassis is completed and painted, the motor can be reinstalled and the work on the superstructure and tender completed as outlined in the

Fig. 7-2 Jewelers' files will remove the marks left on the metal by the molds but don't file-away any details.

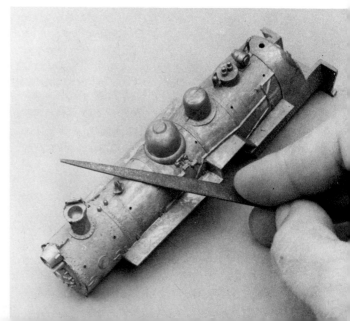

kit's instructions. Decide, before you paint the model, whether you want to add additional piping and some of the accessory brass castings to superdetail the model. You may even want to file-away the piping that is cast into the sides of the boiler and replace it with wire to improve the model's realism.

All the metal parts should be cleaned with a half and half solution of water and vinegar to remove any traces of grease before you paint the pieces (including the frame and driving wheels). There are several brands of undercoating paints you can use to be sure the final color coats will stick to the metal surfaces. The chapter on painting describes the techniques for masking and spray-painting and for applying the necessary lettering and number decals.

Finish the model with a mild bit of weathering if you're modeling the 1920-era, or with a really severe weathering job if you're modeling a steam locomotive from the era when diesels had just about taken over. If the locomotive is one of the metal diesel models, the same general construction and chassis-testing tips would apply (except, of course, for the lack of side rods, main rods, and valve gear on a diesel) right through the painting and weathering techniques—even diesels show signs of road grime and exhaust smudges after just a few days of service on a real railroad.

Save that bottle of black paint for simulating holes that you may not want to cut somewhere; black is a shade that is never used on a steam or diesel locomotive model for the simple reason that it makes all that lovely detail disappear! Even the ''Engine Black'' and ''Locomotive Black'' shades that are sold by Scale-Coat and Floquil are a bit on the dark side. I would suggest mixing-in some white, a drop at a time, until you get a very dark grey. Use the dark grey for ''black'' on diesels, trucks, and the like and for the boiler and cab on modern steam locomotives. The smaller detail parts like piping, air compressors, and tanks can then be painted a shade lighter to make them ''pop out'' more realistically. Apply only the barest amount of weathering to the locomotive, mostly in the form of light grey calcium deposit dribbles and oil or rust stains in appropriate colors. You'll be amazed at the added realism such ''artistic license'' will bring to any steam locomotive miniature.

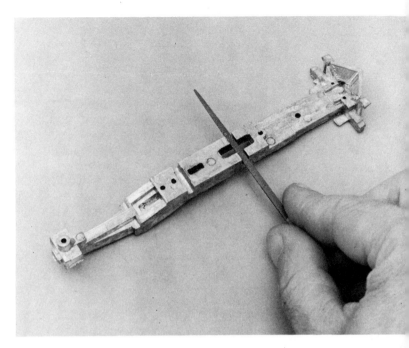

Fig. 7-3 Spend some extra time smoothing the bearings and checking the smooth-rolling qualities of the running gear.

Fig. 7-4 The mold flash on this gear retainer plate can be removed in a moment if you take the time to find it.

VIII

Painting Striping and Lettering

Painting and decaling techniques are, perhaps, the two model building skills that have applications on just about any type of railroad model. It is possible to build a model railroad layout using only ready-to-run equipment but the buildings, even if they are pre-colored plastic, should be painted; and you won't be a model railroader for long before you'll want to try your hand at building one of the craftsman kits that requires both painting and decal lettering. There's a good chance, too, that you'll find some particular locomotive (like the Burlington diesel in Figs. 8-2 to 8-7) that you just can't find as a pre-painted ready-to-run model.

The true secrets of painting and decaling are the paints themselves and a variety of special fluids that can make a decal look like it was hand-painted on the model. Invest a few dollars in the right materials and study the techniques needed to use them.

There are two popular brands of paints for model railroads: Scale-Coat and Floquil. Both are special formulas that provide an ultra-thin coating of paint which won't obscure the finest rivet or wood grain details on your models. Floquil offers a choice of the regular line of lacquer-base paints under the Floquil label and a line of water-base paints under the Polly S label with similar colors in both lines. All these model railroad paints are available in special colors like Scalecoat's Locomotive Black and Floquil's Engine Black as well as authentic railroad colors like Boxcar Red, Reefer Yellow, Coach Green, Penn Central Green, and dozens of others matched to color chips from the prototype railroads.

There are also several other brands of model paints intended for static model aircraft and military miniatures from firms like Testors, Pactra, Imrie Risley, Floquil, and others that may have the colors and shades you are looking for to match some prototype freight car or structure.

All of these paints can be applied, with excellent results and seldom a brush mark, if you use quality sable-hair brushes. Some of the colors are available in aerosol cans to make the work even easier for some modelers. I would suggest, however, that you avoid the temptation to buy anything but a primer color (AMT's model car black lacquer primer is one good one and some of the automobile primers dry with an unusually thin and color-covering coat) and the glossy or flat (nongloss) clear coats which you'll want to preserve and protect the lettering or weathering on the finished model. It is extremely difficult to get a smooth, even finish on something as small as an HO scale model with a spray can; the individual paint droplets are too large and there's too much air pressure and too much paint. You'll have far better and more consistent results if you use a brush for all the color coats.

AIRBRUSHING TECHNIQUES

I've briefly mentioned the artists' airbrush in other chapters, but this is the time to seriously consider the purchase of this rather expensive tool. The airbrush can be adjusted to provide what amounts to a scaled-down version of a regular spray gun's pattern so, in effect, you are using a model spray gun on models.

The airbrush is most useful when you want to control both the amount and color of paint to a fine degree; that's what makes it such a useful tool for weathering models and for

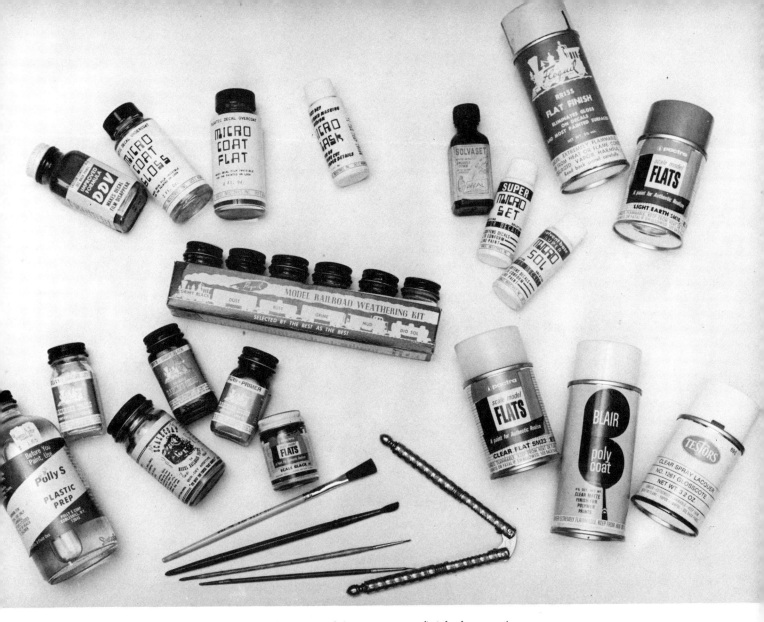

Fig. 8-1 Use model railroad paints on all your models to ensure a finish that won't obscure any of the fine details.

painting complex miniatures like wooden trestles or steam locomotives. It takes some practice to find the right air pressure and paint flow adjustment and to determine the right amount of thinner for each type of airbrush and for each brand of paint.

Most paints, with little or no thinner, can be sprayed to a matte finish with about 40-pounds-per-square inch (psi) of air pressure (adjust it at the air compressor), while paints that have been thinned more than 50-percent can be applied with a smooth and almost glossy finish with about 20 psi. Start with those air pressure figures and work your way downward until you get the effect and coverage you desire. Buy a dozen or so extra

empty paint bottles so you can keep the best mixtures of paint and thinner separate from the unthinned, brush-on paint in the factory bottles; label the bottles with the mixture formulas and the date.

The general idea, in airbrush painting, is to apply just enough paint so that it won't dry before or puddle after it hits the model's surface. If there is too much thinner, the paint won't cover well and it may even attack the undercoat or previously applied colors. Too little thinner will show up as an orange-peel effect on the surface, and it may be so thick as to clog the nozzle of the airbrush. You can get almost the same effects with too little or too much air pressure; too much air will cause the

63

Fig. 8-2   Decals can be used to back-date models to match prototypes no longer available.

Fig. 8-3   Bend a wire coat hanger to serve as a handle so your hands never touch a model that is being painted.

paint to dry before it can adhere firmly to the surface, and too little air pressure can cause the paint to splatter.

A few minute's practice is all you'll need to obtain perfect results with a good airbrush. Be sure to clean the airbrush and nozzle by using pure thinner in the airbrush between every color change and when you're ready to store it. A pipe cleaner, dipped in thinner, can be used to swab away any traces of paint that remain around the bottle attachment, pick-up tube, or nozzle.

MASKING FOR TWO-TONE EFFECTS

The only difficult thing about two-tone paint schemes is the line where the two colors meet; few modelers (or artists) are skilled enough to paint that edge freehand without producing what looks more like a river than a straight line. There are two materials that the modeler can use to make that color separation line nearly perfect: Scotch Magic tape and one of several brands of latex-like liquid masking fluids. For most masking jobs, the two materials can be used in conjunction with one another to take advantage of the best features of both.

Many modelers have had trouble, when masking-off a two-color paint scheme, with the first color coming off as you lift the masking tape. Usually, the paint-lifting problem occurs because the model wasn't thoroughly cleaned (in detergent for plastic models or in vinegar for metal models), rinsed, dried in the air (rag-drying leaves lint and causes static electricity that attracts lint), and then painted with a good primer coat.

The primer coat and the first color coat should be perfectly dry and that can take a matter of days even with lacquer-based

paints; even slightly tacky paint will often lift off along with the tape you use for masking. The tape itself must be removed by pulling it back over itself (as shown in Fig. 8-5) so it will peel, rather than pull, away from the surface.

Always spray (or brush) the lightest colors first; it is always easier to hide a lighter color with a darker one than vice versa. The lighter color may be the smallest area on the model, perhaps even just a 1/8-inch band, but the rule still applies.

When that first color has dried overnight (or longer), the Scotch Magic tape can be applied to "mask-off" the lighter color. Run the edge of the tape about 1/16 inch away from the line that will eventually be the point of color separation and press it down firmly, using a rubber eraser to dab it down over

Fig. 8-4 Masking fluid, applied along the line that will separate a two-color paint scheme, will yield professional results.

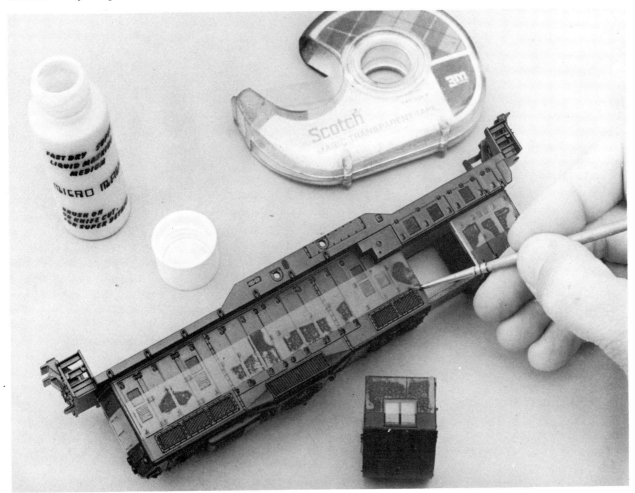

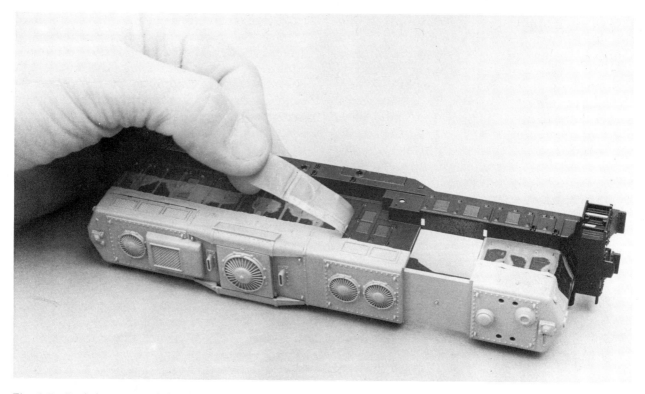

Fig. 8-5 Peel the tape and the dried masking fluid back at a steep angle so the paint doesn't peel off with them.

details. The Magic tape has a unique advantage for masking in that the tape is cloudy until it is adhered, so you can have a visible check as to where it has stuck and where it has not. Cover the 1/16-inch line with two or three coats of a masking fluid like Micro-Scale's "Micro Mask" or Cary's "Magic Masker," but don't worry about leaving a straightedge as you apply the fluid. The masking fluid should actually overlap the eventual color separation line by about 1/16 inch. Let the masking fluid dry for an hour or so.

Then, using a hobby knife and a metal straightedge as a guide, slice through the masking fluid along the exact line you want to serve as the color separation line. Peel the now-dry masking fluid from the still-to-be-painted portion of the model, leaving the remainder on the model to mask the area between the line and the Magic tape. The model is now ready to paint with the second color. The advantage of the masking fluid is that it will seal tightly around the tiniest details and lines, and you'll find it far easier to trim a straight line with a hobby knife and metal

straightedge for a guide than to lay that line down with the edge of the Magic tape. The whole masking process takes just a few minutes (in addition to the drying time for the fluid). If the surface is very large and perfectly flat, you can use the Magic tape alone without the masking fluid.

The Magic tape and the masking fluid are far superior to any type of conventional masking tape because either process leaves a particularly thin covering with a really smooth edge; masking tape is far too thick and the gum on its edge leaves a ragged edge in the color separation line when the tape is removed.

The second color should either be brushed-on or applied with an artist's airbrush. The critical area is the color separation line; the paint must be as thin as possible along that line or a very visible step will be apparent. If you use a brush, apply the paint right up to the line with just the barest trace of color overlapping onto the masked areas. Paint the color separation edge first and then fill-in with the rest of the color.

Use the same procedure with an airbrush;

you can adjust the spray pattern to lay a line that is less than 1/16 inch wide to paint along that color separation line. Allow that second color coat as much time to dry as you did the first; then slice along that color separation line once again with a hobby knife guided by a steel ruler so you don't have to tear through the paint layer when you remove the masking. The Magic tape can now be peeled away back over itself and most of the masking fluid will come off with it. The masking fluid that remains on the model can be picked away with a fingernail or a toothpick, and the masking job is complete.

DECAL LETTERING AND STRIPING

Decals are not supposed to look like shiny plastic with some letters on them but, unfortunately, that's just what they do look like on far too many models. There are some simple methods with which you can avoid that stuck-on look, make that decal-look disappear, and make the letters look as if they were painted right on the model.

A decal is nothing more than a few layers of colored paint (the letters and numbers) and clear paint (the backing that holds the letters together into words). This dried paint has a certain flexibility, so it will curve around a tank car body, for example, but nothing like the cover-all flexibility of wet paint. There are some decal-softening compounds available through any good model railroad shop that soften the decal and its clear film enough so that the decal will snuggle-in around the smallest details almost as well as wet paint. The final touch, in the decal-disappearing act, is to spray the entire model with flat (nongloss) clear paint so the decal film's sheen disappears.

Every brand of model railroad paint currently on the market dries to a perfectly flat, nongloss finish. They're great if you're using dry transfers (although they really don't like to stick to flat finishes very well themselves) or if you're building a model of a structure or assembling a kit with pre-painted sides so you only have to touch-up the paint. That nongloss effect is achieved by having the paint surface dry to a rough texture like microscopic sandpaper.

Decals, even when softened with solvent,

can't find a smooth surface to stick to. One of the reasons a decal may have a cloudy film after it is dry is that the decal isn't really adhering to the surface at all. The solution to the problem is to apply a very light coat of high-gloss clear paint to the areas that will be covered with decals, but that clear coat must be very thin indeed or it will fill-in around the tiny details. You really can't get the glossy clear paint layer thin enough with an aerosol can of clear; the gloss coat should be applied with a brush or, better, with an airbrush.

Micro-Scale has developed a special, predecaling, clear paint that doesn't seem to attack most brands of model railroad paint, but try it on a sample before applying it to a finished model. Sometimes even the clear paints with the same brand label as the colored paints you use have a formula that will attack and soften or etch the color coats. I keep hoping that some model railroad firm will offer a line of high-gloss colors for those of us who rather use decals but, so far, you'll have to settle for that pre-decaling clear gloss coat.

The individual decals or groups of decals, like railroad names, number series, and blocks of dimensional data for freight car sides, should be trimmed from the decal sheet with scissors or a sharp hobby knife. A few firms, like Micro-Scale, stop the clear film at the edge of each group of letters but most others have a solid sheet of clear film over the entire set of decals. If you hold a sheet of Micro-Scale decals so that the light reflects from the surface, you can see exactly where the clear film ends to determine where to cut each separate decal. Other brands should be trimmed as close to the edges of the letters as possible with a razor blade guided by a steel ruler.

Do not touch any surfaces that will be covered with decals; your fingers leave a trace of grease that may prevent the decal from adhering properly. Handle the decals with tweezers until the model is completed and they are protected with a final coat of clear matte-finish paint. Dip the first three or four decals in water just long enough so the water can reach all corners of the decal; immediately remove the decal from the water and rest it on a piece of paper towel. Let the decals sit on the paper towel for a few minutes until the water soaks through the paper backing to dissolve the

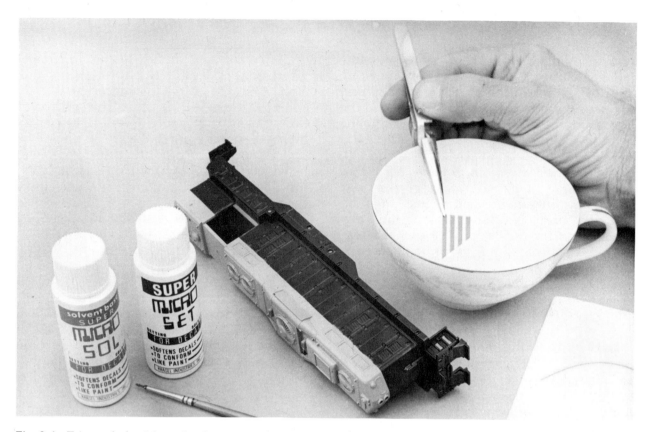

Fig. 8-6 Trim each decal from the sheet and just dip it into water, then set the decal on a paper towel to soak.

Fig. 8-7 Hold the decal in place with a knife tip while the paper backing is pulled from beneath it with tweezers.

glue that holds the decal to the paper. You'll know that the glue is dissolved and the decal is ready to apply when you can move the decal without moving the paper backing.

Brush the thinnest possible layer of decal-softener over the areas where those first three or four decals will be applied. Micro-Scale recommends their "Micro-Set" decal-softener for use beneath the decals or you can use Walthers' "Solvaset" or Champ's "Decal Set." Hold the decal, while it's still resting on its paper backing, over the exact spot where you want the decal to rest. Use the tip of a hobby knife to hold the decal itself while you pull the paper backing from the decal with the tweezers. If the decal seems to float on the layer of decal-softener, you can sponge the excess softener away from the area by gently dabbing a tissue near the edge of the decal. Use the knife tip and a soft paintbrush to move the decal and place it where it belongs.

Apply the other decals to that one side of the model in the same manner but resist any ideas about pressing the decals down on the surface; the softening fluid will do that for you. When all the decals have had time to set for about half an hour, inspect each of them for any signs of trapped air bubbles and prick each bubble with a sharp needle point.

Apply a final coat of softening fluid (Micro-Scale's "Micro-*Sol*" or an additional application of "Solvaset" or "Decal Set") over the surface of each of the decals with a sable hair brush. Apply at least two coats of this final application of decal-softener and allow it to dry for about 12 hours. Inspect all the decals once again for any signs of air bubbles or to find any areas where the decal has not snuggled tightly over details or into grooves or panel lines; and if necessary, apply another coat or two of decal-softener and allow it to dry for 12 hours. Gently rinse the model's surface with water to remove any decal or softener residue and allow it to dry in the air (or blow it dry with an air jet from the air compressor you use for your airbrush).

Finally, spray the entire model with a light coat of clear, matte-finish, enamel like Testor's Dull-Cote or, if you have an airbrush, with Micro-Scale's Micro-Coat Flat.

These same techniques can be used to apply the stripes that appear on modern diesels and streamliners or to apply the gold filigree decals to older passenger cars and steam locomotives.

Benchwork, Trackwork, and Wiring

There is absolutely no exaggeration to the statement that the roadbed which supports the tracks of a model railroad is every bit as important as the roadbed which supports the trackwork on a real railroad. Also, the surface of a model railroad must be firmly supported with the smoothest possible transitions from straight and level tracks to curves or grades. There, though, the similarity between prototype and model ends.

The model railroad must be elevated and the hills and valleys added after the track is in place. Model railroaders face a less obvious problem as well; miniature trains are entirely too noisy, with a tendency to rattle too much if the trackwork is laid directly on any wooden surface, whether soft pine or plywood. There are dozens of types of acoustical panels that can (and have) been used for the roadbed base on various model railroads, but nearly all of them are too soft to hold the small brads needed for some sectional tracks or the scale spikes needed for most other types of model railroad track.

The very best material for any model roadbed is a particular brand of wallboard called "Homosote," but only a very few lumberyards in major cities carry Homosote as a stock item; just about any lumberyard can order the 4' x 8' sheets of ½-inch thick Homosote that are best for model railroad use. Homosote has about the same consistency and the same color as plain grey cardboard. I recommend it without hesitation as the first purchase you should make when you're ready to build a model railroad layout of any size in any scale. The Homosote is not strong enough, however, to be self-supporting; even an unsupported 6-inch span of the material will sag and warp in time and will produce a dip in the track. Most model railroaders support the material with medium grades of ½-inch thick plywood (B grade with filled-in knot holes on one side and C grade with unfilled knot holes on the under side is the best bargain). The Homosote can be attached to the plywood with a few nails or, better, with contact cement. The plywood/Homosote "sandwich" must, then, be supported by some type of tablework to elevate it from the floor.

The only drawback to using Homosote for roadbed is that the material must be cut into strips and curves just a bit wider than the

Building Roadbed and Tablework

ends of the ties and then tapered to simulate the ballast shoulders of most prototype trackwork. The flat sheets of Homosote are fine for yards, but tapering the edges for tracks through the "countryside" is a real bother.

There are three alternate solutions to the taperededge roadbed problem: cork roadbed strips are available with a color and texture that simulates ballast; Campbell offers elevated roadbed pieces with the ballast shoulder and a support to compensate for the thickness of the ties in N and HO scales; and Tru-Scale has a complete milled-wood roadbed and tie section, in HO scale only, that is available either as plain wood or prepainted to simulate the ballast and ties with the track already spiked in place.

Several books recommend the use of the cork roadbed but I have found it to be far more trouble than it's worth. The major advantage of the cork is that it is flexible so you can form curves or cut wedges for switch locations. The Campbell and Tru-Scale wood roadbeds must be purchased in either straight or curved sections with appropriately sized support blocks for switches.

Fig. 9-1 A cross section of well-laid track on individual wooden ties with ballast on a Homosote roadbed supported by pine.

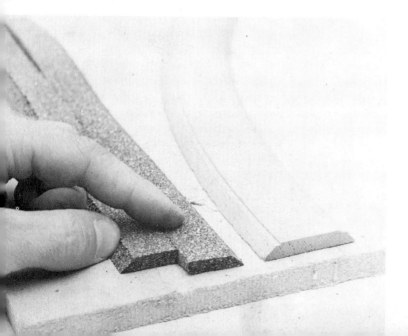

Fig. 9-2 Cork roadbed strips or Campbell brand milled wood roadbed (right) can be used to duplicate main line ballast shoulders.

Semi-flexible sections of both Campbell and Tru-Scale roadbed are available, but their cost is almost double that of the standard straight sections and the switch blocks and other pieces must still be cut to fit. The cork roadbed is too soft to hold track spikes so it is totally impractical for use with individual ties and hand-spiked rail and not much better for use with sectional track. The cork roadbed can be glued or nailed directly to the plywood sub-base but the Campbell or Tru-Scale road-beds should be applied over the top of the Homosote layer. Most modelers who use the Campbell or Tru-Scale roadbed prefer plain sheets of Homosote for areas, such as yards and industrial developments, where the track is heavily concentrated.

BUILDING THE BENCHWORK

The type of benchwork you use to support your roadbed should depend on the type of railroad you envision. If most of your layout will be yards and other perfectly flat areas, then a simple flat-topped table will do nicely. If you expect to have only about one-third of your trackage traveling through "country," then the open grid style is the best choice.

Open-grid benchwork is nothing more than the sides and some crossbraces that would support a normal tabletop except that there isn't any tabletop; the Homosote and plywood roadbed is cut into strips just a fraction of an inch wider than the ends of the ties with curves and straights that follow a pre-planned track plan. Short risers of 1" x 2" or 1" x 4" lumber raise the roadbed about 6 inches or more above the top edges of the benchwork to allow complete freedom for the location of rivers and fills and other scenic features below track level.

It is essential that you have an accurate track plan if you use the open-grid style benchwork because the plywood and Homosote roadbed must be cut to match the location of the actual trackwork. In any case, a plan is a good idea. The roadbed should be wide enough, too, to support any lineside structures like stations or industrial buildings.

Some books advise the use of what is called "cookie cutter" construction: a flat-top table with a plywood and Homosote top. A saber saw or keyhole saw is used to saw through both the Homosote and the plywood *after* all the track is in place so the track and roadbed can be elevated as a unit in the "country" portion of the layout. The major problem with this technique is that the act of sawing, even

Fig. 9-3 This partially completed HO scale layout combines tabletop construction (in the yard) and open-grid benchwork (rear).

Fig. 9-4   Use a pilot bit in an electric drill to speed-up the assembly of benchwork joints; the bit matches the screw size.

with a hand-held keyhole saw, will vibrate the track enough to loosen spikes and ballast and to possibly ruin what might have been a smoothly operating railroad. If you're frightened by the thought of all that careful pre-planning, I'd suggest you start your first layout as an industrial area or yard, perhaps as a module that can become part of a larger layout later.

The benchwork that supports the roadbed should be assembled from the best possible lumber. Bargain priced lumber is often green or full or knots that can cause the entire tablework to warp and bend and shift over the years and can present constant track-alignment problems. Select (knot free) pine, 1″ x 3″, is adequate for most of the supports for the tabletop (or the open grid itself) with cross members spaced a minimum of 2 feet apart. The scrap ends of the 1″ x 3″ pieces can be used for the risers to support the roadbed on an open grid-style table. You can use 1″ x 4″ select-grade pine for the legs if they are braced properly, but 2″ x 4″ pieces are much better. Space the legs no more than 4 feet apart and, if possible, set them back a foot or two from the edges and ends of the benchwork. Thread a ½-inch square-head wood screw into the bottom of the 2″ x 4″ legs to provide a means of making tiny up and down

adjustments to keep the benchwork level; it's amazing how much even a hardwood floor can undulate. The legs should be bolted with ¼-inch carriage bolts and nuts with steel washers between the nuts and the wood.

The benchwork on a large layout (anything larger than 4′ x 8′ should be constructed so it can be disassembled into smaller tables of no more than 4′ x 6′ so you can transport them if you move to a new home. Juggle the size of these take-apart sections so that none of the seams fall across complex trackage like yard throats.

Place the seams on the plywood and Homosote roadbed supports so they fall somewhere within an inch or so of these take-apart seams and splice the joints with a piece of ½-inch plywood attached from the bottom side with wood screws. Assemble all the joints between the benchwork cross members and the points where the track support risers join the cross members with 1½-inch long number 8 slotted-head wood screws. The wood screws will allow you to make major (or minor) adjustments in the benchwork or in the height of the risers without pounding and prying. Try to locate *all* the wood screws so they can be reached from below the layout—the top sides may well be hidden by scenery or roadbed when the layout is completed.

Better hardware dealers can supply special pilot bits that fit a ¼-inch electric drill and cut the exact-size hole needed to install the wood screws without danger of splitting the wood. You may also want to rent or buy one of the Yankee-brand self-driving screwdrivers; this tool makes the task of driving the screws a simple push-in operation with the tool doing the turning. The Yankee screwdrivers are reversible, too, to make screw removal just as easy. The pilot bit and the Yankee screwdriver make screw-assembled benchwork far faster and easier than hammer and nail techniques, and the joints will be far more reliable.

Plan the plywood and Homosote roadbed for your model railroad so you can get the maximum amount of roadbed from each 4′ x 8′ sheet. Cut the curves and straights and wider blocks for switches, double-track areas, or industrial or station locations at one time. Curves, for example, can be cut into so many complete circles or fractions of a circle with a bandsaw or a sabre saw. Don't worry about

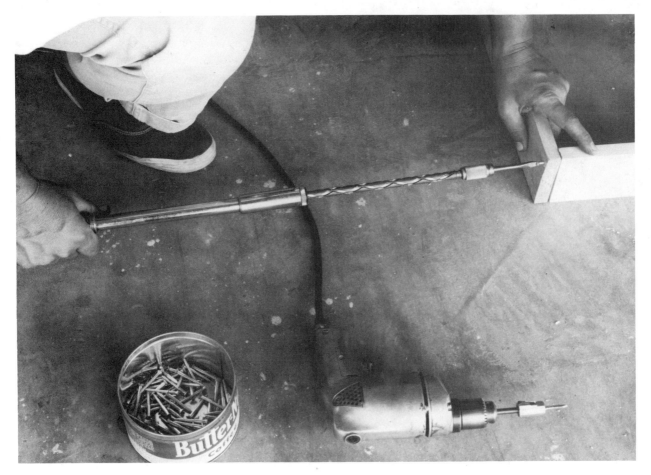

Fig. 9-5 Push on the handle of a Yankee brand screwdriver and the tool does the twisting for you.

Fig. 9-6 Cut the Homosote and plywood roadbed to match the track plan and support it on 1″ x 4″ risers above the open-grid members.

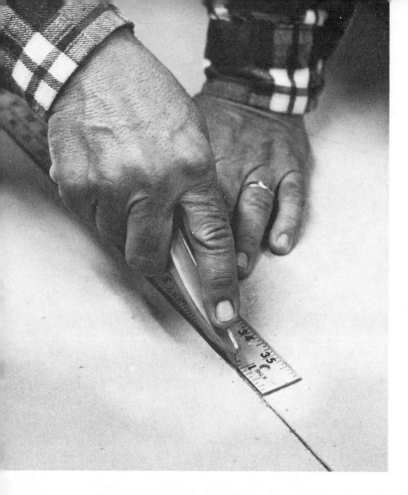

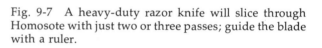
Fig. 9-7 A heavy-duty razor knife will slice through Homosote with just two or three passes; guide the blade with a ruler.

Fig. 9-8 Turntable pits and future bridge locations should be pre-planned so they can be cut before the track is laid.

the length of each curve or straight section of plywood or Homosote roadbed, but do cut about 10 percent more of each size curve and each width straight than you figure you'll need. The pieces can be cut to fit as you install them on the risers that will support them above the basic benchwork grid. You'll likely have to install a few more 1" x 3" cross-members to match the locations of some of the support risers—the plywood and Homosote roadbed should be supported by a riser at least every 24 inches.

The Homosote is just soft enough to allow you to cut it with a heavy-duty razor knife. Two or three passes with the knife is usually enough to slice right through the cardboard-like Homosote. Adjust and align the ½-inch plywood roadbed base to perfectly match the track plan before you attach the Homosote to it. Be particularly careful, if there are any changes in the track's elevation above the benchwork, to see that the valleys at the base of any grades and the humps at the tops of each grade are so smooth and broad as to be barely perceptible changes to the eye.

If your track planning efforts were thorough enough, you should be able to accurately locate any holes or gaps in the roadbed that will later be filled with bridges or turntables. Attach the risers that must support the roadbed on each end of any bridge (and the extra benchwork cross-members that will likely be needed to support the risers) and cut through the plywood and Homosote so you won't disturb the trackwork when you're ready to install the turntable or bridge. A few gussets of ½-inch plywood can be installed with wood screws from beneath the roadbed to hold these sections in place until you're ready to build the bridges or turntables that will replace them.

The height of the tracks above the floor should be decided before you build the benchwork; but if you were wise enough to bolt the legs in place, you can change your mind later and replace the legs with longer or shorter ones. As a general rule, the wider the layout is, the lower it should be for two reasons: to be able to see the tracks and trains near the back of the table and to be able to reach them. You'll find that you can reach much shorter distances as the layout level is raised. For example, you can bend at the waist to reach nearly 4 feet if the layout is only about 3 feet from the floor but you'll only be able to reach about 2 feet if the layout is 5 feet above the floor.

I prefer what is called an "eye level" layout; one that is somewhere between 48 and 58 inches from the floor. The models are closer to the operator so the details can be observed and action, such as steam locomotive side rod motion, coupling, and the like, is more apparent to the eye. You should adjust the minimum and maximum height levels (on a layout with uphill and downhill grades) so they are most comfortable to you, but don't make it so high that a short adult cannot even see the tops of the rails.

Using Sectional Track

The various types and brands of snap-together track sections are, at one and the same time, the boon and the curse of model railroading. Track sections allow a newcomer to assemble the trackwork for a layout in the shortest possible time, but they also place severe limits on the design and the general feeling of flow and grace. I really can't recommend the sectional track, even for a beginner.

I would, however, suggest that a beginner use the switches from the assortment of sectional track but that he substitute the flexible track sections for the smaller straight and curved pieces of track. The many operational disadvantages far outweigh the advantages of using the small pieces of snap-together track.

For example, every rail joint is a potential source of operation problems if it loosens so that it stops the flow of electrical current. Each of those joints is also a potential point where the track can be slightly misaligned and can result in a sharp jog that could derail the locomotives and cars. The sudden transition from straight to curved track can cause extra-long cars to derail when the couplers bind as the car ends are offset when entering the

curve; at best, this sudden transition gives the train a toy-like appearance.

The flexible track sections can be curved to provide an ever-decreasing radius (called a "transition curve") that gradually decreases the radius from nearly straight to that of the rest of the curve. There are several complicated formulae for determining the exact centerline of a transition curve (one method is listed in the *NMRA Data-Pack* book under "Easements"). The easiest way is to use a piece of ¼" x 1" wood lathing placed on edge with the one end parallel to the straight and, a foot past the end of the straight, the other end held to match the curve's radius with the start of the curve about ½ inch in from the straight. Trace the path of the lathing strip with a pencil right on the tabletop and bend and spike the curvable track to match.

The switches that are supplied with most brands of sectional track (except for "scale" trackwork like the Lambert brand and Atlas' Custom-Line series in HO scale) have the curved portion of the track built into the diverging route to present the "transition" problem at each and every switch location. Models of prototype switches (usually identified by a number indicating their degree of sharpness, #4, #6, or #8) have transition or easement curves built into them. Only a few of the AHM switches, the Atlas Custom-Line switches, and Tru-Scale's switches have these easement or transition features and, just incidentally, these three brands are also some of the few HO scale switches (and flexible track sections) that are available in nickle silver rail to add the more reliable electrical pick-up feature of the rail to their attributes.

The Lambert track, with the optional code 70 rail size (in HO scale), is the most realistic of all the various brands of ready-laid track; but the smaller rail can give problems with the oversize wheel flanges used on some of the European-import ready-to-run equipment. Virtually all N scale trackage has grossly oversize rail, but most brands do offer those numbered switches as well as flexible track. The Atlas and AHM brands of snap-together O scale track are about the equivalents, in terms of oversize rail and too-sharp switches, of the average HO scale brass track; but both brands use nickle silver rail and flexible track sections are available. Most O

Fig. 10-1 The snap-together track systems have switches designed to replace standard curved and straight sections.

Fig. 10-2 A Lambert brand ready-laid switch (top) and a Precision brand switch kit with temporary rail-spacing clamps.

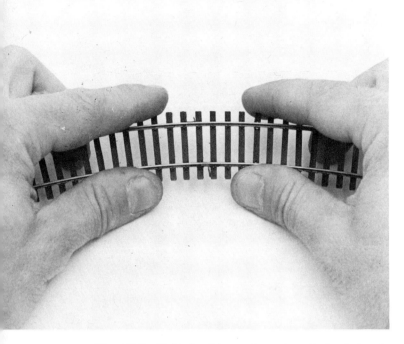

Fig. 10-3 Hold flexible track sections in both hands and "walk" the outer ties apart to form smooth-radius curves.

scale modelers prefer the realism of hand-spiked rail on individual ties so there isn't much choice of ready-laid track in O scale.

There are several track-planning booklets that detail how to use the various brands of snap-together sectional track. With all these systems, there is a certain geometry based on the fractions of a circle that the curved track and switches provide (that's one of the reasons why they have a toy-like appearance) and you must follow the pattern if you expect the ends of the track to line up properly.

Fig. 10-4 The Baumgarten curve gauges fit tightly between the rails to ensure constant-radius curves.

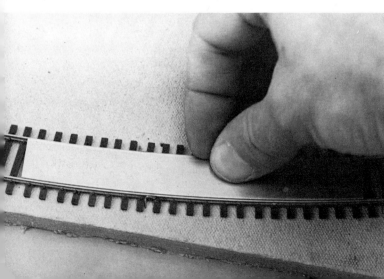

Most of the switches, for example, are designed to replace a section of 9-inch straight track and/or a section of 18-inch radius curved track so you can insert a switch into the plan without having to shuffle a lot of the track sections around. The numbered switches of the more-correctly scaled types of track require a slight offset in each curve that would completely disrupt the geometry of the typical sectional track system. The ends of most brands of HO and N scale track (except for the N scale Rapido track) will mate with one another, but the geometric systems can vary from one brand to the next so you'd best be careful with alignment if you do decide to mix brands of snap-together track.

The various brands of flexible track all use a similar system to achieve their flexibility; every other tie-connecting bit of plastic beneath each rail is cut through so the adjacent ties can spread as the track is bent from a straight to a curve. These flex track sections are furnished as straights so they can be used as-is for tangent track and bent to whatever radius (or transition) desired. Hold the track between the thumb and first finger of each hand and gently 'walk' the outer ties apart while you exert a gentle pressure to force the track into a smooth-radius curve. All the track centerlines should be marked on the tabletop whenever you're using sectional track (or laying separate ties and rail for that matter), so you can use the curve you've marked with a trammel as a guide to determine that the radius is constant all the way through the piece of track you are "curving." Baumgarten has a series of alignment gauges in aluminum that fit snugly between the rails of HO scale track so you can be sure you have a smooth and consistent radius throughout the curve. The Baumgarten line is available to dealers through Wm. K. Walthers.

It's much easier to curve any type of sectional track if you start at one end and work your way toward the opposite end. Try to incorporate the transition from straight to curve in one single section of flexible track whenever possible to minimize any misalignment problems. You'll find that curving the flexible track moves one of the rails so that it protrudes past the ends of the ties at the end of the track section. Chances are, you'll want to cut that section somewhere in the center to fit a switch in place; if not, the pro-

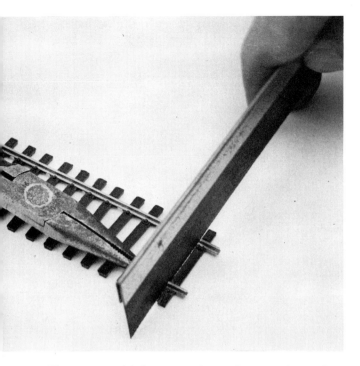

Fig. 10-5 Hold the rail with needle-nose pliers while cutting it to length with a razor saw so the ties aren't damaged.

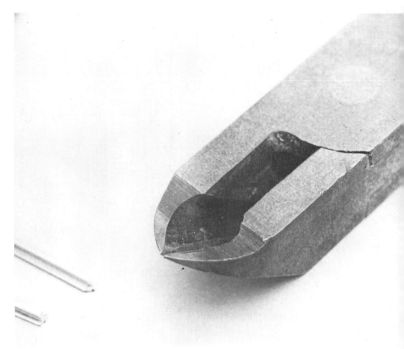

Fig. 10-6 The Lambert brand "Rail Nippers" cut the rail perfectly on one side with all the taper on the opposite side.

truding rail end should be cut so it is just a bit longer or a bit shorter than the next rail so the rail joints won't be directly across from one another. Staggering the ends of the rail helps to avoid kinks in the track, especially on curves.

The rail can be cut with a razor saw but be sure to hold the rail tightly with a pair of needle-nose pliers so the rail isn't ripped from the plastic ties by the force and vibration from the saw teeth. The Lambert Rail Nippers are diagonal wire cutters especially designed to cut model railroad rail; the cutters snip-off the rail with a perfectly flat cut on one side and a much-tapered one on the other. The tapered side of the cut should, of course, be on the scrap end of rail. The plastic tie tops should be shaved enough to allow the rail joiner to fit without creating even the smallest hump in the track. Slice between the bottom of the rail and the tops of the ties with a hobby knife, and shave-away enough material to give ample clearance for the stamped-metal rail joiner. The ends of the rail that have been cut, with either a razor saw or the Rail Nippers should be filed smooth so the rail joiner can slip smoothly in place. Squeeze the

sides and top flanges of the rail joiner tightly against the base of the rail with needle-nose pliers to assure a tight and electrically sound joint.

You'll find that you must do a lot of fitting and piecing-together to complete a layout with flexible track sections. The track plan should first be transferred directly to the tabletop (or roadbed). You can use the switches

Fig. 10-7 Slice and shave the tops of the ties so the rail joiners will fit without forcing the rail upward.

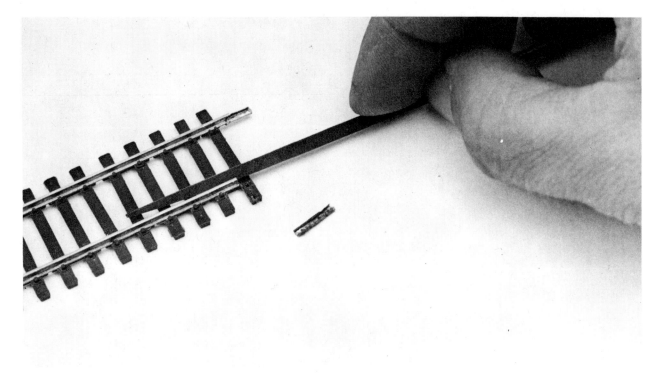

Fig. 10-8   File any cut rail ends so the rail joiners will slide smoothly into place and to remove burrs from the rail head.

Fig. 10-9 Slip the rail joiners in place and squeeze them tightly against the base of the rail for a positive joint.

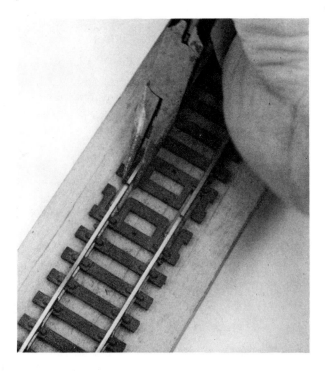

themselves as templates or lay a piece of paper over the switch rails and rub the tops of the rails, through the paper, with a soft lead pencil to transfer the outline of the rails to the paper. The outer ends can then be cut with scissors along those rail lines to provide a paper switch template to use when laying out the full-size track plan on the Homosote.

When it comes time to actually lay the track, begin by positioning each of the switches. In some cases, a portion of the ties and the rail must be removed from the ends of one or two of the ready-laid switches so they will fit the track plan. Do that rail-cutting and fitting first and then spike the switches in place, using the technique with scale-size spikes outlined in the chapter on laying individual ties and rails.

There are holes for spikes on each side of the rail at about every fifth tie on the plastic switch and flex-track ties. You can drill a few additional holes beside the switch rails or near the ends of the track sections if you need more places to put spikes to keep the track in perfect gauge and alignment. Buy two or

Fig. 10-10 An exaggerated example of the type of misalignment that causes derailments; use spikes to force the rails over.

three track gauges from your dealer so you can check the gauge (the width between the rails) at every rail joint and double-check again using the NMRA Standards Gauge (follow the instructions furnished with the gauge).

The flexible track sections can be spiked in place next, but remember to carefully curve and fit each section before even starting to spike it down. Ballast can be applied later by simply spreading it between and around the ties with a brush and then dropping on a so-lution of two parts water to one part Liquitex Matte Medium (a latex-like liquid cement) with an eye dropper. The Matte Medium will spread itself throughout the ballast and beneath the ties to bind the track to the tabletop and to the ballast itself. I prefer the Matte Medium to cements like white glue because the Matte Medium is more flexible to help absorb sound and because it allows the track to be relocated by simply forcing a putty knife under the ties.

XI

One Tie at a Time

The thought of actually laying track with individual wooden ties, spikes, and rails may sound like the absurd excess of a hobbiest who's gone just one step too far in his search for realism. The process, however, isn't really that time-consuming thanks to some clever tie-laying jigs and ballasting techniques that have been developed in the hobby during the last few years. It is certainly the most realistic way to lay track and, surprisingly, it is the least expensive method as well.

The individual tie, spike, and rail system also allows you to provide a most prototypically smooth flow of track through switches and transitions from straight-to-curved track far easier than with flex-track sections. If you can afford to purchase one of the Kadee spikers (it works much like a staple gun with special staples which split into two realistic "spikes"), you can lay this type of trackwork as quickly as any other.

This do-it-yourself track-laying system begins, like any other track-laying system, with an accurate scale track plan and the transfer of that plan to the Homosote roadbed. Draw the centerlines of the track first and note that with this system (again, as with any sectional or

flex-track system) the locations and exact alignment of the switches and any crossings is the critical step. I would suggest that you draw both of the rails at each switch location right on the Homosote in the exact position you want them. You can cut a few paper templates (as outlined in the previous chapter) to help locate switches that are grouped closely together; it's far easier to erase a mistake and redraw it than to rip-up and re-lay the track. You can use just the centerline for the individual tracks or you can draw the rail locations there too. Use a trammel (a wood stick with a hole for a pencil and nail holes located at the various radius sizes you use) to locate the curves accurately too, because you will be using those lines to guide your rail-laying later on. Most modelers apply ballast right after they lay the ties, but I would suggest you wait to apply the ballast until all the rails are in place and checked for proper operation with trains.

There are several brands of ties available in all the popular scales and the HO scale modeler even has a choice of fir, redwood (they don't *have* to be stained), or hard balsa wood ties. Most brands are sold without a stain coloring but you can buy pre-stained ties if you desire. Most of the ties are an exact scale length and width but their height is reduced so you don't have to apply such a thick layer of ballast. You'll need some of the extra-long switch ties as well; the ties on prototype switches get progressively longer as the tracks diverge until the ties are almost double length and then two separate sets of ties begin.

The ties sold as "switch ties" are all the same length, the longest likely to appear on any prototype switch. The modeler must cut them to the various lengths required, using a ready-laid switch or one of the commercially made paper templates as a guide. Don't forget to mark the exact location of the switch points so you can provide the two extra-length ties to support the switch-operating stands that appear on the prototype. The ties at crossings are usually laid-out in ever-increasing lengths much like switches, so determine their lengths and locations and cut switch ties to the proper lengths.

When prepared, you can dye the switch ties and the standard ties in a commercial tie stains like Campbell or Simpson or prepare your own stain from black and brown Rit

Fig. 11-1   You can stain just one tie at a time but it's quicker to hold them in a strainer to
dip dozens into the stain.

clothes dye or from a concoction of shoe polishes. The "black" dyes and polishes are often more on the blue or purple side, however, so try several samples before you stain a whole batch of ties. Prototype tie colors range from a light grey to a reddish/brown shade of fresh creosote, so you can color the ties to suit your own ideas. It's not unusual to see stretches of prototype track with an assortment of newly creosoted ties and older weathered grey ones, so you can do the same type of thing on your miniature trackwork if you like.

The plastic tie and rail-spacing jig by Ramax (available to dealers through Walthers) is an excellent tool for the HO scale (or HOn3) modeler because it provides both a jig for spacing the ties and, on the reverse side, slots to hold the rail while you spike it in place.

The Ramax jig is flexible so it can be used for straight or curved rail-laying; but it will not work with the Kadee Spiker gun, only with individual spikes. The tie-spacing feature, however, can be useful even for those who use Kadee's Spiker tool.

You can make your own tie-spacing jig by cutting slots in a 1" x 3" board or by gluing spacer blocks to the top of the board. Prototype ties are usually spaced about 21 inches apart; subtract the width of your ties (in *scale* inches) from 21 *scale* inches and buy some of the stripwood that is sized in scale inches for the blocks that will space the ties in the jig (3/64" x 1/8" stripwood is about right for HO scale tie-spacing jigs). Cut the stripwood into pieces that match the length of the ties you are using and glue them to the wide side of the 1" x 3" board. Cut enough of the spacers (and a long strip of the 1″ x 3″ board) to space about 2 feet of ties at a time. Glue a single strip of the spacer-size stripwood to one end of the spacers to serve as a stop so you have a piano keyboard-like jig similar to the one in Fig. 11-2.

Place each tie into the slots in the jig with the tie's broad side down and with one end butted against the backstop. When all the ties are in place, press a length of masking tape tightly over them so it touches each tie. Roll the tape over the ties with your thumb so the ties don't shift from side-to-side in the jig. The strip of masking tape, with ties attached, can now be lifted gently from the spacing jig. Coat the roadbed with some undiluted Liquitex Matte Medium (glue), covering an area about ¼-inch wider than the ends of the ties; and while the Matte Medium is still tacky, press the strip of ties in place so they are centered precisely over that track centerline you drew on the Homosote roadbed (the pencil line should show through the Matte Medium). Hold the ties down with a board while you pull the masking tape straight up and away from the ties. Remove the board and reposition any of the ties that might have

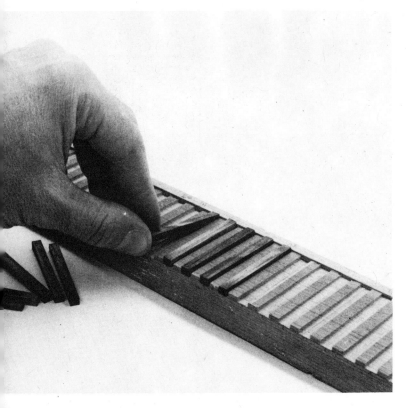

Fig. 11-2   Build a tie-spacing jig like this one and slip the stained ties into each slot with their ends against the stop.

Fig. 11-3   Gently lay a piece of masking tape over the tops of the ties in the tie-spacing jig and press the tape down.

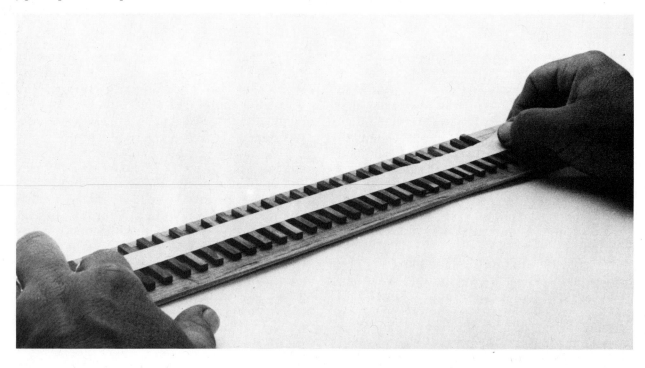

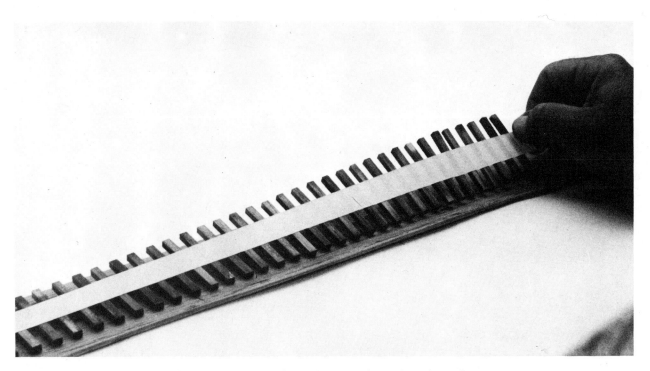

Fig. 11-4   The entire string of ties can be lifted from the jig without disturbing their spacing if you're careful.

Fig. 11-5   Brush some Liquitex brand artist's Matte Medium over the roadbed where the string of ties will rest.

Fig. 11-6   Place the ties and tape in place on the roadbed and hold the ties down with a board while the tape is removed.

Fig. 11-7 After the Matte Medium has dried, sand the tops of the ties lightly with a sanding block.

moved during the process. There is a slight stagger and misalignment on all prototype ties so your model ties don't have to be in perfect alignment, but they should be pretty close to perfect.

The next step if often overlooked by modelers who are in too much of a hurry to get the rails laid. Wrap a piece of fine-grade sandpaper around the rounded corners of a 2" x 4" scrap of lumber to use as a sanding block. The rounded corners will prevent the sanding block from picking at the ends of the ties and knocking them loose. When the Matte Medium has dried overnight, the tops of the ties can be sanded with this sanding block. Work back and forth across the track (along the grain of the sides) with light pressure; all you're doing is sanding-off the tops of those ties to even them off. You'll notice, after just a bit of sanding, that some ties have no stain remaining while others haven't even been touched by the sanding block. You can stop sanding when about one out of every three ties still has a fresh-stained appearance. Touch-up the ties with stain, using a paintbrush dipped in whatever you used for tie stain; now, the ties are ready for the rails.

There's something strangely satisfying about laying model railroad track the same way the real railroads do—with individual spikes. This is the best way to hold the track in place whether it's the snap-together sectional track, flex-track sections, or the "ultimate" of laying one rail at a time.

The prefabricated types of track often have holes in the centers of the ties to accept small nails but those nails are far more noticeable than you would expect; the spikes do just as good a job and they are positioned where they should be. The spikes are essential, of course, to lay individual rails (there is a gluing method we'll discuss later) but they are even more essential to align the cut ends of the flexible track sections.

Most model railroad dealers carry a variety of different spike sizes and lengths. Buy the smallest wire-size spike you can with a length of about 3/8 inch for HO or N scale trackwork and about ½ inch for O scale trackwork. Buy just one box and try them; some brands have a weak design that allows the spike heads to snap-off while you're driving them in place so you may want to try another brand. If you are laying individual rails on hand-laid wooden ties, I would recommend the purchase of Kadee's Spiker. This tool is a special model railroad product that operates like a staple gun to drive two spikes at a time, one

XII

Hand-Spiked Trackwork

on each side of the rail. This not only speeds-up track-laying but provides a spike head that is small enough to be truly realistic. Kadee sells their superb line of couplers, trucks, and N scale equipment through hobby dealers but the Spiker is sold only direct to the customer from Kadee Metal Products, 720 So. Grape Street, Medford, OR 97501. The Spiker is an expensive tool but it will last a lifetime. The chances are you'll want to drive spikes in every tie with the Kadee tool, so be sure to order plenty of them.

Needle-nose pliers provide the best tool for driving conventional spikes. Grip the spikes at a slight angle as shown in Fig. 12-1 and press them in with downward and a bit of sideward force to be sure they grip the rail tightly. Press the spike into the tie until the pliers' tip touches the rail; then use the tip of the pliers, in the closed position, as a punch to push the spike down. The tip of the pliers can be used to push the rail and the spike a fraction of an inch to correct slightly out-of-gauge or out-of-alignment rails. Flexible track and matching ready-laid switches, like the Lambert brand, have tiny pre-punched holes for spikes at about every fifth tie.

Fig. 12-1   Hold track spikes just behind the head in the tips of needle-nose pliers.

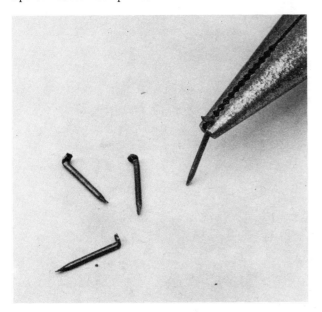

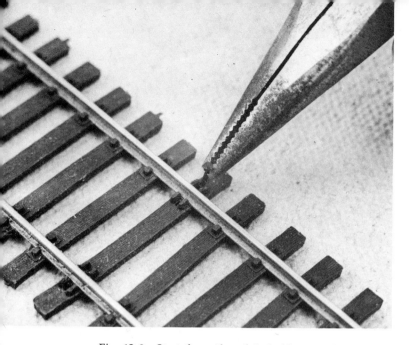

Fig. 12-2 Start the spike while holding it, then push it home with the closed tip of the pliers.

Fig. 12-3 The Kadee Spiker works like a staple gun to drive two spikes at a time almost as fast as you can squeeze it.

The ends of the ties and the pencil lines discussed in the previous chapter should provide enough guidance for laying individual rails on wooden ties *if* you are patient enough to wait to lay the ballast. Buy three or four of the three-point style track gauges for this type of track laying. The three-point gauge automatically widens the track gauge a few thousandths of an inch if you remember to place it on the curve with the single point toward the center of the curve. Alternate the positions of the gauges, as shown, for spiking straight track or switches. Use a steel ruler, at least 12 inches long, to guide the Kadee Spiker (or your hand-held needle-nose pliers) along any straight stretches of trac; and sight down the rail frequently to be sure it is going down straight. Get that first rail perfect and the second one will go down much faster.

Some modelers attach one of the three-point track gauges to a wooden trammel with a bolt for the pivot point of the trammel so they are sure that their curves are precise; a process I recommend. The track gauges will only be necessary when you're ready to lay that second rail; they provide accurate spacing (gauge) between the two rails. You can practice spiking on straight and curved sections of track to learn the techniques but don't connect the rails to within 2 feet of any switches at first. Once you know how to handle the Kadee Spiker (or the needle-nose pliers and individual spikes), the switches and all the short stretches of track that connect the switches to one another should be spiked in place.

Switch "kits" for hand-spiked track are available (in HO scale) from Precision Scale Models, Box 74, Far Hills Branch, Dayton, OH 45419; or you can buy the Simpson, Railcraft, and other brands from your dealer. These kits have pre-assembled frogs, points, and pre-bent guard rails. Spacer bars are attached to the tops of the rails to hold the various parts in alignment while you spike the switch rails in place. If you're skilled in the use of a soldering iron and file, you can fabricate your own switches to the standards and dimensions in the *NMRA Data-Pack* book, from lengths of straight rail. Many modelers use ready-laid switches (like the Lambert brand) to avoid the alignment and fitting problems in those areas with wooden ties and use individual rails for the other trackwork.

Some rail sizes are too small to allow the use of spikes because the wheel flanges will hit the spike heads. N scale modelers who want to hand-lay their own track with code 70 rail and HO scale (and HOn3) modelers who want to match the light rail used on the prototype branch lines (there are spikes small enough to allow the use of rail as small as code 55 in HO if you're very careful) find that they have to actually glue the smaller rail sizes to the ties. It's a tricky process but it can be done with practice and patience.

You'll need a tie-spacing jig like the one described in the previous chapter or one of the Ramax jigs (for HO or HOn3). Insert the ties in the jig and be sure that they are all butted against their stops. Next, apply a thin bead of Goodyear Pliobond cement to the bottom of a piece of rail. Hold the rail above the ties and gently touch it to the ties and apply a tiny dab of the Pliobond to each tie where the rail will rest; then lift the rail away to apply a second thin bead of Pliobond to the bottom of the rail and press the rail permanently in place on the ties. Let the glue dry for at least an hour and then pick the piece of rail, with the ties attached, from the tie-spacing jig and glue it to the Homosote roadbed with Liquitex Matte Medium as previously described. You'll likely have to realign some of the ties that were too thin to stick firmly to the rail. Let the Matte Medium dry overnight and then apply the second rail, with a half-dozen track gauges to keep in alignment with the

Fig. 12-4 The Ramax track-laying jig holds and spaces ties on one side and grips and gauges the rails on the other.

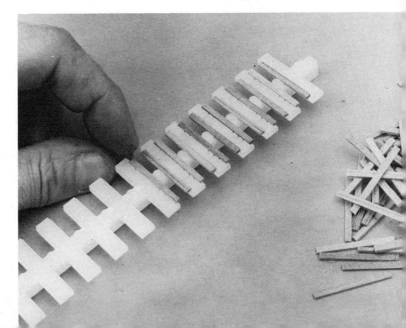

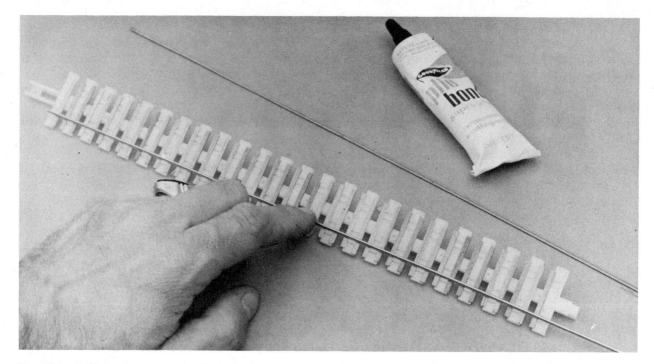

Fig. 12-5   Rail that is too small to be spiked can be glued with Pliobond cement to the ties in the Ramax jig.

Fig. 12-6   Glue one rail, lift the rail and the ties from the jig, and glue them to the roadbed before adding your second rail.

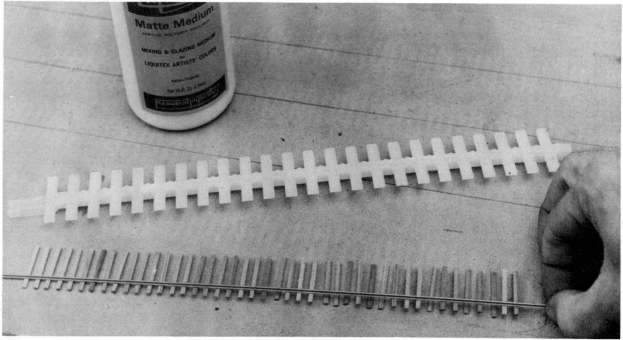

first rail, using the same two-coat Pliobond glue procedure. If the rail must be adjusted after the Pliobond has dried, you can do so by heating the rail slightly with a soldering iron to heat and soften the Pliobond.

BALLAST APPLICATION TIPS

Your model railroad dealer should be able to supply a wide choice of specially prepared scale model ballast in a wide range of colors from several different suppliers. Pick a color that you feel is most appropriate for the area and type of railroad you are modeling. Prototype ballast varies in color from a light grey "fresh" granite to a "dirty" dark grey to the almost black shade of cinders (in the steam locomotive era) to the beige or red color of local rock.

The size of the model ballast particles varies with the intended scale—O scale ballast is larger than HO scale and N scale ballast is smaller than HO scale. The N scale ballast seems more appropriate for HO scale (to my eyes) and the HO ballast seems best on O scale track. You may even want to use a finer, almost dust-size ballast sifted through a fine-mesh strainer using genuine dirt. However, with a magnet, check any dirt you may want to use to be sure that it doesn't contain any magnetic particles that could be picked up by the locomotive's magnets.

Pour a tiny pile of the ballast down the center of the track and brush it into place with a soft-bristle paintbrush. You may have to apply some more Matte Medium to the sloping sides of the roadbed to get the ballast to stick, but do *not* apply glue anywhere near the working parts of any switches. Carefully brush every last speck of ballast away from the switch frogs, guard rails, and the moving switch points and their throw bar.

Apply a few drops of oil (be sure to use the LaBelle brand that won't melt plastics around any plastic track) to these same parts of the switches. Thin a half-pint of the Matte Medium with two parts water to one part Matte Medium and apply the fluid to the ballast with an eye dropper. You'll be able to see the Matte Medium work its way through the ballast. Do not actually touch the eye dropper to the ballast or the ballast will stick to it and

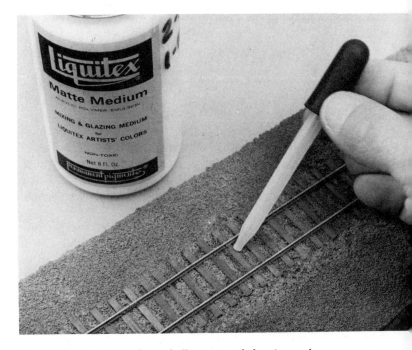

Fig. 12-7 Spread the loose ballast around the ties and the edges of the roadbed with a brush, then apply the glue.

you'll have a real mess, and try to keep the fluid away from the tops of the ties and from the switch points and throw bar. If the fluid puddles on top of the ballast, rather than soaking its way in, you can add two or three drops of Ivory Liquid detergent as a wetting agent to the thinned Matte Medium.

Let the Matte Medium dry overnight and vacuum the trackwork to remove any excess ballast. If you use a clean bag in the vacuum you can salvage the ballast that is vacuumed away. You may find several spots where the Matte Medium didn't reach; these can be recovered with fresh ballast and more drops of Matte Medium applied to complete the job.

The Homosote roadbed should have been coated with one layer of the Matte Medium to seal it when you laid the ties. If you missed that step, you'll find that the ballast isn't bonded to the Homosote but only to itself and it will form a crust that will soon crack and disintegrate. If that happens, vacuum away the ballast: apply a sealer coat of the Matte Medium with an eye dropper to the areas between the ties; and repeat the ballasting operation all over again.

SUPER-DETAILED TRACKWORK IDEAS

Study any stretch of prototype trackwork and you'll find that it doesn't look much like your carefully laid and ballasted track. The real rails are always rusty and the ballast and ties are spotted and stained with drops of oil and sand (sand is dumped on the rails in front of the locomotive's drive wheels whenever extra traction is needed). Chances are, there are also a few weeds and a bit of debris. It's time, once again, for you to look at the world through an artist's eye.

Finely sifted light-beige sand can be applied over the ballast (in a few spots) if the ballast is wetted with the thinned solution of Matte Medium—just be sure to vacuum-away any excess sand so it doesn't get into the oily locomotive and car bearings. Well-thinned black paint can be dabbed here and there near the rails to simulate those oil dribbles and a few spots of "earth" colored paint (to match whatever color you expect to use on the surrounding scenery) can be sprayed lightly to simulate wind-blown dust.

The switch frogs and guard rails and every rail joint abound in bolt heads. These can be simulated with tiny bits of 0.005 or 0.010-inch thick plastic with the "bolts" embossed into the backside with a nail point. Glue these simulated rail joiners and bolt plates only to the outside of the rails (so the models' wheel flanges won't hit them and derail) with Pliobond. You can even make a light saw cut

Fig. 12-8   You have to know what the prototype *really* looks like before you can recreate the subtle shadings in miniature.

Fig. 12-9 This HO scale track has four Kadee spikes per tie, simulated bolt-on rail joiners, and "rusty" rails.

across the tops of the rails every 16-scale feet to simulate the prototype's rail sections (unless you're modeling one of those modern railroads that use nearly endless lengths of welded rail); any simulated rail joiners should be centered over the saw nicks.

The most important detail touch, however, is to paint the sides of all the rails with a rust color. Floquil's "Flo-Paque" series of craft paints includes a brown that is about the right shade (it's number F-71) or you can blend and mix the orange shade of Floquil's model railroad rust color with some boxcar red or roof brown to get the shade that seems best to your eyes. Use a number-one paintbrush and just drag it along the sides of the rails. Some of the rust will spatter on the

spikes and ties but that happens on the prototype too.

Don't worry about any specks of paint that get on the tops of the rails; the paint can be scraped away quickly with a razor blade after it dries. Do be careful to keep the paint away from those moving switch points and their connecting bar, however. The only part of this track-detailing process that takes any significant amount of time is the fabrication of those bolt plates and simulated rail joiners, and they can be omitted if you're in a hurry. The other detailing steps can be accomplished in an evening or two and the results are nothing short of astonishing; after all, track is really the most important "scenic" item on your railroad.

XIII

Remote Control Switches

One of the Christmas-time dreams about around-the-tree trains is to be able to change the train's path around the track by remote control. Real railroads do use remote-control switch operation but only on the main line's tracks; the industrial spurs and all the switches on branch lines are operated right at the switch. Both types of control have their place in model railroading so consider the manual operation seriously before you decide that remote control is really what you want—it may not be worth the bother or the expense.

The modeler has the same three choices of switch control as the prototype: (1) electric switch machines located near the switch but controlled by push buttons or toggle switches some distance away; (2) controls by rods or cables to a switch lever panel away from the switch, perhaps in a control or interlocking tower; or (3) manually operated switch stands that appear beside the switches.

Each switch on a model railroad, however, is even more complex than the prototypes because the miniature switches must carry electrical current (without creating a short circuit)

as well as provide the choice of diverging routes for the trains themselves. This dual role is probably the single major bugaboo in any model railroad system; a problem only if you ignore it in hope that some manufacturer of switches has solved it for you—and only one has, Lionel with their three-rail system.

The switch controls, whether remote or beside the switch, control the switch and the flow of electrical current, so I'm going to have to jump ahead a chapter or two and introduce you to the fundamental principle of model railroad wiring for two-rail trackage: namely that one rail supplies the power (call it "positive," if you like) and the other rail returns the power (call it "negative"). If the two rails touch, as they can at a crossing or a switch, there's a possibility of a short circuit *if* the electrical connections are made so the power flows *in* from either of the diverging routes. Proper wiring and gaps (cuts in the rail with a bit of insulation inserted in the cut to provide an electrical current-flow "gap") must be used to prevent such short circuits.

The electrical current that flows through those rails, however, is directed toward the diverging routes at each switch just as the trains are. The operating (and sometimes short circuit) problems usually develop on the diverging route that the switch is *not* set for; if some additional wiring and gaps are not provided, no other train can operate on any trackage along the "dead" route.

The "fixed control" types of switches provide that flow automatically because both diverging routes always have power available, through the switch rails, regardless of which way the switch points may be set. Most of the N, HO, and O scale track switches in the snap-together lines of sectional track have this type of "fixed control"; but most of these brands can be easily modified into the "selective control" type of switch, if the modeler is willing to run a few extra wires.

The "selective control" switches are generally a better choice for the model railroader who wants to operate trains and switcher-type locomotives. The frogs in these types of switches are gapped and insulated so the electrical power flows only down the rails in the direction that the switch points have been set to direct the trains. The alternate route's trackage is electrically "dead," so no trains can operate on it unless the modeler provides some additional wire connections (and some gaps to prevent short circuits).

In many cases, the selective control type of system will simplify wiring because the switches can turn sidings on or off automatically without having to push buttons or flip toggles on the control panel. You can, for example, have two locomotives on the same layout by "parking" one on a siding while you operate the other. When it's time for the second locomotive to be operated, the first engine is simply run into a siding and the switch thrown for the main line; the switch to the "parked" locomotive's siding is then thrown to the siding route and that locomotive receives the electrical current. Most of the switch kits for hand-spiked track have this selective control feature, and the snap-together switches often have instructions that show how to modify them from fixed control to selective control.

TWO SWITCHES FOR TWO JOBS

The point of this digression into "selective control" and "fixed control" was to impress upon you the importance of the switch points in directing electrical current as well as the trains. If those switch points don't make a firm contact against the rail, neither type of switch will provide any electrical power flow beyond those switch points! The switch points may press against the rail firmly enough to allow the locomotive and car wheels to roll without derailing but not firmly enough (because of a speck of lint or some oxidation) to allow the flow of electrical current.

This electrical flow problem will plague you, at every track switch, until you install a separate set of electrical contacts at each and *every* switch so that the track directs the trains and the electrical contacts direct the current.

Fig. 13-1   The ready-laid switches, like N-scale Bachmann, Life-Like, and Rapido-brands, mount the switch machines *on* the table.

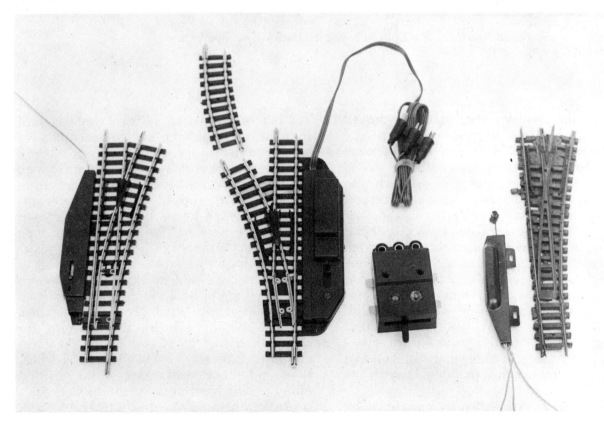

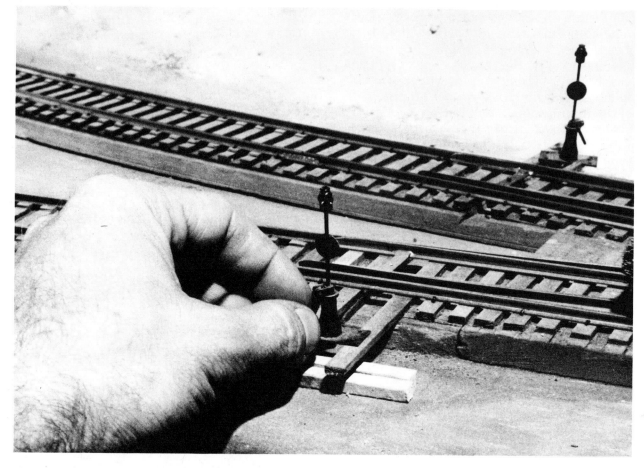

Fig. 13-2 Most models of switch stands are placed beside the track just to improve the realism but these operate the switches.

(Few of the snap-together or do-it-yourself switch kits have this feature; you have to add it to your trackwork and wiring system yourself.) The extra contacts are a bother to install but they will eliminate so many headaches in years to come that I must recommend that you install them as soon as you possibly can after each switch is in place. The same control that moves the track switch's points can be used to actuate the electrical contacts that will direct the electrical current. You will have to run wires (beneath the table) from the two incoming rails and from both of the rails on both diverging routes (a total of six wires), but they will help to simplify future electrical wiring and virtually guarantee that you won't be bothered with switches that don't switch the power.

The accessory "switch machines" sold by Lambert, Kemtron, ConCor, Pacific Fast Mail, and others have these electrical contacts built into the machine (the switch machines for snap-together track switches do not); or if you want to control your switches manually, you can buy a separate set of such contacts from any electronics supply store. The tabletop-mounted switch levers like the ones shown here (or the popular "George's Pet" cam-type levers) are a bit more difficult to adapt to actuate an under-the-table electrical contact as well as the track switch, but it can be done if you're willing to fiddle with extensions from the switch or the switch lever. The electrical contacts should be below the table (or enclosed in a dust-proof box beside the track and hidden by scenery or a removable structure) and that's also where you'd position either a switch machine or the linkage for a manually operated remote-control cable, rod, or lever.

Fig. 13-3   The Slim Gauge Guild uses automobile choke cables to actuate most of their switches by manual remote-control.

MANUAL REMOTE CONTROL

The most popular and least-expensive method of controlling track switches (and hidden electrical contacts for them) is the simple choke cable like you may remember using on an older automobile. These cables can be purchased for $2 or less (if you shop in surplus and discount stores) complete with a knob and, often, a mount for the working end of the cable.

The "Anderson" type of turnout (switch) linkage (shown in Figs. 13-8 and 13-9 with the ConCor switch machines) works just as well with a choke cable. The linkage transfers the choke cable's pull through the table and to the switch points' throw bar. The Slim Gauge Guild devised a sliding-style linkage above and below the table with a stiff wire or rod to connect the two. They use a tiny electrical switch called a "micro-switch" (available for less than a dollar from surplus stores) to direct the electrical power through the track rails; the same action that actuates the switch linkage nudges the lever on the micro-switch to change the electrical current flow from the main line to the branch line. You'll have to make your own version of the Slim Gauge Guild's sliding action linkage from square brass tubing sizes that telescope inside one another; but the Anderson linkage is sold through model railroad dealers under the Eshleman label.

Modelers have adapted electrical switches (the microswitch is just one such example) for years, but Fred Miller was the first I've seen to adapt the newer slide-type electrical switch for use as a set of contacts beneath a model railroad track switch. His system was described in the June 1969, *Model Railroader* magazine. I've tried several such systems myself and seen others on model railroad layouts so I know it works. It is, perhaps, the simplest way of combining a choke cable (Miller used just a length of brass rod), electrical contacts, and a positive, spring-action setting for the switch points themselves. The linkage requires one of the better-quality D.P.D.T. type slide switches ($3 or so from an electronics supply store), 2-inches or so of 0.025-inch steel piano wire (a common model airplane material—you can substitute a length of hairpin); and some 0.010-inch thick brass for the mounting bracket (you may find a small angle, like those from toy Erector sets, in a surplus store that will work).

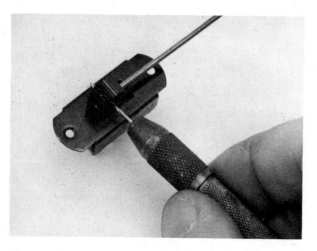

Fig. 13-4 A spring-loaded, slide-style, D.P.D.T. switch can do double duty as a circuit-selector and switch linkage.

Fig. 13-5 A short length of 0.025-inch spring steel wire moves the switch points whenever the rod moves the D.P.D.T. switch.

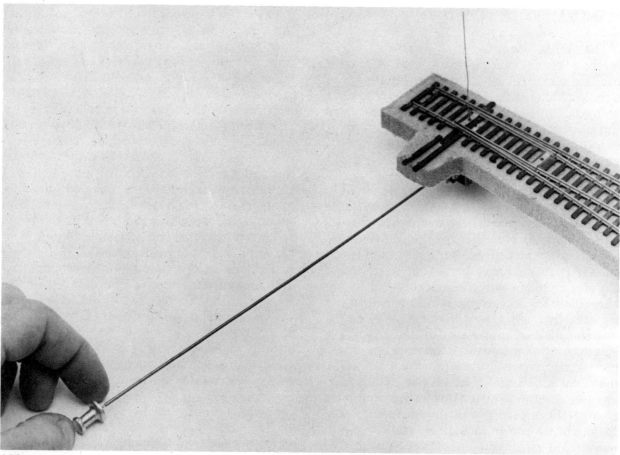

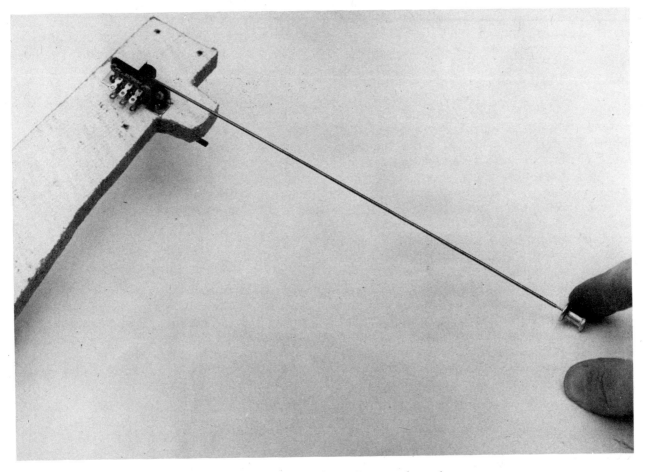

Fig. 13-6   The D.P.D.T. switch is mounted on its side with tiny brass angles and screws directly below the switch points.

The D.P.D.T. switch is mounted on its side so the lever travel coincides with the direction of the switch points' actuating rod. The lever on the D.P.D.T. switch is drilled, as shown in the photos, with a number 72 drill bit to fit the 0.025-inch wire that reaches through a hole in the roadbed to move the switch points. A second hole, to match the diameter of the choke cable you are using, is drilled at right angles to the number 72 hole. You'll need to buy two of the tiny screw-type collars to clamp the choke cable firmly to both sides of the hole in the D.P.D.T. switch. I used a piece of 1/16-inch brass tubing because this particular switch was less than a foot from the edge of the table. The number 72 drill bit was used to drill through both the lever and the brass tubing to lock the tubing into the lever, but the two screw-lock collars will be needed if you use a choke cable. Drill a ½-inch hole through the roadbed so it is centered directly under the switch points' throw bar. It's best to drill the holes before you lay the switch, but it can be done from beneath the table if you are very careful. The D.P.D.T. slide switch is then mounted to the underside of the roadbed (or the plywood support for the roadbed) so the 0.025 wire protrudes through the ½-inch hole in the roadbed and on through a hole (or through the hollow rivet in this Lambert switch) drilled in the center of the throw bar. Test the action of the switch before you insert the screws to permanently mount the switch.

The better-quality slide-type D.P.D.T. switches have a spring-loading feature that snaps the lever into either position, and that same snap-action will hold the switch points firmly against the rail if you position the D.P.D.T. switch properly. The choke cable or brass tubing can then be inserted in the switch and the excess length of 0.025 wire trimmed so it only protrudes about 1/32-inch above the throw bar.

The next step is to connect the electrical wires to the D.P.D.T. switch. Solder a length of wire from the rail leading into the track switch to one of the *center* posts on the D.P.D.T. switch. Solder a wire from that same rail (as it would be followed by a locomotive wheel through the switch in both diverging routes) to one of the D.P.D.T. switch's posts on the same side as the first and solder the wire from the "diverging" rail to the post on the same side but on the *opposite* end of the D.P.D.T. switch. Solder three more wires from the entering and two diverging routes) of the opposite rail to the three posts on the opposite side of the D.P.D.T. switch. The D.P.D.T. switch will connect the two wires from that incoming pair of rails to the appropriate pair of rails on the diverging route as its lever is moved from one position to the other to throw the track switch. Do *not* connect any wires from any one of the D.P.D.T. switch's posts to any other (as you would if you were cross-wiring to the two pairs of end posts to make the switch into an electrical current reversing switch); the wires from the two pairs of end posts lead to the track's four rails on the diverging-route side of the switch, and the center pair of posts leads to the rails on the entrance (or point) side of the track switch. Pulling or pushing the knob at the end of the choke cable (or map pin knob that was pressed into the end of the brass tube) actuates both the track switch and the D.P.D.T. switch.

SWITCH MACHINES

Switch machines are nothing more than electrical solenoids (such as those used in doorbell buzzers) that have been designed expressly for use in actuating the track switches on a model railroad. Most of them operate on the 16-volt a.c. current that is usu-

Fig. 13-7 A simple brass rod and the hairpin-style spring furnished with this Lambert brand switch machine link it to the points.

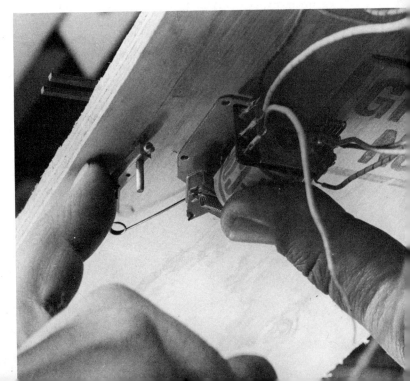

Fig. 13-8   The Anderson style linkage uses a brass lever on the top of the roadbed connected to a through-the-table pivot rod.

Fig. 13-9   A square brass rod connects the Anderson linkage pivot rod to the switch machine beneath the table.

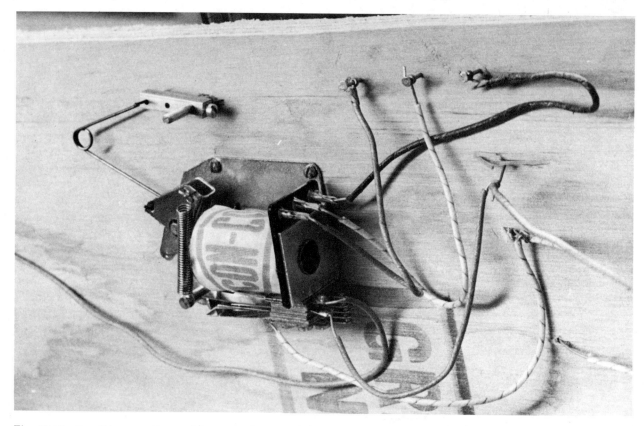

Fig. 13-10   Small brass nails provide an on-site terminal strip to connect the wires from the switch machines to the control panel.

ally available on the back of any commercial power pack so their wiring and voltage are completely independent from the 12-volt d.c. current that operates the locomotives on your layout.

The switch machine itself must be supplemented with a pair of push buttons or a momentary-contact toggle switch at the control panel. If you mount the switch machine on the top of the roadbed, beside the track switch, you can likely use the wire clip furnished with most such machines to move the track switch's throw rod. Wiring instructions and installation tips are included with most switch machines but few of them tell you that you need to buy (or fabricate) an additional bit of linkage like the Anderson type to mount the switch machine beneath the roadbed. Mount the Anderson linkage through a hole beside the switch (as outlined in the instructions furnished with the linkage) before you install the switch machine. The brass bar on the bottom of the linkage provides a degree of adjustment to allow the

switch machine to be placed on any side of the linkage pivot. Hold the machine in place, temporarily, while you operate it manually to be sure that there is equal pressure on the switch points in both directions. Fiddle with the switch machine location until the switch points snap shut with an identically loud click in either direction; then mark the locations of the switch machine's mounting holes with a screwdriver to be sure the mounting screws place it where you want it. Try the action, again, after the machine is mounted firmly and adjust the linkage if necessary.

A few brass nails, driven into the underside of the roadbed or tablework, can serve as terminal posts to make wiring simpler—chances are you'll remove the switch machine at least once in its lifetime to clean and adjust it and the electrical contacts. A nonoperating "dummy" switch stand can be placed beside the switch to improve the realism if you desire; there are several brands of such switch stands available through your dealer.

A power pack is all that's needed to control a one-track oval but the moment you add one remote control track switch, you have the beginnings of a control panel. The power pack is the heart of the model's electrical system with 12 volts of d.c. for the rails and 16 volts of a.c. for accessories like switch machines available from the pack's ability to convert the normal 110-volt house current into the type of power that is used on today's model railroads. The power pack also incorporates a circuit breaker (fuse) to protect itself from short circuits and the speed control, reversing, and on-off switches that are grouped under the general heading of "throttle" controls.

The low to medium-priced power packs use a wire-wound rheostat for speed control; the expensive (and best) power packs substitute transistors for the rheostat to provide smoother starting and better slow-speed control over the locomotive. The capacity of the power pack is generally indicated in its rated amperage availability. Most N scale motors (in the locomotives) require a maximum of about one amp, HO scale motors require one to two amps, and O scale motors can demand up to as much as four amps; you'll need that much power for every locomotive you intend to operate at the same time on your layout. You'll usually just run one locomotive at a time, but there may be occasions when you want to "double-head" your trains with two locomotives and you need double the amperage capacity if you expect to be able to control the two and if they are to deliver anywhere near their maximum pulling power.

The power packs that incorporate two complete sets of "throttle" controls should have enough amperage to handle the motors in at least two locomotives or, if you double-head both trains, enough amperage capacity for four motors. Most power packs are designed so the a.c. amperage for accessories like switch machines is "deducted" from the locomotive's available power; you might want a bit of extra amperage if you plan on having a number of lighted buildings (switch machines draw power only for the few moments they are used to move the switch points).

If you plan on building a large layout, one where three or four people may be operating trains at the same time, then you'd be wise to buy a separate power supply pack without

XIV

Power Packs and Panels

the throttle controls but with 6 or more amps rated capacity (for HO scale). Individual throttle packs are available without any power supply, so you can buy as many throttles as you expect to have need for.

THROTTLE CONTROLS

The power pack (or power supply and throttle controls) may likely be the most expensive single investment you will make in this hobby, so select them wisely. I've mentioned the advantages of transistorized throttles before but there are several different types to choose from. Some of the best brands have a separate adjustment for the amount of acceleration and another adjustment for the amount of braking (plus a "panic" stop switch) in addition to the actual speed control knob. These acceleration and braking controls can be set so the train takes as much as 10 feet to get up to top speed and takes that long to stop regardless of how fast you screw-on the speed control; that's about the way a full-size locomotive performs. With the acceleration and braking adjustments set to zero, the train will respond instantly to whatever setting you have on the speed control knob with no delayed acceleration or braking other than the "engineer's" ability to move the speed control smoothly on or off.

The acceleration and braking adjustments are bonus features that make operation more interesting, but I consider the basic transistorized throttle as essential to the enjoyment of the hobby as the locomotives themselves. The transistorized throttle, whether part of a complete power pack or a separate throttle package, must have adequate amperage ratings to handle your locomotive (or a doubleheaded pair of locomotives).

CONTROL PANELS

The control panel may or may not incorporate the throttle controls but, by its very definition, should incorporate all the switches that control the different operating blocks which have been electrically isolated for multiple train operation, the reversing loop wiring, and those blocks which are necessary just to avoid short circuits on layouts with several track switches. The push buttons or toggle switches or choke cables that operate the remote-controlled track switches should also be part of the control panel.

Most modelers follow a system similar to that in the control towers of full-size railroads. A schematic (simplified) diagram of the trackwork and switch locations is painted on the face of the control panel (or applied with ¼-inch wide drafting tape), and the block control switches and switch machine controls are placed on the track diagram directly over the portions of the track that they control.

Fig. 14-1   Two separate power packs control this layout with nine Center-Off D.P.D.T. switches to select which pack for each block.

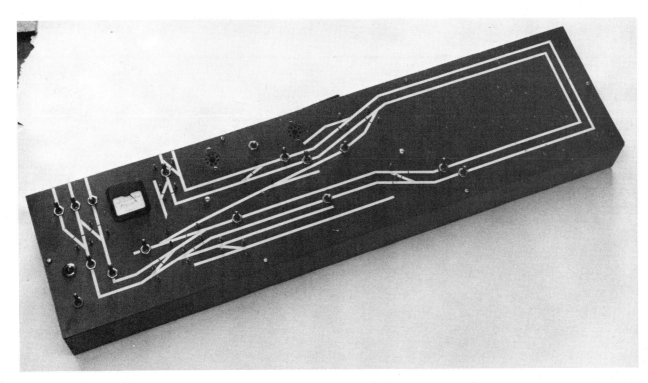

Fig. 14-2 The control panel should have a diagram of the track so switch and block controls can be related to what they control.

Fig. 14-3 A backside view: the switches are D.P.D.T. Center-Offs and the nail-like items are Kadee brand switch-control buttons.

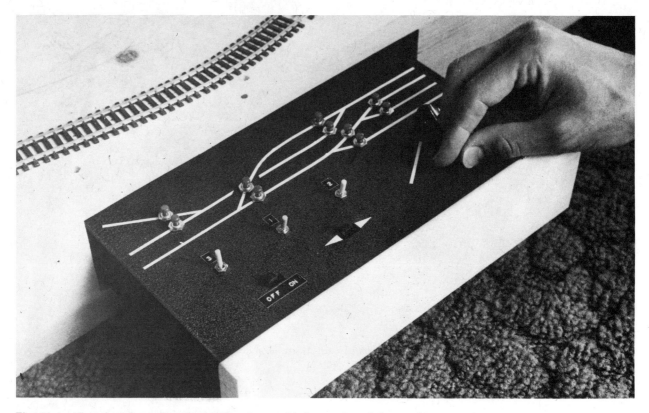

Fig. 14-4   The control panel on Dan Wilson's portable layout is a slide-out drawer with throttle and track controls.

The control panel itself can be assembled in an evening with 1" x 4" lumber for the frame and a hinge-down front of Masonite. The back of the control panel can quickly become a maze of wiring, so it's best to use different colors of wire for each block or switch machine and to number the blocks and switch machines with corresponding numbers on their operating switches. The wires themselves can be grouped together in insulated hooks to keep things neat and simple. The wires from the control panel should lead to a terminal strip (available from electronics stores and some model railroad shops) rather than directly to the layout. The wires from the layout are then connected to their mates along the opposite side of the terminal strip. The connecting points on the terminal strips are screws rather than the usual soldered connections so the control panel can be removed from the layout for moving or rebuilding without having to cut every wire on the layout. Leave enough extra wire length, on both sides of the terminal strip, so you can hinge the front of the control panel open or move it

a few inches without pulling any of the wires and breaking their connections.

WALK-AROUND CONTROL

The most enjoyable and satisfying type of locomotive and train control is called "walk-around control"; it enables you to walk around the edge of the layout to follow the progress of the train. The system works best on a medium to large, around-the-wall type of shelf layout, but it can make operation on even a 4' x 8' island layout far more fun. The heart of the system is a control box (available at any electronics supply store) with the speed control, reversing switch, and on-off switch removed from the power pack and installed in the box.

The wires that connect these components into their normal positions in the power pack are extended to a cable long enough to reach to the farthest ends of the layout. There is no central control panel (with the block on-off switches and the push buttons or toggles for the switch machines); rather, these controls

Fig. 14-5   You can walk along beside your train if the throttle is in a separate box with a lengthy extension cord.

Fig. 14-6   The PFM brand control panel includes an entire console for supplying *sound* signals to speakers in the locomotive.

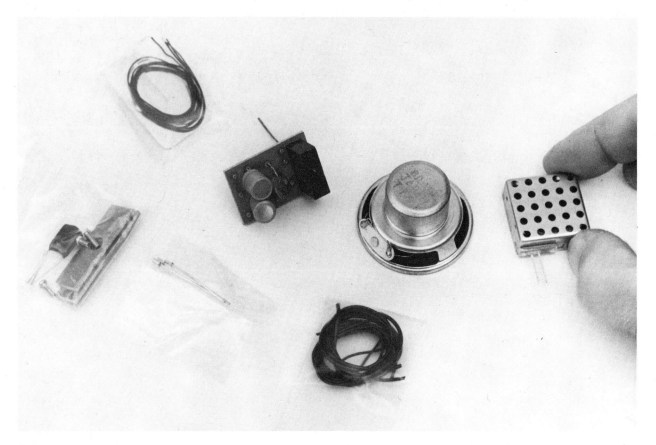

Fig. 14-7   The tiny square speaker or the round one next to it and these other electrical parts are mounted in the locomotive and tender to complete the PFM brand sound system.

are placed around the edges of the layout table as near to the blocks and switches they control as possible. The block and switch controls may still be placed on a small schematic diagram of the track plan in their area, particularly where there is complex trackwork like a yard. The walk-around system places both the train and the controls within easy reach and sight of the "engineer" to make operation, especially switching around yards and industrial spurs, even more enjoyable and life-like.

HEAR THE WHISTLE BLOW!

Modern model railroads can take advantage of several different types of sound systems that simulate the whistle of the steam locomotive; the horn of a diesel; or the wide range of exhaust, steam, and the clanging bell of the typical steam locomotive. Most of the systems, like the Modeltronics brand, mount a speaker in the locomotive or in the tender and reproduce just the chuffing and steam sounds. The superb (and expensive) Pacific Fast Mail model railroad sound system, however, uses that locomotive-mounted speaker to transmit virtually all the steam sounds plus the sound of a bell and a whistle. All of those sounds are adjustable from the PFM combination power pack and sound console with a delicate transistor throttle for locomotive speed control. The PFM system is, perhaps, the ultimate if you can afford it.

Simply stated, the wiring on any model railroad becomes proportionately more complex every time a switch or a reversing section (like a P-shaped loop or a triangular-shaped wye) is added. The complexity increases, too, when the modeler decides that the layout should be wired so that two or more trains can be controlled independently. You can do all of that with the basics in this chapter, and you can wire switch machines with the instructions included when you buy the machines.

If electronics is your thing, and you have a desire to provide automatic train controls with relays or wiring so that there can be three or more separate throttle and control panels, then I would suggest you buy one of two very fine books on wiring: *How to Wire Your Model Railroad* (Kalmbach Publishing Co., Milwaukee, WI 53233) or, as a second choice, Paul Mallery's *Electrical Handbook for Model Railroaders* (Carstens Publications, Inc., Newton, NJ 07860).

I prefer to keep my wiring as simple as possible—even to the extent of avoiding the potential problems of electric switch-control machines by substituting manually operated choke cables for remote switch control with the route-selection wiring right at the switch in the form of a D.P.D.T. slide-switch which is actuated by the same choke cable that operates the switch. Wherever possible, I let the track switches control the on-off flow of power into industrial sidings or yard tracks. There are enough things that can go wrong with a model railroad's operation, I feel, without adding any electrical complications that aren't absolutely necessary.

BASIC WIRING TIPS

A transformer and rectifier, inside the power pack, convert the 110-volt a.c. from any wall plugs to the 12-volt d.c. required to operate a model railroad locomotive. A rheostat or transistor throttle is added to that transformer and rectifier, along with a directional-reversing switch and an on-off switch, to complete the basic control system. All of these items except the transformer and rectifier can (and, I feel, should) be mounted in a separate throttle control box with enough wire length to allow walk-around control.

XV

Wiring Your Railroad

Wires 1 and 2 in Fig. 15-1 lead to the transformer and rectifier (the basic components of a power supply pack) and wires 3 and 4 lead to the track. Wires 5 and 6 must be added, at exactly the points shown, if there are any reversing loops or wyes on the railroad; these two wires lead to the reversing portion of the track in these wyes or loops and to a separate D.P.D.T. switch to control the train direction in that reversing section. The wires leading to the tracks should be about 14-gauge to minimize any voltage drop or loss, but short pieces of 24-gauge wire can lead from the rails to the underside of the baseboard to be less conspicuous where they are attached to the rails.

Every wire joint (except those to a terminal strip on the control panel, as mentioned in the previous chapter) should be soldered with noncorrosive solder like the Ersin brand. If both the rail and the wire are filed to remove any oxidation, an inexpensive soldering gun can be used for the wire joints with a quick enough bond so that even plastic ties won't melt.

A single pair of wire connections are enough to provide power to a simple loop of

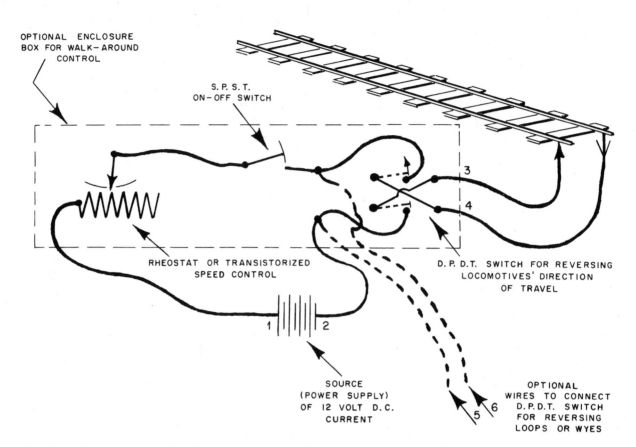

OPTIONAL ENCLOSURE
BOX FOR WALK-AROUND
CONTROL

S. P. S. T.
ON-OFF SWITCH

3

4

RHEOSTAT OR TRANSISTORIZED
SPEED CONTROL

D. P. D. T. SWITCH FOR REVERSING
LOCOMOTIVES' DIRECTION
OF TRAVEL

1 2

SOURCE
(POWER SUPPLY)
OF 12 VOLT D.C.
CURRENT

5 6

OPTIONAL
WIRES TO CONNECT
D.P.D.T. SWITCH
FOR REVERSING
LOOPS OR WYES

Fig. 15-1 Power pack and throttle electrical wiring. (Note: wires are numbered to correspond with their locations on other wiring diagrams.)

Fig. 15-2 Solder any wire connections to the outside of the rails (or below them before the track is laid) to clear wheel flanges.

Fig. 15-3 Typical wire connections for simple oval-type track layout.

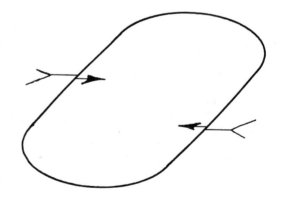

114

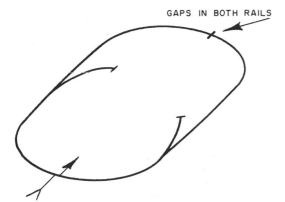

GAPS IN BOTH RAILS

Fig. 15-4 Locations of feeder wires and rail gaps for "facing" and "trailing" switches on simple oval layout.

track like Fig. 15-3, but I would strongly suggest that you add a second pair of wires to help overcome any current loss through the track's rail joiners. Short pieces of 24-gauge wire should be soldered across *any* rail joints on any hidden or inaccessible trackage (with a bit of slack in the wire to allow for expansion of the rails due to the weather) to ensure positive electrical current flow across the rail joint.

When you add switches, to even a simple loop layout, the location of the electrical feeder wires becomes extremely critical. The wires to any switch on the layout should feed from the point side of the switch or a short circuit or lack of power in some portion of the layout will always result. The addition of those switches adds a further complication due to the basic model railroad practice of using the rails themselves to carry the electrical current. The rails must be cut (gapped) and an insulation placed in the gap (common Ambroid or Testors household cement will do) so the electrical current cannot flow across if the track expands in hot weather. The gaps themselves need only be as wide as the cut a razor saw blade will make; or if you have one, the gap can be cut with an abrasive cut-off disk in a motor tool. The knack of supplying electrical current to each of the two rails on a model railroad is a fairly easy process if you think each step out logically, keeping in mind that a short will result every time one rail touches the other (at the frog of a switch, for example) unless a gap is cut somewhere or the feeder wires are relocated. A gap will also be needed to electrically isolate each passing sid-

Fig. 15-5 A cut-off grinding wheel in a motor tool is the easy way to cut electrical gaps without shifting the rails.

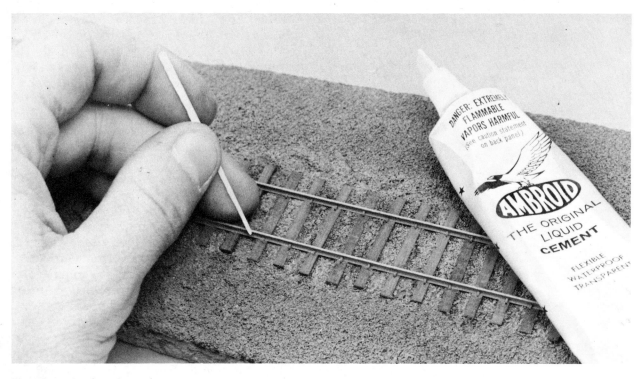

Fig. 15-6   Apply a drop of cement to any rail gaps to serve as an insulator and spacer so the cut ends cannot touch.

ing and to divide any long stretches of the main line into train-length segments *if* you expect to operate two or more trains at the same time. Additional feeder wires, connected to some type of an on-off switch, will usually be needed to provide power to those electrically isolated blocks.

A short circuit will result whenever two switches face each other, as shown here, un-

less at least one gap is cut in the inside rail. If the distance between the two facing switches is shorter than a train-length, then just one gap will be needed and the jumper wires shown in Fig. 15-7 can be omitted. The distance between the gap and the switch is dead, you'll note, whenever that switch is set to align with the diverging (curved) track route. By cutting two gaps, as shown, close to each

Fig. 15-7   Rail gaps and extra wires allow train operation between two facing switches.

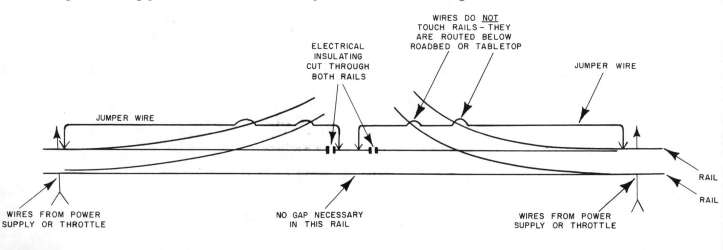

switch and with a pair of jumper wires from *both* switches' inside rails to the electrically isolated block, you will be able to operate trains (for switching purposes or whatever) regardless of how the *unused* switch on your route is aligned.

Wires like these can eliminate a lot of head-scratching when a train stalls for no apparent reason; you won't have to go all around the layout throwing track switches to find out which one was set "wrong."

I described additional switch wiring in the chapter on remote-control switches to ensure that the power flow did not relay on the track through the point area of the switch; please note that the jumper wires for facing switches are to be used in addition to the normal switch wiring I suggested. If you avoid the installation of any reversing loops or wyes

and if you can keep one rail and its wires separate from the other, then the problem of facing switches is about the only track wiring and gapping bugaboo you need worry about.

TWO-TRAIN CONTROL

You do not need two completely separate power packs to control two trains as long as you have adequate amperage. You will, however, need a second set of throttle controls, including a speed control, reversing switch, and an on-off switch (plus an additional reversing switch if there are any of those bothersome reversing loops or wyes in the track plan). You will also need some method of selecting which of the two throttles will control any given section of track. Two-man

Fig. 15-8   Wiring diagram for basic walk-around throttle control for two-train operation.

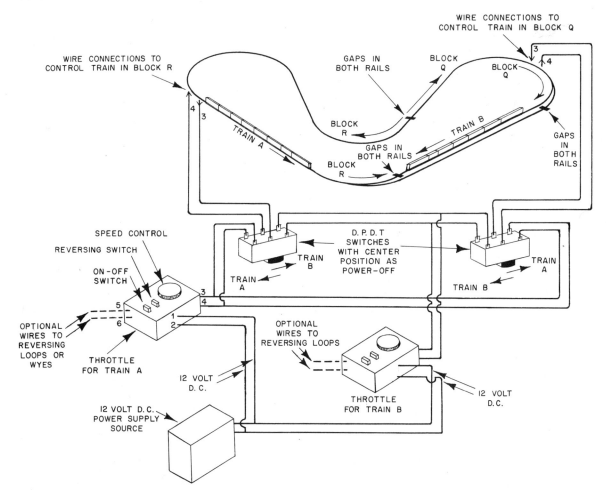

control is adequate for most home layouts (clubs sometimes need to provide enough control positions for a dozen trains and engineers), particularly if there is a yard or two to occupy a third or fourth engineer with switching to make-up and break-down trains. The yard area can have its own throttle control separate from the two (like those in Fig. 15-8) for the main line.

A standard type of toggle switch called a D.P.D.T. switch with a center position for power-off (called a D.P.D.T. Center-Off switch) can be used as the on-off and throttle-selector switch for each of the electrically isolated sections of tracks (called "blocks"). The operators *must* be trained to turn the block they have just vacated to the center-off position so there's no chance of a short circuit resulting from another train just entering that block.

There should be a minimum of three blocks on even the smallest layout so there can be one "dead," or "off," block between any two trains, but the passing siding in the diagram serves that same function. The D.P.D.T. Center-Off toggle switches would be located on the edge of the table as close to the blocks they control as possible. These basic two-block wiring diagrams can be expanded to include an infinite number of blocks. If you wish to be able to use three or more operators, each with his own separate throttle

control, then you could substitute the multiple-position rotary-selector switches that are available at electronics supply houses; but the cost and the wiring complexity would be many-times that of this simple system.

REVERSING LOOPS AND WYES

One of the very best types of track plan is that which routes the trains along a single track (with a few passing sidings) from one terminal to another. There should, however, be some way of reversing the trains when they reach the terminals at the ends of the line and that, from a wiring standpoint, complicates things.

The first step, in wiring any reversing loop or wye, is to locate just exactly which part of that trackage will be used for the actual reversal of the train. At a wye, for example, the train may reverse direction by backing into the stub-ended leg of the wye. Some wyes (like the one at Basalt, Colorado) are incorporated into the junction of a main line and a branch line so that only the tight curve portion of the wye, which connects the main and branch lines, serves as a reversing area. Once you find that reversing area, gaps must be cut through both rails near the locomotive end of the train and, again, near the caboose end of

Fig. 15-9   Special wiring is required for all reversing loop tracks.

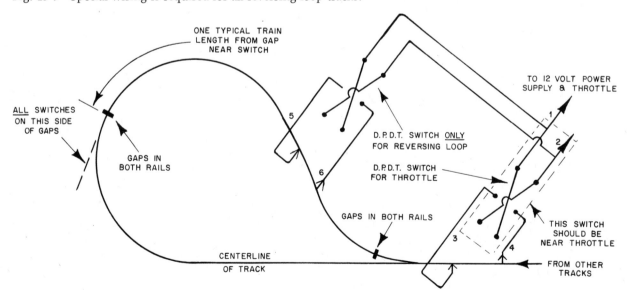

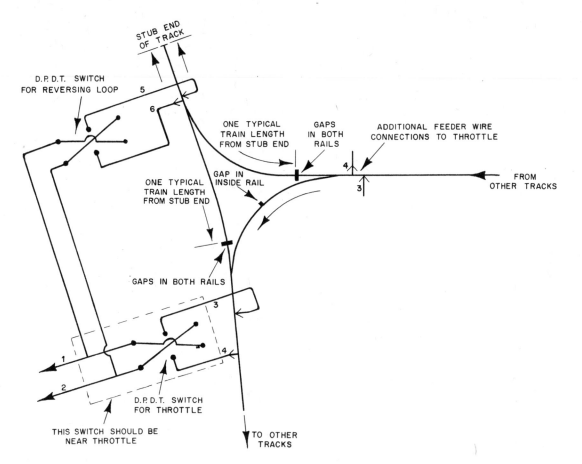

Fig. 15-10   Wiring for stub-end reversing wye tracks.

Fig. 15-11   Wiring for wyes between main line tracks and diverging branch tracks.

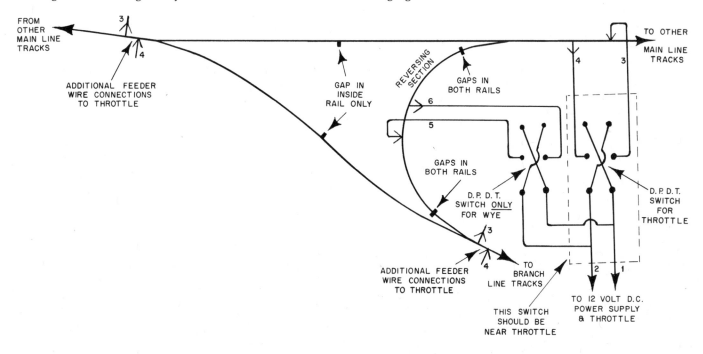

the train to give a trainlength section of track that is electrically isolated from all other trackage on the railroad. Two separate wires (numbers 5 and 6 in most of these diagrams) are then connected to this section of track. Both of these wires lead to the center posts on the back of a D.P.D.T. switch. The two posts on the far ends of the D.P.D.T. switch are cross-wired so the switch will reverse the flow of current (all "reversing switches" are this type). One wire from the end of the D.P.D.T. switch connects directly to the 12-volt power supply source and the other goes to the wire in the throttle which leads from the speed control to the "normal" reversing switch.

The three diagrams in Figs. 15-9, 15-10, and 15-11 show the most common situations where a reversing switch should be located; the same type of switch and wiring must also be used for turntable track. With this type of wiring, a train can travel around the reversing loop or wye without stopping, because the operator has time to throw the reversing switches, on the blocks the train is *about* to enter, to the proper direction. You may have to study some track plans carefully to locate reversing loops or wyes; ess bends with switches on either end are often reversing sections if the train's path is traced through every possible alternate path on the layout. Tracks branching out suddenly from a switch may also eventually connect to a common third track to form a wye.

Do not, by the way, confuse the "wye" type of reversing section shown in these track plans and wiring diagrams with a single track switch that is also called a wye. The wye switch is merely a standard switch where both diverging tracks curve away rather than the one straight, one curved route of a conventional switch. The wye switch is used to save space in complex track plans; and often, one or more of the three switches that are in the corners of a reversing-type wye are wye switches!

Planning and Operation

Model railroading is far more fun today than it was less than a decade ago—thanks to a few breakthroughs like relatively oxidation-free nickle silver rail, transistorized throttles, the walk-around control concept and an automatic coupler (by Kadee) that is truly automatic. Virtually all the inexpensive, ready-to-run locomotives and cars are supplied with an X 2F style "horn hook" coupler if the equipment is HO scale, a similar-style coupler on most O scale ready-builts, and a grossly oversize hook-type coupler (developed years ago by Arnold-Rapido) if the equipment is N scale. The Kadee couplers must be added to this type of equipment and to most kits by the modeler.

Kadee makes couplers for N, HO, and O scales as well as a special coupler for HOn3 modelers; several firms modify the HO couplers for use on S scale and on On3 equipment. The Kadee couplers add less than a dollar to the cost of each locomotive or rolling stock and that's the best dollar you'll ever spend on the hobby. The Kadee coupler looks very much like a prototype coupler except that the Kadee air hose is a piece of steel wire that hangs from the coupler rather than the underframe of the car.

XVI

Hands-Off Coupling and Uncoupling

Fig. 16-1 The X 2F style "horn hook" couplers mounted on the bottom of the car and Talgo-style on the truck itself.

Fig. 16-2 Kadee makes conversion to their couplers easy with a choice of complete underframes, Talgo trucks, or replacement couplers and coupler pockets for N scale equipment.

CARS COUPLED   UNCOUPLED OVER MAGNET

DELAYED SET TO DROP   UNCOUPLED AND DROPPED

Fig. 16-3 The Kadee uncoupling action is the same for any line scale—magnets do the work.

Fig. 16-4 The letters A, B, C, and D are typical locations for Kadee uncoupling ramps.

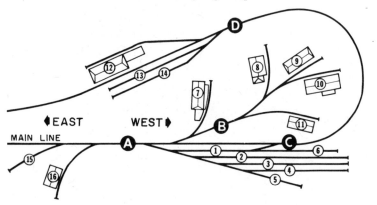

Kadee supplies a variety of "ramps" to actuate their couplers to the uncoupling position ("coupling" is a matter of gently pushing two couplers together anywhere on the track). These ramps are magnets that repel the steel "brake hoses," forcing the steel hoses toward the outside of the car to open the coupler. The actual uncoupling can occur at the ramp if the locomotive pulls away from the car, but it can also take advantage of Kadee's clever "delayed action" feature by simply shoving the now-open coupler (and the car) down the track to the desired position; the coupler won't recouple so the locomotive can then back away to leave the car. A single Kadee ramp at a yard throat, A in Fig. 16-4, is all that is required to 'spot' a car on any of the sidings to the right of A. The locomotive must pause and, sometimes, back up just a fraction of an inch over the ramp at A to cock the couplers between the car and the locomotive into the delayed position; the locomotive can then push the car to any of those sidings and leave it without having to use another uncoupling ramp.

There's nothing electronic and the couplers couple or uncouple with almost complete reliability if they are installed precisely the way Kadee recommends in their instructions. The

Fig. 16-5 A jewelers' screwdriver, inserted and twisted between the Kadee coupler knuckles, will allow manual uncoupling.

couplers can also be uncoupled by hand, using the point of a jewelers' screwdriver or, better, one of the special uncoupling "picks" sold by GH Products.

Kadee offers dozens of different types of mountings for their couplers with kits, particularly in HO scale, to fit most cars and locomotives. Their HO and N scale couplers are also sold mounted on freight and passenger trucks (Talgo style trucks) for use on model railroads with smaller-than-normal curves. Most of the imported brass locomotives are designed to accommodate Kadee couplers on the tenders and on the pilots of switching locomotives; but you may have to fabricate a mounting channel, from sheet brass, like the one on the pilot of this PFM brand Santa Fe 2-8-0 to fit the couplers to the front of some steam locomotives. The couplers are even more realistic if they are painted in various shades of rust; but don't get any paint on the sliding faces or the pivot points.

Some types of operation allow switching of entire strings of cars rather than just one car at a time. You can save a few dollars by equipping such strings of cars with Kadee couplers

Fig. 16-6 The brake hose that moves the Kadee coupler knuckle must clear the locomotive pilot so the coupler can operate.

Fig. 16-7 These four N scale ore cars are permanently coupled with Kadee couplers on each end car only.

on the end cars, like Ben Davis did with these four Atlas N scale ore cars (see Fig. 16-7). Ben removed one of the stock Rapido style couplers from the end of each car and cut the faces of the remaining couplers flat so they would slide into the now-empty coupler pocket of the next car; the technique allows N scale cars to be coupled closer, like the prototype, than with the stock couplers. Kadee couplers on both ends of all the cars would accomplish the same close-coupling realism.

The standard Kadee magnetic uncoupling ramps mount between the rails so their surface is about flush with the tops of the rails. Most of these ramps can be disguised as highway crossings. Kadee also makes what is called a below-the-ties ramp for locations where you would want the ramp to be invisible. The roadbed must be cut away to match the thickness of the ramp and the ramp inserted in place, preferably before the trackwork is in place.

Before you build your own, try to operate someone else's layout with Kadee couplers and ramps so you can get the first-hand experience it takes to locate the ramps while your layout is still in the planning stages. The most obvious locations are at the entrances to multi-track yards (near the yard "throat") and on industrial sidings with the ramp far enough along the siding so the cars that are uncoupled there don't foul the main line trains. The ramp locations on the 5' x 16' (in HO scale) layout of the Colorado Midland's trackage at Basalt, Colorado, are marked to give you an idea of some typical Kadee ramp locations.

Kadee couplers' reliable operation allows switching operations that exactly match those of the prototype railroads (providing you locate the ramps in the proper places). Most modelers find that the switching moves to make up or break down trains in the yards and switching cars in and out of industrial sidings is far more enjoyable than just running trains around and around.

With an operating system like that described in the next chapter, you can actually move "loaded" and "empty" freight cars in and out of the various industrial tracks and then make up trains of such cars for transport to imaginary distant cities. The key point in such switching operations, however, is reliable coupling and uncoupling; and the Kadee coupler is the only one that provides that reliability and a realistic appearance.

Fig. 16-8 Conventional Kadee uncoupling ramps mount between the rails but this one is hidden beneath the ties.

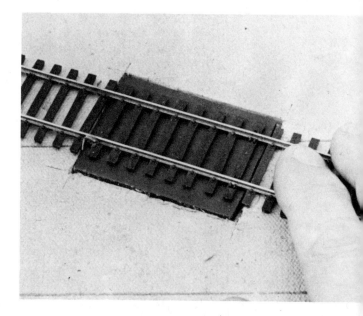

The locomotives, the rolling stock, the structures, the track, and even the scenery on your model railroad can be a faithful and remarkably realistic miniature of the prototype in every respect. Transistor throttles can allow starts and stops so slow that you can barely tell the train is moving except for the slight clatter as the slack is taken between the couplers of each car. The locomotive may chuff and whistle it's way down the main line.

All that realism, though, is wasted if you don't take advantage of what it promises: actual operation patterned after real railroading. Most club layouts (and a number of private layouts) have one operating night each month where trains are run, right on schedule, just as though the "Midnight Flyer" really had to arrive at midnight. These modelers generally use a speed-up clock that turns an hour into 5 or 6 minutes to compensate for the shorter distance the models have to cover as compared to the prototype; but the arrival times and destinations are as real as those on

XVII

Real Railroading

Fig. 17-1 Timetables, like this 1902 Colorado Midland copy reprinted by the Colorado Railroad Museum (in Golden, CO), can be simulated for interesting operation on any model railroad.

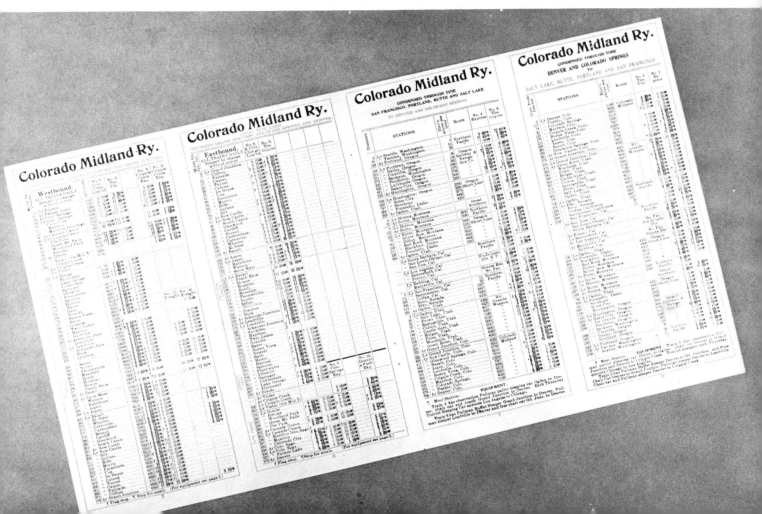

this Colorado Midland timetable (see Fig. 17-1).

A few simple gear changes will often be enough to speed-up an electric clock and the weights can be removed (even easier) from a wind-up clock so it will pass one hour in 5 or 6 minutes. You can establish a timetable for even a simple oval layout by timing the trains around one lap (on the "scale-time" clock) and by establishing imaginary stops; on a larger layout, those stops and times can have some real meaning. When there are two or more operators, each "engineer" must see that his train is on time so it can meet the other train at a passing siding rather than with a head-on crash out on the main line somewhere. The trains that are switching industrial sidings must get their moves completed or partially completed so they can clear the main line in time for the "express."

If the timetable is arranged like a prototype's, the coming and going of the models takes on a realism that has to be seen to be believed. Try to arrange your work or vacation schedule so you can visit a club layout sometime to witness timetable operation in action and see why so many modelers use it on their home layouts.

TRUE-TO-LIFE TRACKWORK

There's a lot more to realistic trackwork than just ballast and some painted-on rust. The realism should begin while your layout, no matter how small, is still in the planning stages. Kadee automatic couplers and improved track-laying methods promise realistic operation, but the tracks have to be laid in some life-like pattern of sidings and switches to allow the best of the prototype's action on your layout.

Only a club layout would have the room for a yard as large as those on the full-size railroads, but even that maze of trackwork can be condensed into a size that can be used on a medium-size home layout. The track plan in Fig. 17-2 is a condensed layout of the full-size Colorado Midland Railroad's yard at Leadville, Colorado, in about 1906. The length has been compressed from the prototype's miles and a few of the sidings that are duplicates of those on the plan have been left out to adapt the yard to model railroad space limitations.

The purposes that each track serves, however, are the same whether it's a model or the prototype; and the yards on the most modern railroads have virtually the same general layout but they are even larger. The four "through freight" and "local freight" tracks would most likely be part of a "hump yard" on a modern railroad. The hump yard is just what is seems to be: a series of yard tracks with one end elevated to form a hump. The switch engine need only switch the cars to the top of the hump (it would be located on one of the "switch leads" on this plan) and gravity and remote-controlled switches would direct the cars (or cuts of several cars) into the appropriate siding. Huge lengths of steel "retarders" press against the cars' wheel flanges to slow them on their way down the hump so they roll to a stop in the yard; these retarders are operated from the same tower that controls the switches. Hundreds of model railroaders have incorporated hump yards in their layouts, some with even the remote-controlled reatarders.

The yard engine (a "switcher") sorts the cars from incoming trains on those four "freight" tracks with cars destined for industries and towns on the "local" tracks; and cars that will continue their journey to destinations on some other railroad down the line are

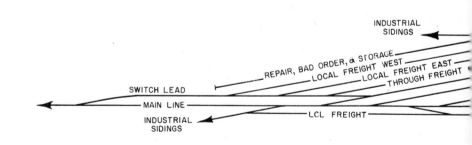

Fig. 17-2 Classification yard (condensed to model proportions).

spotted on the "through" tracks. The switcher may also spot new cars at industries near the yard and pick up others to be spotted on the appropriate "freight" track.

When a train is ready (according to the timetable) the switcher will pull a caboose from the "caboose track" and add it to the end of the train so the train is ready for the "road" engine to couple-on. Notice that the two "switch leads" are about as long as the yard tracks, so the switcher can pull train-length cuts of cars in and out of the various tracks without interfering ("fouling") with the main line tracks. Notice, too, that all four of the "freight" tracks have switches on each end (like a "passing siding") so that the engines on arriving or departing trains can run around their train to couple on either end and so that the switcher can work either end of the yard. This particular yard is a "through" yard because trains arrive and depart in both directions from both ends of the yard. The plan could be condensed even further, for a model railroad, by making the yard a "stub yard" with most of the tracks on the left ending in stub-end tracks with bumpers so that all traffic arrives and departs from the right side of the yard. Space could be saved, too, by making the roundhouse smaller, or the yard could be condensed by making a single track serve as both "east" and "west" in the freight yard area.

THE FIDDLE YARD

Frankly, there are darn few model railroads large enough to accommodate the most condensed versions of yards like the Colorado Midland's Leadville facility. Model railroaders in England, often even more cramped for space than American modelers, have devised the ultimate in condensed yards: a single spur track! Sometimes that single track is connected to a series of removable tracks where entire trains can be stored, but it can lead to a simple area where cars (and locomotives) are added or removed to simulate the arrival or departure of cars and trains from cities on "other" imaginary railroad connections.

The trains are broken down by lifting the cars from the rails and placing them on storage shelves; and new trains are made from the available assortment on the shelves and are placed on the "fiddle yard" spur track. Nearly all the functions of a full-size yard can be carried on, but only in your imagination. The trains that enter and leave that fiddle yard spur, however, are the same trains, with the same changes in their consists, that would enter or leave a real yard. O scale cars can be re-railed fairly easily by hand but the HO scale re-railing track sections and the separate re-railer ramps furnished with N scale sets will make the train make-up job quicker and easier.

You'll notice several "holding tracks" and "hidden yards" on the track plans in later chapters. These hidden sidings serve much the same function as the fiddle yard, allowing you to run one train *into* the yard with a different train *exiting* the yard. A switch can be added to any of these hidden storage tracks to bring a track close to the edge of the table to easily remove or replace individual cars or complete trains; so there may be a constant flow of cars from "cities" far removed from the locale of your layout.

THE OPERATION-UNLIMITED SYSTEM

I think you'll find, as I have, that switching cars in and out of trains in a large yard like

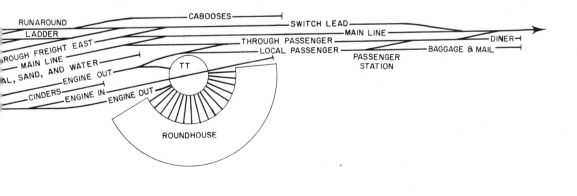

Fig. 17-3   HO and N scale re-railers make it easy to get cars or locomotives on or off the track at a fiddle yard spur.

Leadville is a luxury that just isn't worth the precious space available for most home layouts. The area occupied by even that relatively small yard would be better filled with a dozen individual industries at, perhaps, two different towns and with individual spurs to serve those town's industries.

Industrial buildings lend a large degree of credibility to your railroad's operations by providing a visible source for freight "revenue" (there's that imagination at work again). Passenger stations help to create the same illusion of need for passenger service and, if you're clever enough, you'll provide a siding at most passenger stations to accept a diner, baggage car, or express reefer so your passenger trains can do some switching rather than just chase their own observation cars around the layout.

The best way to "plan" your industries is to take an inventory of the types and numbers of

freight cars you have (or plan to buy or build). For example, if you have a lot of tank cars, then you'll need to create a number of industries that can be served by sidings where tank cars can be spotted. There's room for two or more bulk oil dealers on any layout; locomotive servicing facilities use oil lubrication if not for fuel as well. Some manufacturing plants use oil by the carload for lubrication or fuel or (in modern times) to make plastics; and there are other, similar users of chemicals that are delivered by tank cars.

Resist the temptation to model a huge industry like a refinery and, instead, imagine that the refinery is located somewhere off your railroad so that the tank cars originate on an "interchange" track (or, for that matter, on that fiddle yard track). Similar lists of potential industries can be made to demand deliveries or shipments by boxcar, reefer, flat car, stock car, gondola, or hopper.

130

You don't have to build any of these industries until you're ready; just mark their names and locations on the tabletop beside the siding that will serve them. You can find room for a dozen such industries, served by half that many sidings, on even a 4' x 8' layout. Remember to include at least one passing siding somewhere on such a small layout so the locomotive that is switching those industrial sidings can "run around" its train to shove cars into the sidings that face the direction of travel.

You can make things a bit more difficult for the switching crews by locating two or more industries on the same track and by having one or two sidings that can only be reached by traveling over another siding; the cars that are spotted by the industries on the main line ends of these sidings will, then, have to be moved out of the way to reach the industries further on down the track and then replaced—all by the switch engine, of course. The industries on prototype railroads are often located in groups like this, to the grief of the switch crew in a hurry but a delight to the model railroad operator. You can switch cars in and out of these various industries at random, but the operation-unlimited system that follows is even more fun.

The operating system I call "operation-unlimited" is really a collection of operating ideas that dozens of other model railroaders have used since the 1930s; I have revised and updated them with later ideas of my own and

Fig. 17-4   These few stationary supplies are all you need to set up the permanent paperwork for "operation-unlimited."

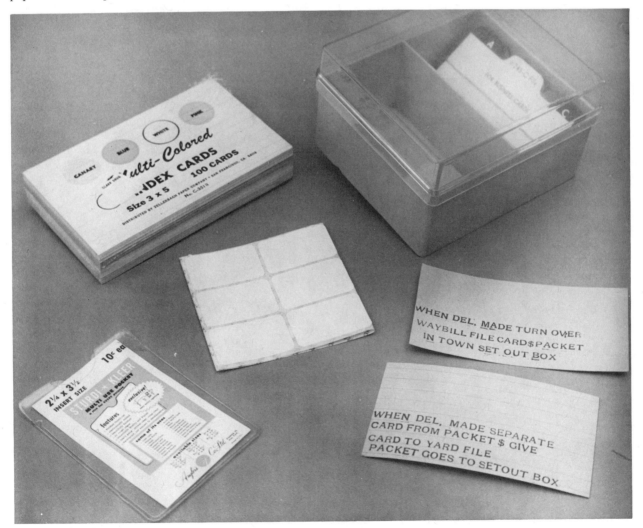

others. I'd have to give credit to a list of thirty or more model railroaders for their ideas, but people like the late Frank Ellison, Dr. Roy Dohn, Doug Small, Terry Walsh, Linn Westcott, and Doug Smith contributed most of the basic concepts.

The first step was to provide enough industries to coincide with your "mix" of freight equipment so that you could keep most of

your tank cars in action. You'll need to visit a well-stocked stationery store to purchase enough 2¼" x 3½" clear plastic envelopes (at about a dime a piece) to match the number of freight cars you have or plan to have. Buy about five times that many file cards and at least that many self-adhesive ½" x 1" white labels. If you have more than about twenty cars, you may also want to order two rubber

Fig. 17-5   The waybills slip inside the plastic envelopes so the operating instructions are visible below the car number tag.

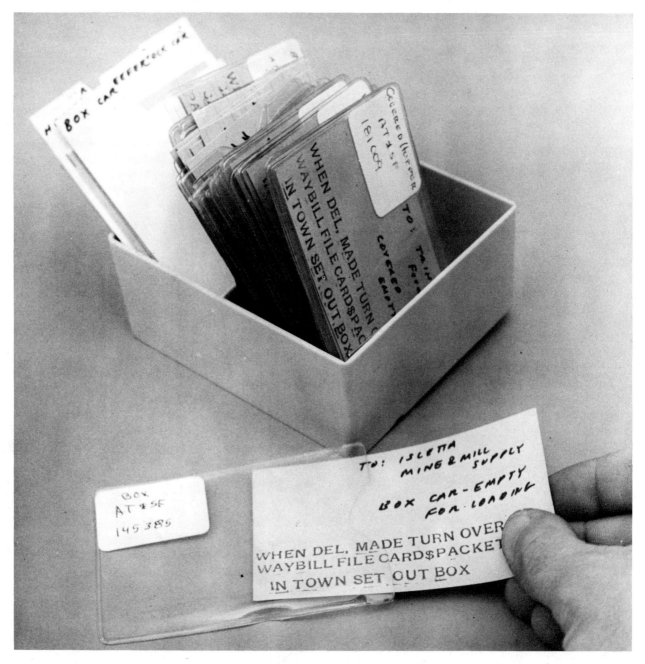

stamps (at a few dollars each) so you don't get writers' cramps; one should read: "When delivery is made separate card from packet and place card in Yard File—packet goes to Setout Box." The other rubber stamp should say: "When delivery is made turn over waybill file card in packet and place packet and enclosed card in Town Setout Box." Buy a file box big enough to hold all the plastic envelopes and you'll now have the basic materials for the operation-unlimited system.

Use the self-adhesive labels to mark one plastic envelope to match each of your cars. Print (so anybody can read it!) the type of car, the initials of the railroad name on the side of the car, and the car number as it appears on the side of the car; stick the label in the upper left hand corner of the plastic envelope. Label one envelope for each of your cars. These envelopes will "follow" the car around the layout—in the engineer's hand when that particular car is in a train and in the storage file box when the car is "spotted" at an industrial spur or in the yard (or on your shelf). The full-size railroad cars usually have a pocket or waybill tackboard of some kind, but it's too small to be of any use on a model so we'll substitute the plastic envelope and remember to move the envelope every time we move the car. The plastic envelope will hold a simplified and modified version of the "waybills" that are used to route the cars on the prototype railroads. When the plastic envelope has a "waybill" in it, that car is "loaded" with some commodity; when the envelope is empty, then the car is "empty" and available for "loading"; that's why the clear envelopes are used (so you can tell at a glance if any particular car is "loaded" or "empty").

There is some more paperwork to prepare for the operation-unlimited system, but be consoled by the fact that you only have to do it once before the "system" is set up. You will have to make new envelopes to match any new cars that are added to your layout and a few new "waybills" if you add more industries; but the purpose of both the cars and the industries should be to add more operating interest, and the small amount of initial paperwork preparation will multiply that operating interest many-times over.

Cut the file cards (so they fit inside those clear plastic envelopes and make enough of them so there are at least five cards) for each industry on your layout (include any "interchange" tracks with other railroads in that count of industries—any yard, including the fiddle yard, counts as at least one "interchange" track). Stamp the bottom of one side of each card with "When delivery is made separate card . . ." and the other side (near the bottom of the card) with the "When delivery is made turn over . . ." stamp.

Now, it's time to think like a railroad's traffic salesman in search of new customers. Pick one of your railroad's industries and try to imagine what type of products it might ship (and what type of car they would need) and what type of products those industries might *receive* (and what types of cars those products would need). Make one list of "shipments" and another of "arrivals" for *each* industry. Wherever possible, try to include other industries that are on your layout as sources for both shipments and arrivals to and from each other. When that is not possible (as in the example of the oil refinery), mark the source or the destination as "interchange" and imagine that the freight traffic originates (or is destined for) industries on some "other" railroad. Those lists, when completed, can be transferred in this manner (by printing so *anybody* can read them) to the file cards you cut to fit the clear plastic envelopes (leave the upper left corner of each card blank so the car label won't cover any of the words on the "waybill" card):

FROM: (the name of the town on this first
        line)
        (the name of the *shipping* industry or,
        in some cases, "interchange")
TO: (the town and then the name of the
        industry that will *receive* this
        shipment)
CARLOAD OF (whatever this industry *ships*)

(This rubber stamp goes at the bottom):

WHEN DELIVERY IS MADE SEPARATE CARD FROM PACKET AND PLACE CARD IN YARD FILE—PACKET GOES TO SETOUT BOX (the "packet" is that clear plastic envelope with the type of car, RR name, and number label)

Write the following information (from your industries' lists of shipments and arrivals) on the opposite side of that *same* card (leave the upper left corner blank so the car label won't cover any of the words on the "waybill"):

TO: (the name of the town where the industry is that will fill this car with the products it *ships*)

TANK CAR—EMPTY *FOR* LOADING (or boxcar, or reefer, or any other car that would be used to transport this particular product)

(This rubber stamp goes on the bottom):

> WHEN DELIVERY IS MADE TURN OVER WAYBILL FILE CARD IN PACKET AND PLACE PACKET AND ENCLOSED CARD IN TOWN SETOUT BOX

Make at least five cards for shipments "from" each of your industries (and try to include each of your industries on a total of five or more "to" destinations on the "empty for loading" side of the cards). The "to" destinations on the "carload of . . ." side of the cards should be five or more *different* industries (or interchange tracks). When all the cards are completed on both sides, separate them according to the type of car each card describes and file them with header cards showing car types ("boxcars," "reefers," etc.).

You'll need two small boxes (file card boxes will do) at each town; one to hold the plastic envelopes of the trains that switch in that town and the other box, marked "SETOUT", to hold the envelopes of the cars that are sitting at the industries in that town. Have five or six boxes at any yard (two will do for a fiddle yard) with one box marked "YARD"; the others will be used to hold the envelopes of the incoming and outgoing trains of cars. The switch engine's "engineer" should remove the envelopes of the cars he is making into trains from the "YARD" box and place them in the box with the other envelopes that match the cars all ready in the train. Since only one train can occupy any one yard track, it's easier for the yard operators to keep things straight if there is one box for each yard track—the cars on the storage tracks of the yard are those whose cards are in the "YARD" box. It's also easier to keep track of envelopes and their corresponding cars if you keep the envelopes in the same order that the cars are in the train (and on the storage tracks). The various waybills that are not

"loaded" in car envelopes can be stored in the rear of the "YARD" box.

Operation with the system began when you placed the various car packets in the boxes nearest the car's location on the layout but, so far, all the cars (and all their envelopes) are empty. The "YARD" operator (he may be the same one who switches the yard or, particularly if you're using a fiddle yard, he may be the engineer who will take the train over the railroad) starts every operating session by removing a few of the waybills from the file. His next step is to locate the types of cars that those waybills demand and, then, to make them into trains.

For this very first operating session you can load about half the cars on the layout with appropriate waybills; about half of those with the "carload of . . ." side up and half with the " . . . empty for loading" side up. The first train out has two chores: to deliver the cars in the train (all of which should be loaded with waybills) as instructed by the waybills themselves and to pick up any empty cars on the sidings (cars whose envelopes are empty). Notice that the instruction stamps tell the engineer to return the waybills to the yard. The yard is where *all* waybills are inserted into envelopes; the engineer either turns the "waybill" over or removes it and brings it back to the yard as instructed by the waybills themselves. The yard operator should file the returned waybills at the back of each pack of that waybill type of car to keep as much variety in the system as possible. If you find you are repeating car movements too often, simply make some more waybills with some different "to . . ." destinations on the "from . . ." side of the waybill (be sure to complete *both* sides of any new waybill).

You will find that it takes several evening's operation to understand the system but, if you follow every step exactly as described, it quickly becomes a habit. The effect of the "operation-unlimited" system is absolutely astounding; about midway through the operating session, you suddenly become aware that you are no longer running just trains but a string of loaded (or unloaded) cars with a destination and a purpose—and that is what railroading (real or model) is all about!

This same system can be adapted to passenger train operations by substituting reasons why baggage cars, mail cars, diners,

Pullmans, extra coaches, business cars, and the like should be added or removed from the trains and where. The various books on full-size passenger trains will have the data you need to establish an operation-unlimited system for passenger traffic.

The operation-unlimited system is intended to provide operations for what the real railroads call "way freight" or "peddlers" or "local freights"; but you can use the system to automatically provide traffic for "through" or "express" trains as well. The waybills that are marked with a "to" or "from" destination for "interchange" with some other railroad are the ones that will route the cars into the through or express trains.

If you find that you don't have enough through or express trains to keep enough engineers busy, then make two or three additional waybills for each industry with a "to" or "from" routing to some interchange. Empty cars can be added to the consists of any through freight trains under the guise that they are being returned to their "home" railroads. You can generate still more through and express train action by creating a rule that demands that every car in the yard be moved out (and back in again) on a through or express train during each operating session. The system is flexible enough to be used on any size layout, from an oval to a giant club, and with one or twenty operators; but you'll have to try it on your particular railroad to see how many waybills are needed for each industry to provide both way freight switching (for one or more trains) and through freight operation.

XVIII

Track Planning

Some of the most effective model railroads ever built never had a track plan until *after* the trackwork was in place, but these succeeded only because the layouts were around-the-wall types. A 2-foot wide shelf is, perhaps, one of the best setups possible for a model railroad layout in any scale. The shelf avoids the one major tight spot in any track plan: half-circle curves.

The track that curves around the corners of the room on a shelf layout can easily be laid to something greater than the minimum radius for the scale of the railroad (about 15 inches for N scale, 24 inches for HO scale, and 48 inches for O scale), and the rest of the track-work can wander at will as long as the routes in and out of the switches are in perfect alignment with the switch rails.

The around-the-wall layout does, however, present some drawbacks. If you can run the layout completely around the room, there's the problem of a swing-up or duck-under access to the railroad. If the room is much larger than 14-feet square, the around-the-wall layout uses up only about two-thirds of the potential space for the layout. Finally, there's the problem of providing any method of re-

136

versing the trains; reversing loops or wyes require a table width of about 10 percent more than *twice* the minimum radius.

You can do what Irv Schultz did on his HO scale layout and move the backdrop out from the wall so the "bulge" portion of the return loops is hidden behind the scenery, but that can be a waste of space too. For most model railroad layout locations, a combination of the around-the-wall and the island type of table seems to be the best choice, particularly if the narrow end of the island table can butt against a wall so you can walk around three sides of the table as though it were a peninsula, and if the around-the-wall shelf can connect with the wall end of the table. There is one type of layout design that I can suggest as the *worst* possible choice: a layout that is so wide and so long that the normal operating area must be a cutout (operating pit) in the center of the table. You'll get terribly tired of crawling under the layout to reach that pit (and just as disgusted with trying to hoist and align and lift-up access panels to it) and this type of layout does not lend itself to walk-around control. You can fit just as much track into that space with a single island and an around-the-wall connecting shelf on one or both of your longer walls. However, these "island" and "peninsula" layouts do require track plans so that you can be sure the curves and switches will fit within the confines of the table edge.

BASIC TRACK PATTERNS

A model railroader can capture every detail of the prototypes' locomotives, including smooth performance and sound; he can duplicate rolling stock and structures right down to the last rivet; and he can lay track that looks just like the real thing through grass and tree-covered hills and stream-drained valleys. The one thing that the model railroader cannot do, though, is to bring to his model empire the endless distances the real railroads cover.

The track plan is really the only aspect of model railroading where the modeler must compromise a bit to create a true-to-life miniature. Most curves are just broad enough to permit the longer passenger and freight cars, and the switches are only about a fifth as long as the gently diverging routes of the prototypes'. That compression, however, doesn't affect the appearance of a model railroad as much as you might expect; because our eyes seem to have some sort of telephoto effect which makes train lengths and the spaces between buildings seem smaller in real life than they really are. The trick to model railroad layout planning is to see that even those tight-radius curves really do fit without an offset jog and that the switches really do align with one another *before* any track is laid.

There are several ways that the track can be twisted and curved to fit on any island tabletop, including the obvious oval and figure-eight layouts. Combining these two produces a layout where the trains can run twice as far in about the same amount of space, and there are some obvious points where switches could be inserted to provide reversing loops. If the parallel tracks are separated by a difference in elevation, a track plan like this one won't look anywhere near as crowded in practice as it does on paper.

The prototype railroads do not run around in circles (or ovals or eights, to say nothing of doing it twice-around) and that can be a bother to many modeler's imaginations. You

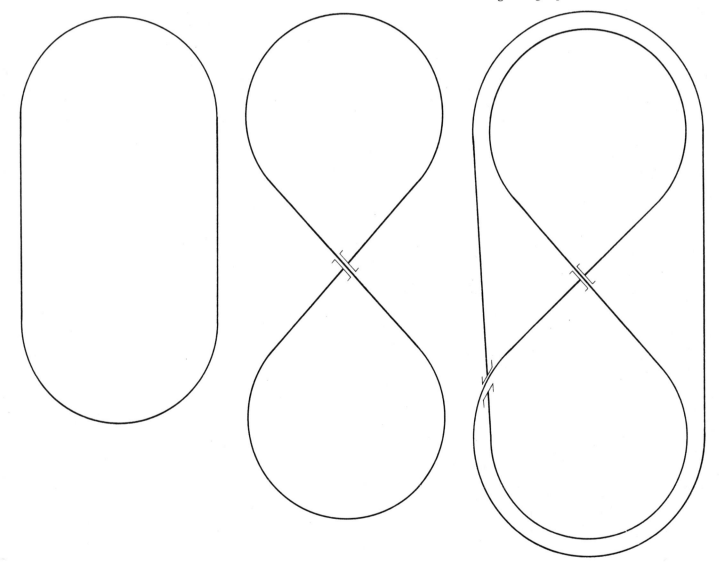

Fig. 18-1 Oval plan.

Fig. 18-2 Figure-eight plan.

Fig. 18-3 Combination oval and figure-eight plan.

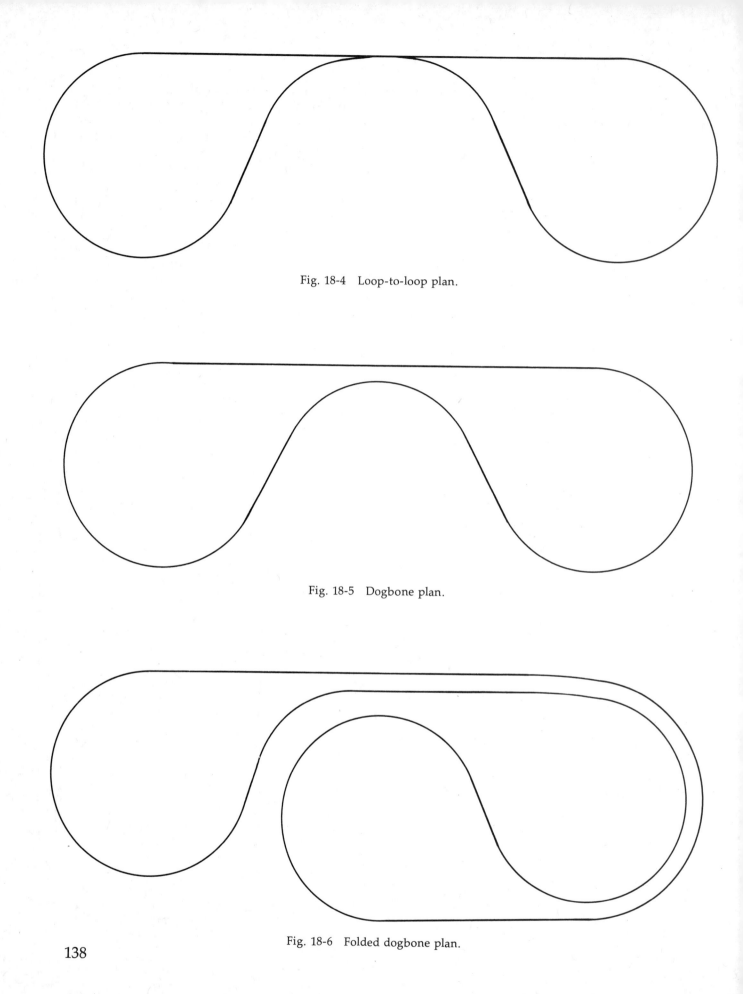

Fig. 18-4   Loop-to-loop plan.

Fig. 18-5   Dogbone plan.

Fig. 18-6   Folded dogbone plan.

can place a siding somewhere along an oval and call that Town A as the train departs, and when the train arrives, you can call it Town B. This is one way to get a lot of operating potential from a simple oval, but it certainly does tax the imagination.

The real railroads run from (or through) one town to the next in what railroad modelers call a "point-to-point" layout. An around-the-wall type of shelf layout that only covers two or three walls is almost automatically a point-to-point layout. You'll soon tire of running the locomotives backward in one direction on any point-to-point layout, and one solution is to install a turntable at each end so the locomotives can be turned. The bother of turning the locomotive and rearranging the train so the locomotive is first and the caboose is last soon gets to be a bore, however; so most modelers add a reversing loop to one or both ends of the layout. The loop-to-loop types of layouts usually have many feet of track and several sidings between the two switches that begin the reversing loops.

If the busy traffic on main line railroads must be a part of your model railroad, then you'll probably want to devise a double-track system so "east" and "west" trains can operate at the same time. With two loops at each end of that double-track system (in a "dogbone" track pattern), you can operate two trains (with the necessary rail gaps and wiring) with little danger of head-on collisions. The double-track portion of the "dogbone" style layout plan can be extended in a "folded dogbone" pattern with at least a portion of the two end loops hidden so that the double-track illusion is maintained. A pair of switches can be added, at either of the loops, to provide a reversing loop if desired; and a few crossovers along the main line can serve as passing sidings so slower trains can be overtaken by the express trains. Other passing sidings, yards, and industrial sidings can, of course, be added to any of these various track patterns to provide greater operating interest and excitement.

PLANNING YOUR MODEL RAILROAD

The first step, in locating the tracks for any home layout, is to determine just how much "right of way" is available for the model empire. A full basement is nice, but most modelers are lucky to find a single basement room or spare room for their layouts. An attic is a logical choice if there is an access stairway and enough headroom, but it must be insulated and well-ventilated or the extreme variations in temperature will expand and contract the rails and the benchwork.

The most common location for railroads in modern homes that lack basements is the garage. The only real drawback to a garage layout is the constant stream of dust and dirt and humidity that can reach the layout. If you can negotiate with your family to use the entire garage area, then the automobile-entrance door should be locked and weather striping applied around all the edges of the door to seal-out the dust and humidity. If you can only negotiate a portion of the garage, then I would strongly suggest that you construct a dust-free partition and ceiling to seal-off the model railroad portion of the garage from the elements.

Since the amount of space you can use will determine, to some extent, the scale you select for your models, try to make your space selection as early as possible. The available space and the scale of your models will most likely be the deciding factors as to what type of layout you design: around-the-wall, island, or a combination of the two—the peninsula layout.

Conventional curves require a table at least 36 inches wide in N scale, 56 inches in HO scale, and a whopping 118 inches for an O scale layout. If the track plan has reversing loops, the table will have to be at least twice as long as those minimum widths. Any double-track routes that go around curves will have to be added to those minimum dimensions. Don't forget to provide access openings on any layouts where the track is more than 24 inches away from the table edge. Normal operating aisles should be 24 inches wide with a minimum of 18 inches, and any aisles where spectators would stand should be 30 inches or wider.

Draw an outline of the available space to exact scale and sketch-in the table-widths and aisles that you prefer. For the final track plan drawing, I would recommend that you use a scale of 3/4 inch equals one foot, so the 1/16-inch marks on the ruler can indicate inches. This 3/4-inch scale is just large enough

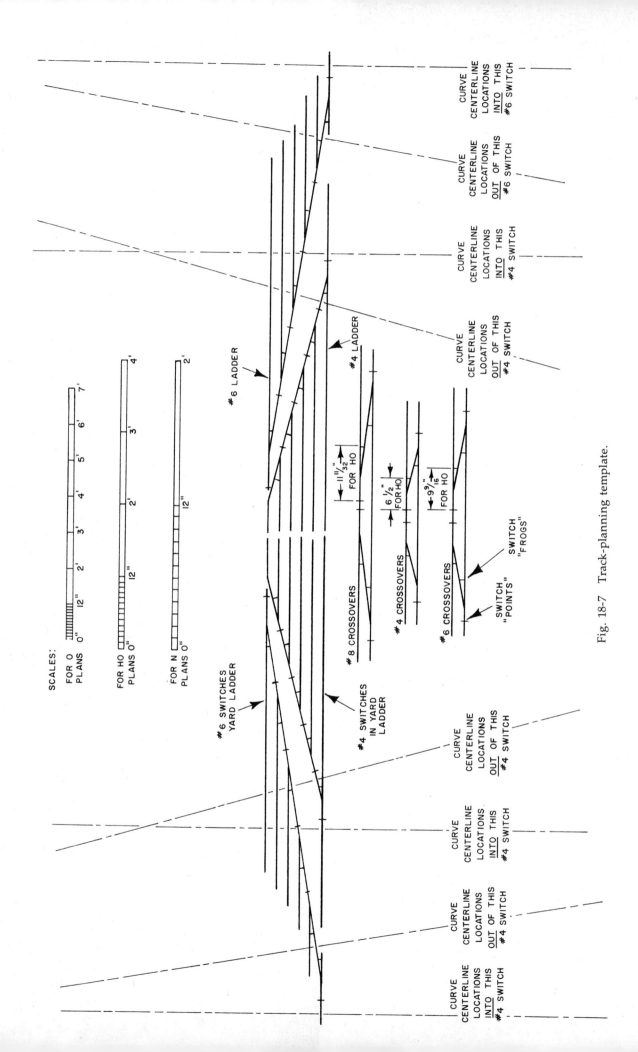

Fig. 18-7 Track-planning template.

Fig. 18-8 Use transparent drafting paper so you can see the switch alignment and curve center marks on the planning template.

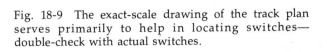

Fig. 18-9 The exact-scale drawing of the track plan serves primarily to help in locating switches—double-check with actual switches.

so errors in track alignment will show up, but small enough to fit on a reasonable-size piece of paper. Drafting supply stores sell triangular rulers with half a dozen different scales, including 3/4-inch-to-the-foot, to make measurements quicker and easier. Use a clear plastic drafting triangle to be sure you get the corners of the room and the track's radius centers square. I use an inexpensive drafting compass but the 25-cent toy kinds will work just as well if you remember to set the compass to the marks on the ruler, not to the marks on the compass handle, when you draw the curves. It may sound like you're well on your way to becoming a professional draftsman but it's really not that complex, and your work doesn't have to be letter-perfect—the primary purpose of track planning is just to be sure that the plan you envision will actually fit in the space you have available.

The angle and position of each of the track switches is almost as critical as finding space for the curves. The problem areas are those where several switches may be located too closely together in a yard or industrial area. If you are using snap-together type track and switches, you can literally lay out the layout on the floor to see where the edges of the benchwork should be located or, at the very least, you can connect a variety of switches to see if there is room for the switch complex you plan.

The various booklets that deal with specific brands of snap-together track can be a big help too. All but one of the plans in this book have been drawn to accept the more realistic switches like number 4s, 6s, or 8s. The switch number, by the way, is determined like the percentage of a grade; the diverging tracks in a number 4 angle-away from each other one-unit for every four-units of track length. That

Fig. 18-10   If your layout is a complex array of grades and overlapping track you'd be wise to build a model of the model first.

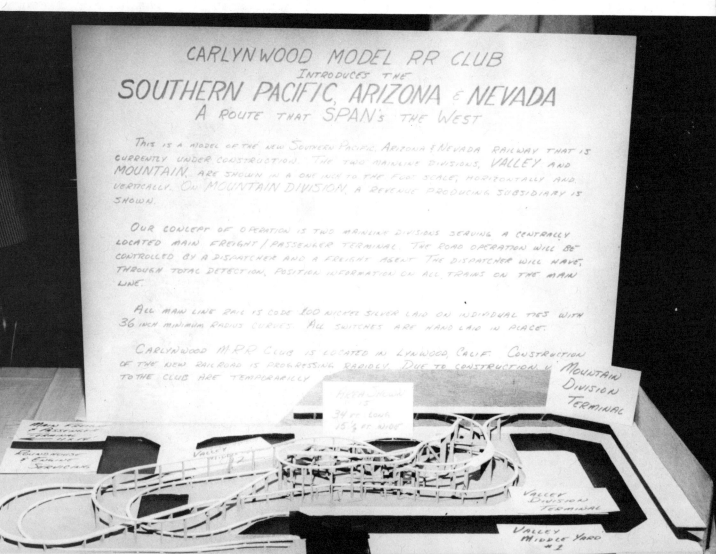

angle, however, requires a fairly severe radius on the curved portion of the track that roughly corresponds to an 18-inch radius curve in HO scale; the number 6 switches are closer to 30-inch radius (in HO scale) so the number 6 should be the smallest size you would consider for anything but a tiny branch-line layout. The number 8 switches are usually used only when the modeler wants the trackwork to look more like the prototype. You can see the difference the switch size makes in the length required for a crossover from one double-track to the other. Number 4 switches can be used for freight yards where only a small switch engine and cars of less than 50 feet will operate. The number 4 switches allow a much steeper angle on the "ladder" track that leads to each yard track, so the yard tracks themselves can be longer to hold more cars.

The track-planning template will help you locate switches and crossovers and double-track or yard positions. A photostat shop can enlarge or reduce the template so you can use it on a 3/4-inch scale track plan or you can simply use the appropriate scale from the template as your layout-planning ruler. The dotted lines will help you to locate the final critical dimensions—the curve centers of curves that begin or end at a switch. If you position the curve center so the curve ends too close to a switch, there won't be room for the switch points to operate or, at best, the actual curve will have to tighten just before it enters the switch—there's no point in using a 24-inch radius curve if the end of it spirals down to 12 inches to fit a switch location. Place the point of the compass on the dotted line and the pencil end on the appropriate switch when using the template. If you use inexpensive drafting paper for your track plans, you can easily trace the switch and curves of the template through the paper. The semi-transparent paper will also allow you to plan critical areas like reversing loops, wyes, and yards on separate sheets of paper so you can juggle them around to best fit the outline of the benchwork.

Fig. 18-11 Percentage grade chart.

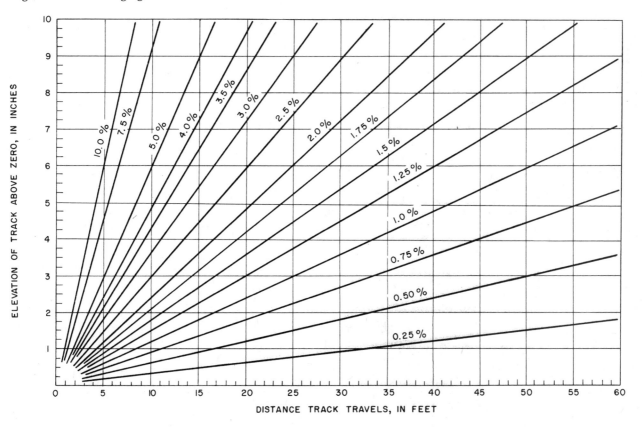

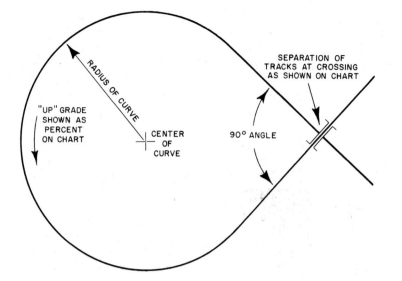

Fig. 18-12   Minimum distances for over and under loops.

FIGURE 18-13

PERCENTAGE OF GRADE CHART FOR OVER-AND-UNDER LOOPS

Radius of curve (in inches)	Separation of tracks at crossing						
	1⅝" (minimum for N scale)	2"	3" (minimum for HO scale)	3½"	4" (minimum for S scale)	5" (minimum for O scale)	6"
8	3.0	3.7					
10	2.4	3.0					
12	2.0	2.5	3.8	4.4	5.0		
14	1.7	2.1	3.1	3.7	4.2		
16	1.5	1.9	2.7	3.3	3.8		
18	1.4	1.7	2.5	2.9	3.4		
20	—	1.5	2.2	2.6	3.0		
22	—	—	2.1	2.4	2.8	4.2	
24	—	—	1.9	2.2	2.5	3.1	3.8
30	—	—	1.4	1.7	2.0	2.5	2.8
36	—	—	1.2	1.4	1.6	2.1	2.4
42	—	—	1.1	1.2	1.4	1.8	2.2
48	—	—	0.9	1.1	1.2	1.6	1.9
54	—	—	—	1.0	1.1	1.4	1.7
60	—	—	—	—	1.0	1.2	1.5
72	—	—	—	—	0.8	1.0	1.2
96	—	—	—	—	0.7	0.8	0.9

MULTI-LEVEL GRADE PLANNING

If any of your trackwork must be elevated so that one track can pass above another, you must determine just how steep the grade must be. The combination figure-eight and oval track plan is just one example of how one track might have to climb a grade to clear another track. It is possible, of course, to make each of those a crossing with both tracks at the same level; but that takes even more space, and it can seriously limit multi-train operation.

Grades are almost always present on the prototype railroads and they can improve the realism of a model railroad in addition to allowing the tracks to be positioned for the best use of the available space. Most model locomotives will pull a car or two up a grade as steep as 10 percent (a rise of 10 inches in a 100-inch length of track), but a grade of 6 percent is about the steepest that a four or five car train can climb. The prototype railroads seldom have grades of more than *one* percent!

Most model railroaders try to limit the steepness of their grades to 2 or 3 percent.

The chart in Fig. 18-13 shows how steep the grade will be for the elevation and the distance up the hill. In situations where one track must climb over itself (a surprisingly common occurrence in many model railroad track plans), the chart for the over-and-under grade and radius dimensions may be a help in your planning. If you use a bridge at the point where the tracks cross, you can get by with the minimum clearance figures; but tracks that pass beneath yards and the like will require about another ½ inch to allow room for the Homosote baseboard beneath the upper level trackwork. The "separation" dimensions are measured from the tops of the rails on the lower track to the tops of the rails on the upper track. You can use the completed track sketches to help in locating the best positions for wiring connections, and gaps in the rails and uncoupling ramps and to help you pre-plan the structures, bridges, and scenery.

XIX

The Master Module Layout

The most satisfying model railroad layouts are those that can grow as your interest in the hobby develops. The modular concept, adding as space and time permit, allows for this type of growth. It is easiest to imagine a layout made from modular sections that grows around the walls of the layout room from either or both ends of the original module, but there are alternative module methods. The late John Allen completed a tiny 4' x 8' HO layout that he incorporated into a 6½' x 20' layout a few years later; and that same 4' x 8' module became a branch line on his last layout, a basement-size giant, some 15 years later.

With some careful pre-planning, your first model railroad can remain with you and become part of any larger system that you may build in the future. A very small yard is, perhaps, one of the best first-time layouts. The relatively large number of tracks will provide plenty of switching action; enough to use the operation-unlimited system or any other operating plan. The tiny yard can later become the terminal for a branch line on a larger layout (like John Allen's 4' x 8' layout) or the base for a smaller railroad's operations.

Fig. 19-1   Only the very rich would drive to Basalt, Colorado, in the spring of 1909; the rest of us would take the Colorado Midland's eastbound Train 4. *(Photo from the Western Collection.)*

Fig. 19-2
KEY TO SYMBOLS
on all layout plans

straight or curved track centerlines

end of track (bumper)

trackage hidden by tunnels, buildings, or scenery

number 6 switch
POINTS   FROG

number 8 switch
POINTS   FROG

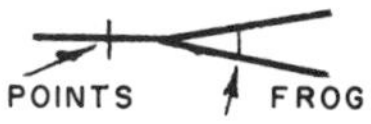

number 6 wye switch
POINTS   FROG

number 8 wye switch
POINTS   FROG

number 8 three-way switch
POINTS   FROGS

curve centers

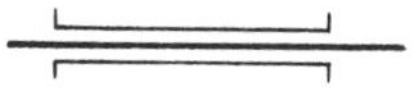

bridge

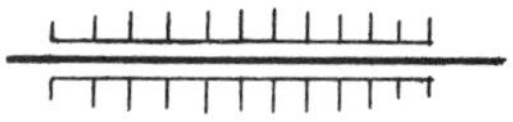

wooden trestle

tunnel portal (or entrance to other hidden trackage)

snowshed (with open sides)

snowshed (with enclosed sides)

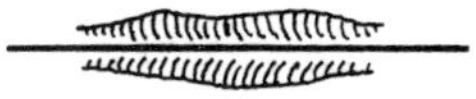

cut (earth rises steeply above track level)

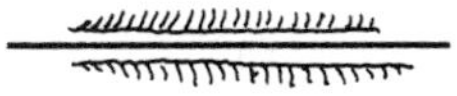

fill (earth falls away steeply from track level)

cliff, ridge, or palisade (steep slope)

hillsides (marks fan out toward *bottom* of slope)

stream or lake

station or freight-loading platform

99
elevation of track above floor or "zero" level

electrical gap in one rail

electrical gap in both rails

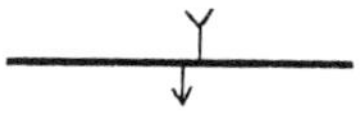

electrical feeders (connections to power source)

uncoupling ramps

Fig. 19-3
KEY TO LETTERS
on all layout plans

AA   points where cross-section drawings would intersect layout
B   points where 2 x 4 wood supports for upper levels must be positioned if upper level cannot be supported from ceiling rafters
C   commercial coal dealer (often used for locomotive refueling)
CI   cinder pit
CT   Coaling tower or trestle for locomotive fuel
D   Dwelling owned by railroad for railroad workers
E   Engine house or roundhouse
FT   Freight house (for less-than-carload lot (lcl) freight)
H   Railroad hotel or eating house

I   Ice house for re-icing refridgerator cars
M   maintenance of way sheds
O   lubricating and fuel oil storage
P   pump house for water supply to steam locomotives
S   freight car or passenger car service shop
SD   sand house and tower for locomotives
SS   snowshed
STA station
TT   turntable
W   water tower or stand pipe
X   track location at transition from upper to lower level
Y   track location at transition from upper to lower level
Z   track location at transition from upper to lower level

Fig. 19-4   Basalt, Colorado, circa 1906.

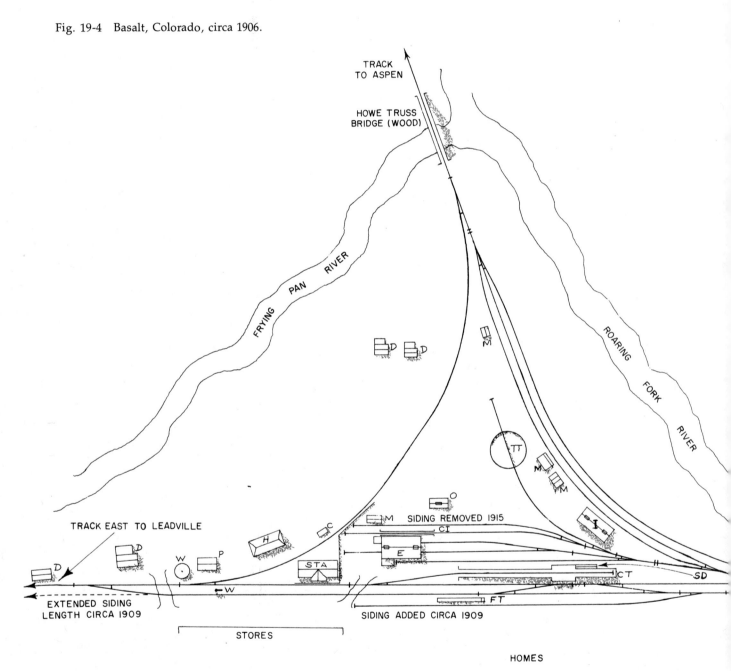

148

The real railroads' yards are definitely not just concentrated at the ends of the line the way most model railroaders seem to imagine. Additional yards are placed along the line about a day's run apart so the trains can change crews. In the days of steam powered trains, these division point yards were used to change engines and the caboose on any through train. When ice was still in use in the refrigerator cars, the ice house to replenish the supply was often located at the division point yard; and in some cases, cattle pens were located there so the cattle could be unloaded for the mandatory rest period on any long-distance animal movement. Dining cars and baggage cars and sleeping cars were added or removed from the passenger trains at these same division points. In all, it is a center of action that could keep any model railroader busy for years. The unusual emphasis on locomotive movement to supply the trains with "fresh" power provides a rare prototypical chance for a modeler to show off a collection of locomotives.

Some of the full-size yard locations were developed at the points along the major railroads where a branch line might join the main line. These junctions might have once been the meeting of just two tracks but, as traffic grew on both the branch and the main line, the junction often grew to a city-size yard in spite of being located in a small town. The track plan in this chapter is based on just that kind of place: Basalt, Colorado, a division point yard on the Colorado Midland Railroad's main line and, at the same time, a yard for the Midland's branch line to Aspen, Colorado.

By real railroad standards, this was a truly tiny yard with just three yard tracks on the far west end and a two-stall engine house; but the site has just about everything a modeler could dream of to provide operating action. As small as the Basalt yard was, it's too large to be modeled in exact scale. The yard tracks on the right end of the drawing in Fig. 19-4 have been shortened by over ½ *mile*; this "tiny" yard would require an 8' x 50' area in HO scale! The condensed version (Fig. 19-4) incorporates all the structures and all but one

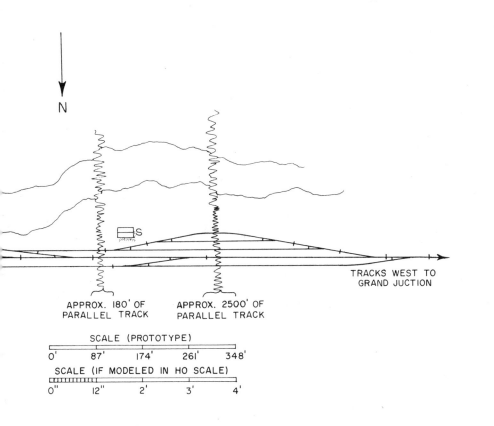

N

S

TRACKS WEST TO
GRAND JUCTION

APPROX. 180' OF
PARALLEL TRACK

APPROX. 2500' OF
PARALLEL TRACK

SCALE (PROTOTYPE)

0'   87'   174'   261'   348'

SCALE (IF MODELED IN HO SCALE)

0"   12"   2'   3'   4'

of the yard tracks so the switching movements that were made on the prototype can be matched on the model.

The three parallel tracks that swing by the ice house and turntable appear to be a storage yard but they were not: the track nearest the ice house was used to re-ice refrigerator cars and for some lcl (less than carload lots)—freight; the center track was the branchline to Aspen; and the track nearest the river was the switch lead for the 0-6-0 switchers that worked the three tracks to the west.

Virtually all the tracks inside the wye's triangular area were used for locomotive storage or servicing, except for the track on the south side of the engine house which was used to pick up cinders from the track just beside the engine house. Cabooses and some passenger cars were turned on the turntable but most locomotives were turned on the wye trackage. The sand house was a bit unusual in that it was suspended on wood posts beside the coaling trestle's storage bins so carloads of sand could be pushed up the trestle (just as carloads of coal were) to be hand-shoveled into the sand bins.

The town of Basalt was (and is) located on the hills along the edges of the trackage to the north. The hills came so close to the tracks at some points, like the area where the Roaring Fork River sweeps nearest to the tracks, that the railroad reduced the number of tracks to fit the available flatland beside the river. The main line followed the Frying Pan Creek (River) almost to its headwaters at the top of the valley to the east and all the way to its connection with the Grand (now the Colorado) River to the west. The line to Aspen followed the far more gentle slope up the Roaring Fork Valley.

Water-level routes like these were very common in the turn-of-the-century period when most of today's real railroads were first surveyed and graded to provide the easiest (and least expensive) route. Notice how the switches are placed very close together, particularly at the entrance to the center of the wye, and the use of several three-way and wye-style switches to conserve space—common practices on real railroads where space is expensive or, at Basalt, where the trackage was added as the railroad grew. I've used number 8 switches on the plan of the prototype just in case you might want to

model it full-size in N scale, most other prototype railroads used even longer switches like a number 10 or a number 12. The three-way switches, wyes, and number 8 switches are available as both kits and as ready-laid units from a variety of model railroad manufacturers.

A DIVISION POINT AND JUNCTION ON A SHELF

The Basalt division point yard is one of the best prototype areas I've ever seen for adaptation to a model railroad. There is no reason why you couldn't create your own plan based on prototype practice; but in this case, the plan actually *is* prototype practice. I've used the Basalt yard in Figs. 19-5 and 19-6 as an example of how such a "nugget" of action can begin as a simple 2' x 11½' shelf layout in HO scale (a 1' x 6' N scale version could fit on a window sill or a dresser top; and the 4' x 20' O scale version could fit along a garage wall). This same tiny layout plan is used on the 5' x 16' HO scale layout in this chapter (Fig. 19-7) and retained in the "lifetime layout" in the next chapter.

With a bit of think-ahead planning about the layout you *might* build someday, you can do the same thing with your very first layout. Don't let the fact that this particular yard happens to be on just one railroad (the Colorado Midland) in one era (1889 to 1923) confuse your thinking. This same track plan could be used for a modern diesel road by simply substituting oiling and washing services for the coaling and water and cinder facilities on the plan; and the 'locale' could be anywhere from California's foothills to the forests of the South to Maine's north woods.

There are two versions (see Figs. 19-5 and 19-6) of the shelf layout for Basalt: one using hand-laid or kit switches and the other with the best of the Atlas ready-laid track (their "Custom-Line" series with nickle silver rails). From these plans, you can see how much the trackage must be modified to allow the convenience of ready-laid track (a few of AHM's wye and three-way switches would help but I didn't want to complicate things for you by using two brands of snap-together track). If the excess track on each end of several of the Atlas switches were trimmed and

An Amtrak streamliner on an
N-TRAK modular layout module.

New cabs, paint, and decals can
transform a Lionel locomotive.

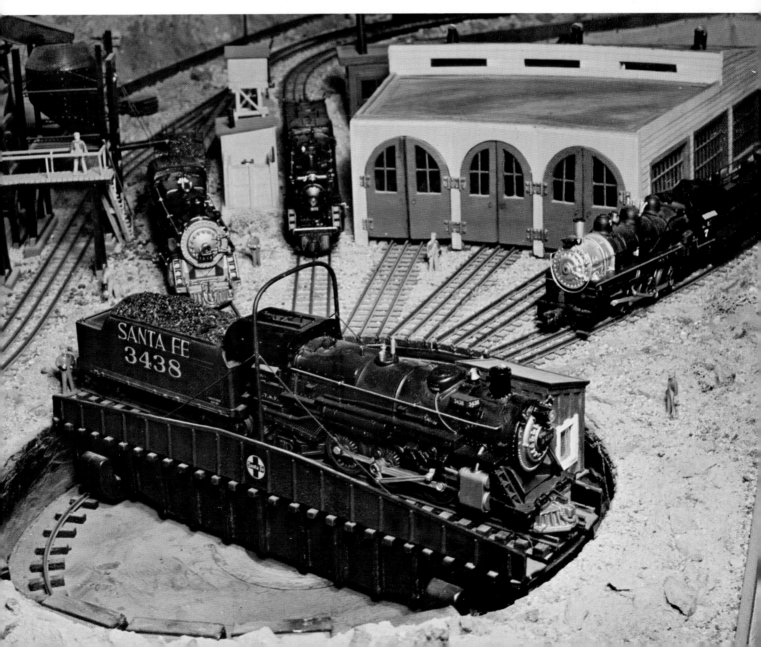

Resin water and a scratch-built sawmill in N scale.

Karen Overgaard's modeling
artistry in N scale.

The mechanisms are toys but the effect is life-like.

The scratch-built "St. Clair" station in HO scale.

Some paint, weathering, and
imaginary smoke in HO scale.

Most of the foliage is foam on Irv Schultz' superb layout.

The Slim Gauge Guild is a mountain man's dream-come-true.

The molded plaster rocks were shaped in latex molds.

A real railroad, gone for decades, but well worth modeling.

Subtle weathering and proper paint disguise any trace of plastic.

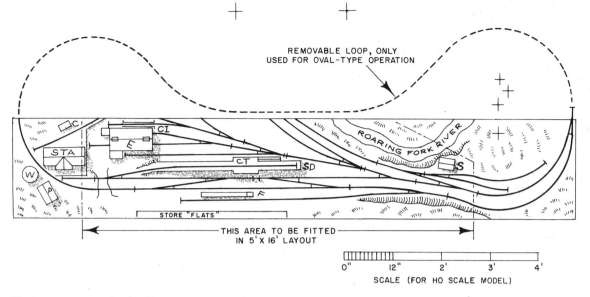

Fig. 19-5   2' x 11½' shelf layout module of Basalt, Colorado (for hand-laid track).

flexible track used in place of the track sections (with some AHM three-way switches), you could just about duplicate the pattern of the hand-laid trackage. You can see, by comparing the trackage on these two plans, whether hand-laid track (or trimming and fitting sectional track) is worth the effort or if you would rather settle for the speed and convenience of ready-laid snap-together track. You would, of course, have the same type of choice to make with N scale or O scale trackwork. The point to remember is that you cannot use snap-together track sections to duplicate most published track plans without making so many changes that the finished railroad just barely resembles the original plan.

The shelf layout requires a few operating changes because there isn't room for a

Fig. 19-6   2' x 11½' shelf layout module of Basalt, Colorado (for Atlas HO scale snap track).

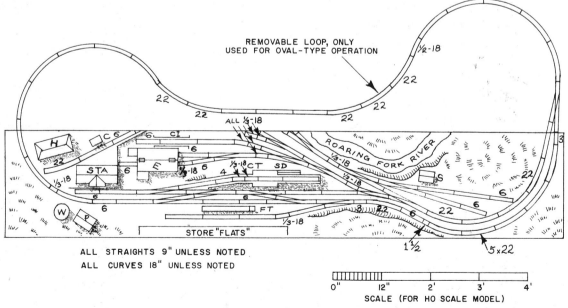

runaround track at both ends of the layout. I've put the switch at the right, but you could make the lower track stub-ended and place the switch on the left or, if you have another foot of length for the layout, put switches at both ends. A passenger train would arrive at the station from the right and the engine would uncouple from the train way back by the sand house (SD). The engine would then run through the crossover and back around so it could come up behind its own train to push it on into the stub-ended track just in front of the station. There is only room for one short coal car and a tank-type switcher (one with no separate tender) in front of the station for switching carloads of sand and coal up onto the coaling trestle.

The track to Aspen could connect with the removable "loop operation" track if you wanted to simulate operations on the branch line. Operations on this shelf-style layout would consist mainly of changing engines and cabooses on any "through" trains (remember this is a division point) and adding or removing diners, Pullman cars, and baggage cars from through passenger trains. Trains could also be made-up and broken down for traffic to and from Aspen on the branch line.

The waybills described in the operation-unlimited scheme should be made out mostly for railroad-related industries on this particular layout so cars can be supplied to carry sand, coal, and lubricating oil; to pick up cinders; to deliver ice to the ice house track; and to carry tools and supplies to the car service shed (S) and the freight platform. A number of local industries that don't have their own sidings would likely receive shipments from the freight platform too.

There is room for as many as six different industries along that track, and others could be positioned along sidings if you wanted to alter the plan to serve the industrial area of a town or city. There's plenty of operating action for at least three locomotives on just this small shelf—a local switch engine, an engine for the through freight train, and another for the through passenger train. If a switch is added to the removable track to simulate operations to Aspen, a fourth engine could be used to power the Aspen-bound branch line freight (or a fifth for the Aspen passenger

train). The two through trains' consists can be altered by using part of that removable track (or the track that runs between the station and the water tank) as a fiddle yard. In all, there's enough operating action to keep two engineers busy for years—and all that on a simple shelf.

THE MASTER MODULE

A 5' x 16' layout is a practical size for just about any home layout. It's big enough to allow trains of twelve to sixteen freight cars and six to eight passenger cars to operate without running into themselves and small enough to fit in a basement room or part of a garage. You won't get much of a railroad in that space if you model in O scale, but twice that area (10' x 32') is considered about average for those in the larger scale.

The layout described and illustrated (*all* those track diagrams show the possible routes trains can take on just this *one* layout) on the next few pages (Figs. 19-7 and 19-8) fits that 5' x 16' area if modeled in HO scale. The layout could be modeled in half that space in N scale, but one of the primary advantages of this small scale is that it allows real world "spaciousness." I would suggest, then, that the N scale modeler use this same basic plan with the same switch locations and siding length but with closer track spacing. The open feeling of the actual trackage at Basalt, Colorado, could almost be matched precisely in this area with N scale models; and the train lengths could be typical of the modern railroads (almost) with thirty to forty-car freights and twelve to sixteen-car passenger trains. If you're considering a layout in N scale, look at plans for HO scale railroads in this same manner rather than assuming you can halve the length and width in N scale; you can, but the layout will be far better if built with HO scale's minimum radius curves and siding lengths. The size of the layout alone is 5' x 16' but be sure you have at least 2 feet of space for an aisle along the "Roaring Fork River" edge of the layout and, preferably, another 18-inch aisle along one end and across the hill-covered back of the layout (so you don't have to crawl under the table to reach the hidden trackage). Those 18-inch aisles will also allow you to have a mine or another small town on the back side of the layout (more possibilities for that back side are given in the next chapter).

The late Frank Ellison was one of the first model railroaders to compare our layouts to an actor's stage—the trains are the actors; the trackwork, the structures; and the scenery, the props. The analogy is a good one because the trains on any model railroad really do "make an appearance" on the layout; for a brief moment, trains from some "other" railroad cross the path of your model trackage bound for some "other" imaginary destination. The timetable (if you use one) defines the various "acts" of the model railroad, and an operating scheme like the "operation-unlimited" concept serves as the "script."

Real railroads are almost always linked to other rail lines to the extent that you'd have to model an entire continent if you didn't chose just one scene or aspect for your miniature empire. There were a few mining or logging or industrial railroads that didn't connect with other railroads but they were exceptions to the rule.

This 5' x 16' layout carries that "on-stage" concept to perhaps its ultimate in duplicating a real place with real trackage and real buildings and even a particular time in history. "Eastbound" trains from Grand Junction, Colorado, travel to Basalt; stop to change locomotives, cabooses, and crews; and travel on toward Leadville (and eventually to Colorado Springs), Colorado. An occasional train drifts down the tracks along the Roaring Fork River into Basalt from Aspen on the end of the branch line to deliver cars or passengers bound for the east or west. The grade to the east is steep enough (a rough-to-climb 3 percent) to require one or two additional "helper" engines on most freight and passenger trains and those, too, are added at Basalt. The helper engines will cut off the trains at the top of the grade (Ivanhoe) to return to Basalt. The helper engines are used on the freight, passenger, and mixed (a freight train with a baggage/coach in place of the caboose) trains to and from Aspen; and all the main line locomotives are serviced, turned, and refueled at Basalt. All this happened daily on the prototype Colorado Midland Railroad from 1888 to 1923 when the line was abandoned; but it can happen in miniature every

evening from now on with the trackage that appears on these pages.

The eastbound trains appear at Basalt from the right side of the plans (at Z) and disappear (after changing locomotives and cabooses and adding or dropping any cars bound for Aspen) at the far left after passing the water tower (W). Westbound trains take the opposite path. The trains to and from Aspen appear and disappear from tunnel X just before the wooden Howe-style truss bridge (Campbell has a kit for one in HO scale) over the Frying Pan River. The plan indicates that there are tunnel portals at the points where the trains appear on the scene, but they really "vanish" into a thick grove of aspen trees at Z, behind a hill just beyond the water tower at Y, and into a deep cut at X. There's no reason why any of these points couldn't be tunnel portals on a model railroad except that that isn't the way it was done on the Colorado Midland's route and there's no point in destroying even that little bit of reality when there are other ways to allow the trains to disappear from the scene. I would go a step farther, with the two yard tracks near Z, to permanently mount a freight car at the extreme end of each of those tracks to serve as an end-of-track bumper. The same grove of trees that hides the disappearance of the main line tracks at Z would hide the area beyond those two bumper cars to give the illusion that the yard tracks continue as they did on the real railroad.

THE HIDDEN YARD

The tracks that disappear at Z and at the water tower can connect with one another beneath the visible tracks to form a simple figure-eight layout (see Fig. 19-8). The track that disappears at X could tie-into the "eight" with a switch inside the tunnel portal. One more hidden switch would be needed to bring together the two tracks that disappear at Z. That simple series of hidden tracks, with two switches, may well be all you would want to build. I would, in fact, suggest that you do just that if your track-laying enthusiasm is nil. The simple figure-eight system will require a bit of imagination to explain why a westbound train that disappeared at Z can

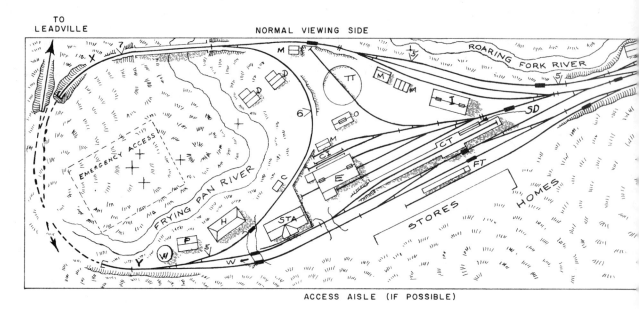

Fig. 19-7   Visible trackage at Basalt, Colorado (for 5' x 16' in HO scale).

Fig. 19-8   Hidden (lower level) trackage at Basalt (for 5' x 16' in HO scale).

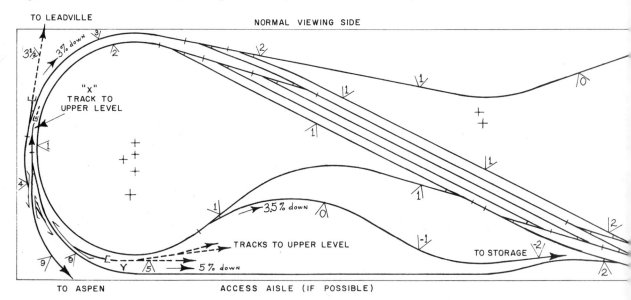

POSSIBLE
SITE FOR MINE
FROM ASPEN BRANCH

0"   12"   2'   3'   4'
SCALE (FOR HO SCALE LAYOUT)

TRACKS
TO UPPER
LEVEL

3% down

0"   12"   2'   3'   4'
SCALE (FOR HO SCALE LAYOUT)

reappear as an eastbound train at the water tower. You'll also have to ignore the fact that trains supposedly headed up the branch line for Aspen appear again on the main line near the water tower. Model railroaders have to imagine-away a lot more things than those, however, and imagination requires far less efforts than does laying the hidden yard trackage.

There is more hidden than visible trackage at Basalt but each of those hidden tracks does serve a purpose. The five parallel tracks in the center of the hidden yard are there so that you can hold the trains until you are ready for them to appear—none of those five tracks serves as a conventional yard track for making and breaking-down trains (there is no uncoupling or coupling in this hidden yard). The array of hidden trackage can be simple flex-track and ready-laid switches without any ballast or other details. All the trackwork should be laid and checked for operation before any scenery is installed. If you use an open-grid type of benchwork, all the hidden tracks will be accessible from beneath the scenery; but you would be wise indeed to place removable chunks of scenery directly above the groups of switches near the two edges of the table.

The plywood and Homosote roadbed for the hidden tracks can be placed on or near the top of the benchwork and the visible tracks elevated above on risers. Only a small portion of the hidden tracks (those with zero elevation marks) could be placed directly on the benchwork; most of the hidden yard has an elevation of one inch, with grades out of both ends of the yard leading to the five-inch elevation of most of the visible trackage. The track to Aspen rises up to 9 inches to pass above the now-hidden Leadville track beyond the water tower. That Aspen-bound track then descends, on a 5 percent grade, to connect with the hidden yard near the back edge of the table. There is an additional track marked "to storage" that can connect to even more hidden sidings if you wish; or that track can serve a hidden fiddle yard to add or remove locomotives or rolling stock. Notice, too, in Fig. 19-8 the *visible* trackage is shown in dotted lines and the hidden trackage with solid lines. The letters X, Z, and Y (near the water tower) are points where the tracks disappear from view so you can better relate how

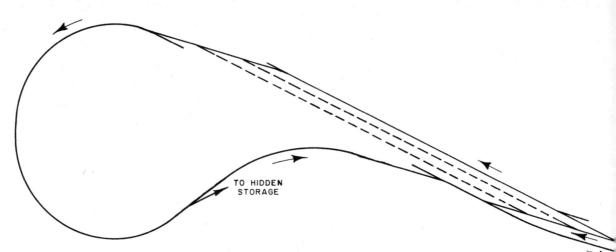

Fig. 19-9   Return loop train routing for "west" (Basalt/Grand Junction/Basalt) operation. (Note: dotted line tracks are for train storage only; solid lines are "through" tracks.)

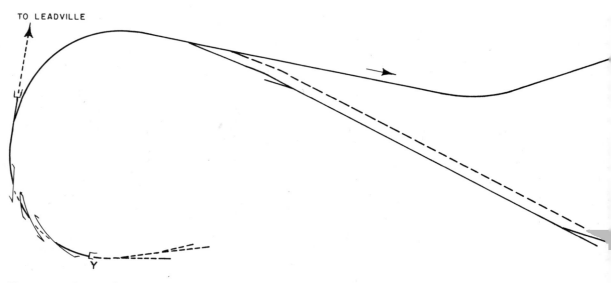

Fig. 19-10   Return loop train routing "east" (Basalt/Leadville/Basalt) operation. (Note: dotted line track is for train storage only; solid lines are "through" tracks.)

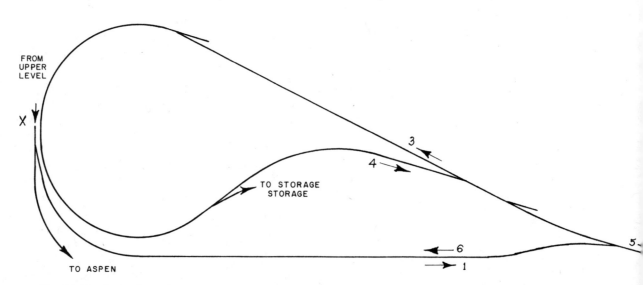

Fig. 19-11   Aspen branch train operating sequence for Basalt/Aspen/Basalt out-and-back operation.

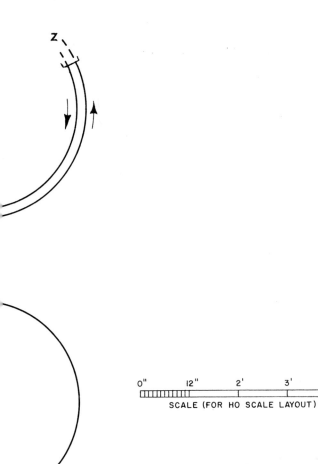

SCALE (FOR HO SCALE LAYOUT)

the hidden trackage connects with the visible trackage. The tracks indicated with dashes in Fig. 19-9 are alternate storage tracks for the trains.

Trains that leave or enter Basalt from the west take this route through the maze of hidden trackage with normal travel in the direction of the arrows (see Fig. 19-9). The westbound trains have a choice of three holding tracks beneath Basalt so the train that just "went west" can be replaced with another eastbound train. The eastbound trains normally leave their particular storage track and head around the hidden reversing loop to reappear on the right hand track at Z. Only the tracks used by the trains that go to and from the west are shown (along with any switches that are on these tracks); the other tracks are used for west and Aspen-bound traffic.

The trains bound for (or arriving from) the east, leave the visible trackage at Y (near the water tower) and take the route indicated by the arrows (see Fig. 19-10) through the hidden trackage. These trains travel through their reversing loop first and then arrive at the track that leads back to Basalt. The dashed line in Fig. 19-10 is a single storage track for eastbound trains. Notice that the solid line track is the same one that the westbound trains would use. This track should normally be left clear (not used as a storage track) so that the eastbound, westbound, or Aspen-bound trains can use it without fear of running into a train that's being held on a storage track. The switch to the "To Leadville" track is optional. It appears on the drawing because that track actually will lead to a miniature "Leadville" someday (and it *does* in the next chapter!).

The trains bound to and from Aspen follow this path (see Fig. 19-11) through the hidden trackage after they leave Basalt to disappear at X. The switch to the track marked "To Aspen" can lead to a mine or another small town on the back side of the layout. (In the next chapter, it really does go to Aspen on the track plans with the hidden tracks serving as "interchange" tracks with the Denver & Rio Grande RR.) The Aspen-bound trains would follow the sequence shown by the arrows and numbers in Fig. 19-11. The train would run down the steep 5 percent grade (behind and below the stores at Basalt) to stop just out of sight near Z. The train must back through the reversing loop (numbers 3 and 4) and on through the switch (at 5) to stop (caboose end first this time) just out of sight at Z. Notice that it uses the outer of the two tracks that disappears (from Basalt west) at Z for all these maneuvers. The train would then run forward (engine first) through the switch (at 5) on up the 5 percent grade (at number 6) on its way back to Basalt. There is no separate storage siding for the Aspen trains, but the track from the number 3 to the next switch can be electrically isolated so one Aspen train can be stored there until the next one enters the hidden trackage (only Aspen trains use that short stretch of track). The length of track between numbers 5 and 2 and that "storage" section just beyond number 3 limits the lengths of the trains that can be operated on the Aspen branch line to 5 feet (if the layout is built in HO scale); but that's long enough for an engine and eight to ten cars. In any case, the 5

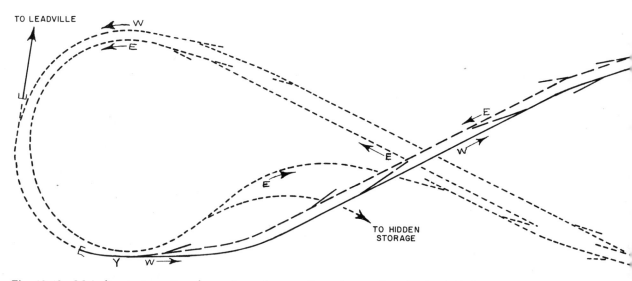

Fig. 19-12   Main line train routing for eastbound or westbound operation. (Note: dotted lines are tracks hidden from view.)

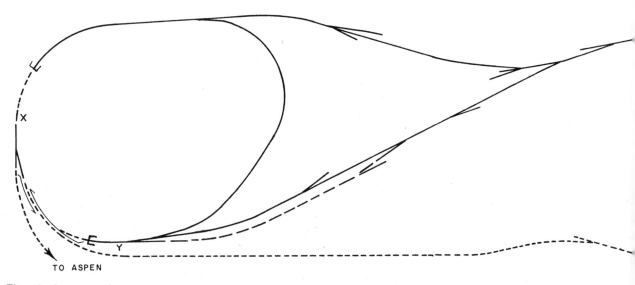

Fig. 19-13   Aspen branch train operating route for continuous (oval) operation. (Note: dotted lines are tracks hidden from view; long dashed line is used for passing only.)

percent grade would limit most trains to that length, because that's about the most that locomotives can pull up so steep a grade.

MULTI-TRAIN OPERATION

The choice of three separate routes (eastbound, westbound, and Aspen-bound) for trains to and from Basalt provides plenty of operation potential for two or three en-

0"   12"   2'   3'   4'

SCALE (FOR HO SCALE LAYOUT)

gineers. One man can operate the switcher in the Basalt yard while the other two operate the east-west through trains and the trains on the Aspen branch. The hidden, track does, however, allow operation of a single westbound train (in a figure-eight pattern) and a single Aspen-bound train (in an oval pattern) with only occasional interference with the visible trackage at Basalt. For a one-man operation, then, three trains can be operated at the same time with an Aspen-bound train circulating around an oval, a westbound train through a figure-eight, and a switcher working the tracks at Basalt. The arrivals and departures of the two circulating trains would constitute an automatic type of timetable that the Basalt switcher would have to watch out for while he worked cars in and out of sidings. That's right, this layout is designed so *three* trains can be operated at once!

The main line train would follow the track pattern shown here for the one-man operation of three trains. In Fig. 19-12, the solid lines indicate the visible tracks that the train would travel; the dotted lines indicate its path through the hidden trackage; the long dashed lines show the visible route that could be used so a westbound (W) train could be reversed to travel eastbound (E). Only that train's path is shown (as well as the switches it passes through); all other trackage is clear, at all times, for use by the Basalt switching locomotive.

The Aspen-bound train would follow the track pattern shown here for one-man operation of three trains. In Fig. 19-13, the solid lines show the visible trackage; the dotted lines indicate the portion of the route that is hidden from view; the short stretch of long dashed lines is an alternate route the Aspen train could take if there is a "main line" passenger train at the Basalt station. Notice that the Aspen train uses the outside track around the right end of the layout so it won't collide with the main line train that might be circulating around the figure-eight. That same outer track is used by the main line train *only* when the operator wants to change its direction through the hidden reversing loop trackage. The Aspen train would use the two legs of the wye that lead to Y *only* to reverse its direction; normal operation would be through the center of the three tracks near the ice house (in Fig. 19-7).

Fig. 19-14   An HO articulated swings its boiler out and around a curve.

A pair of mirrors, one mounted above the hidden yard's switches and the other down near the floor can be used for a visual check on the trains in the out-of-sight yard. An under-the-table light could illuminate the hidden yard when you wanted to check operations down there. As an alternate method, Campbell, Tri-Delt, and others make train-detection devices that can be wired to monitor lights on the control panel.

There is absolutely no standard as to how much time you should spend on any hobby, especially model railroading. Some modelers spend decades completing a single locomotive, others spend that much time just daydreaming (armchair model railroading) about their hobby and still others may fill two or three basements with superbly detailed layouts. What might be a "lifetime" layout to one modeler might be just a month's worth of enjoyment to someone with more leisure time. The 2' x 11½' shelf layout in the previous chapter might be just enough model railroad for some, and the 5' x 16' expansion of that shelf layout might be enough for most. There are a few model railroaders, however, who want a "project" that they *know* will take a lifetime to complete—and that's just what this layout is. This particular "lifetime" layout would fill an average two-car garage with actually *two* HO scale layouts; one with the average track level about 56 inches above the floor, and another layout, immediately above the first, with an average track level about 82 inches above the floor. The upper level is accessible when the viewers and engineers stand on a pair of 2-feet high platforms and that upper level is connected to the lower level by a spiral (or helix or corkscrew) of seven circles of track called a "stacker".

There's enough here to keep any man (and most clubs with half a dozen members) busy for a lifetime. The layout occupies a space that is generally available to anyone—a two-car garage about 18½-feet square. A similar-size area in a basement would do (as long as there is a minimum ceiling height of 99 inches); or the "spiral" could be eliminated and the two levels placed side-by-side in an area about 18½' x 32'. For most of us, this is a project to dream about but never even contemplate completing. Almost any model railroader could, however, complete a portion of this giant withing a few years of leisurely spare time.

This lifetime layout is based on a real railroad, the Colorado Midland, that operated through the Colorado Rockies from about 1888 until 1923 with all the towns and places patterned after those on the prototype. Even the track and switch locations and the buildings themselves are those of the Colorado Midland; so this is one model railroad that truly does go from one place to another like

A Lifetime Layout

the prototype. There is enough trackage and action on either of the layout's two levels to satisfy almost any model railroader so that either level *can* be considered a complete layout.

The portion of the railroad from the town of Basalt to Sellar, up the spiral trackage on the "stacker" inside the mountain to Ivanhoe, and on around (above Sellar and Basalt) to the snow shed just *before* Busk could be modeled as a smaller version of the prototype. These two levels would fill a room about 12½' x 18½'; a portion of the track at Sellar and at Ivanhoe could be removed to condense the size to 12½' x 16' (for HO scale) and still include most of the operating and scenic ideas. If the two-tier idea and the spiral "stacker" scare you (or if your ceilings are less than 99-inches high), then consider building *either* level of this 12½' x 18½' portion of the total plan.

There is yet another way that this "lifetime" giant can be attempted by any modeler with guaranteed success. Build just a portion at a time, beginning with something as small as the 2' x 11½' shelf layout in the previous chapter; and if all goes well, proceed

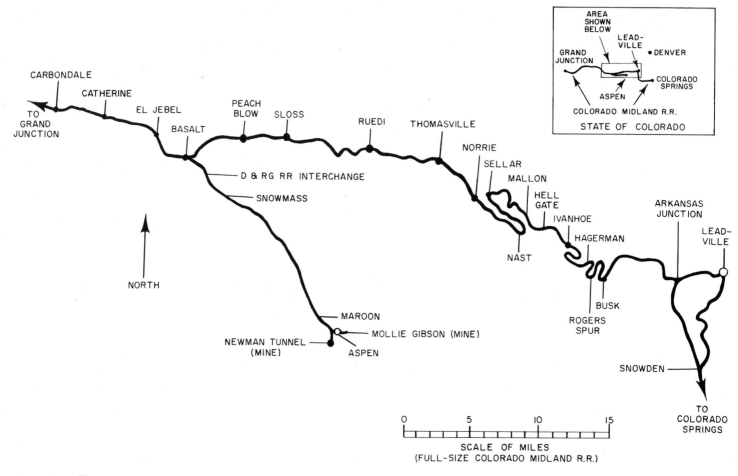

Fig. 20-1   Carbondale to Aspen and Leadville portion of the Colorado Midland Railroad, circa 1906.

to the 5' x 16' layout that incorporates the shelf. The 5' x 16' layout constitutes "stage 1" of the lower level on this lifetime layout; "stage 2" is an extension of the spur track toward Leadville on that original 5' x 16' layout. The legs of the wye at the town of Sellar can be extended (temporarily) to meet each other to form a reversing loop so operations could run from loop-to-loop (from the loop just past Sellar to the hidden, west reversing loop beyond and beneath Basalt). If operation goes well on that "island" and "around-the-wall" layout, then you might want to build the spiral stacker to the upper level and the trackage at Ivanhoe.

The next stage would include the Hagerman Tunnel and loops and would extend over the Hagerman trestle to a hidden reversing loop placed behind the upper level's backdrop. The final stages of construction would

extend the line into Leadville on the upper level and build the branch line into Aspen on the lower level. Even if you never get beyond that 2' x 11½' shelf (or the 5' x 16' "master module") a lifetime layout like this is worth dreaming about; you know there *is* a Leadville and an Aspen in real life *and* as part of a master plan that need never be completed, only started and enjoyed . . . .

This lifetime layout is truly a "master" plan, inspired by master track planners like John Armstrong, who has presented the concept of a two-tiered layout in *Model Railroader* magazine, as well as dozens of layouts based on prototype railroads. The layout is inspired, too, by master model railroaders like Irv Schultz who proved (to me, at least) that a shelf-type layout offers the ultimate in realism—thanks to the panoramic view such a design offers by encompassing your peripheral vision. The "lifetime" plan incorporates the shelf or around-the-wall concept even on the island portion because you cannot see across the island (at Basalt and Snowmass on the lower level and at Hagerman and Arkansas Junction on the upper level) so *all* your attention is concentrated on just the train you are operating. The master modeler ideas, pioneered by the late John Allen (and used so effectively on the Slim Gauge Guild's HOn3 layout), of waist-high mountains soaring to the ceiling appear at the mountain that captures the "Hell Gate" area of the Colorado Midland (incidentally, the same mountain that hides the spiral "stacker" trackage loops from one level to the next).

The lifetime layout was designed to allow, in fact to almost require, the use of walk-around train control so the engineers can follow the trains with throttle controls in hand. Whether you build the entire two-tier layout or just the first two stages, the very best that model railroading has to offer is included here and could very well be in *your* garage or basement!

Please don't let the fact that this particular layout is based on a relatively obscure prototype give you the impression that it wouldn't "fit" your favorite prototype. You could duplicate the plan exactly with either Santa Fe or Burlington locomotives and rolling stock for *both* of these railroads once owned by the real Colorado Midland. There's no reason at all why your miniature railroad has to be in 1923; "your" railroad could have survived right up to the diesel era.

The trackage doesn't have to represent the Colorado Midland either; change a few of the sidings and vary the terrain a bit and the lifetime layout plan could be used to duplicate the Moffat Road's line (now the Rio Grande) from Utah Junction (Leadville on the lifetime plan) to Orestod (Basalt) and Glenwood Springs (Aspen). Leadville, Basalt, and Aspen could be replaced with Toulumne, Jamestown, and Angels, respectively, to adapt the layout to match the famous Sierra Railway in California; or 100 miles north, the Western Pacific's route, scenery, and names could take the place of those on the Colorado Midland with Basalt being replaced by the canyon that is spanned by the bridges and the wye track at Keddie. The route and general format of the East Broad Top Railroad's nar-

Fig. 20-2   The mixed train from Aspen to Basalt had no boxcars of silver ore on this spring day in 1911, only the baggage-coach. *(Photo courtesy of the Colorado State Historical Society.)*

Fig. 20-3 The Colorado Midland's Aspen-bound passenger train used open-platform cars for years after the through trains adopted the more modern, closed vestibule cars. The patrons received a fine view from the Maroon Creek trestle. (*Photo courtesy of the Western Collection.*)

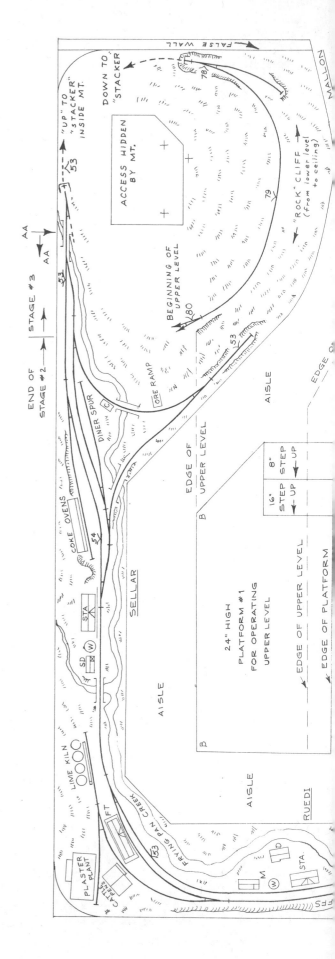

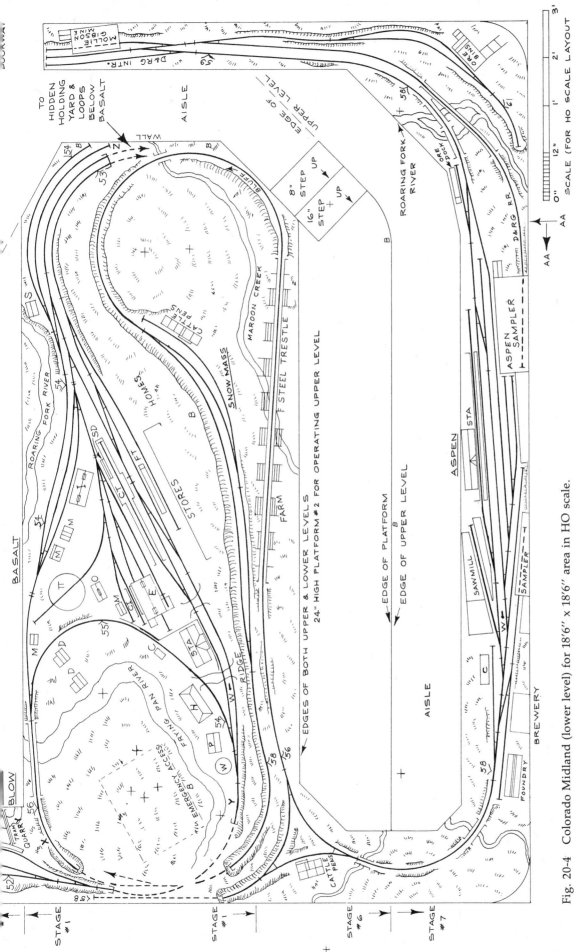

Fig. 20-4 Colorado Midland (lower level) for 18'6" x 18'6" area in HO scale.

165

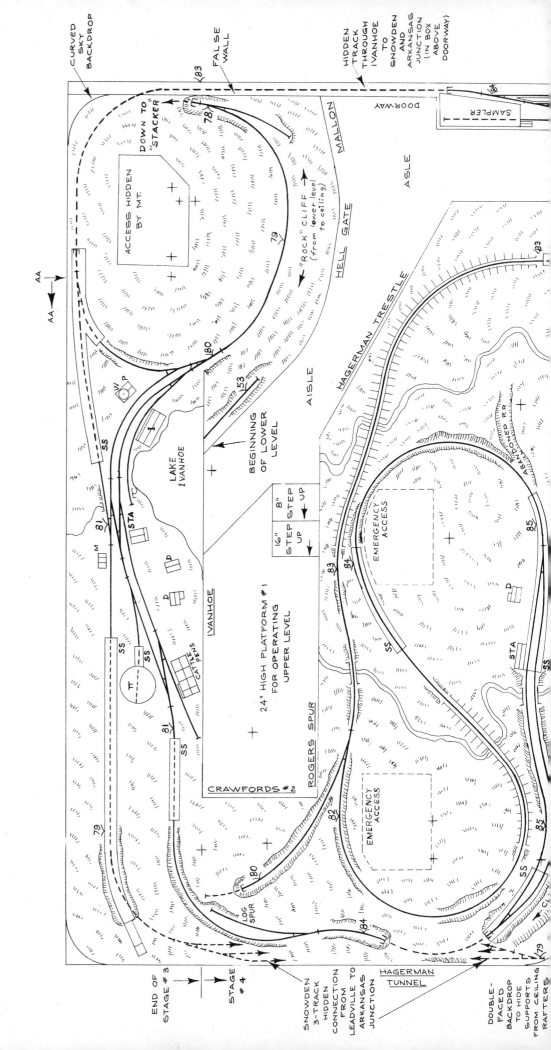

CURVED SKY BACKDROP

83

FALSE WALL

HIDDEN TRACK THROUGH IVANHOE TO SNOWDEN AND ARKANSAS JUNCTION (IN BOX ABOVE DOORWAY)

DOWN TO "STACKER"

78

ACCESS HIDDEN BY MT.

79

"ROCK" CLIFF (from lower level to ceiling)

HELL GATE

MALLON

DOORWAY

ASLE

AA

SAMPLER

83

AA

SS

W P

I

80

81

STA

53

BEGINNING OF LOWER LEVEL

AISLE

HAGERMAN TRESTLE

ABANDONED R.R.

LAKE IVANHOE

M

D

D

STEP 16"
UP
8" STEP
UP
UP

83
84

EMERGENCY ACCESS

85

SS

STA

D

SS

TT

SS

IVANHOE

CATTLE PENS

24" HIGH PLATFORM #1 FOR OPERATING UPPER LEVEL

ROGERS SPUR

CRAWFORDS #2

82

EMERGENCY ACCESS

85

SS

79

SS

81

80

LOG SPUR

84

SS

HAGERMAN TUNNEL

79

166

END OF STAGE #3

STAGE #4

SNOWDEN 3-TRACK HIDDEN CONNECTION FROM LEADVILLE TO ARKANSAS JUNCTION

DOUBLE-FACED BACKDROP TO HIDE SUPPORTS FROM CEILING RAFTERS

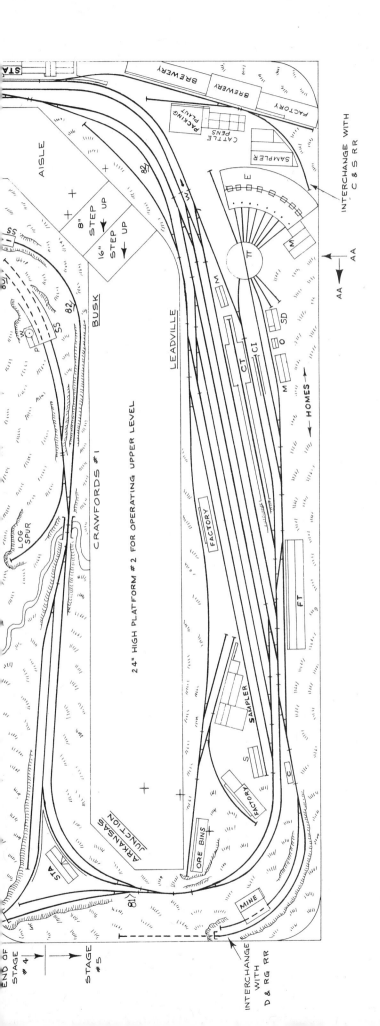

Fig. 20-5   Colorado Midland (upper level) for 18'6" x 18'6" area in HO scale.

167

row gauge trackage—from Mount Union (Leadville) to Orbisonia (Basalt) and on to the mines at Robertsdale (Aspen)—could replace the details of the trackage on the lifetime layout. A surprising number of full-size railroads had wye-style junctions much like Basalt; use your own favorite prototype places and equipment on a near-duplicate of any or all of this giant layout.

Don't overlook the idea, either, of creating your own railroad with its own name and herald and paint schemes and caboose styles. The railroads of men like W. Allen McClelland and the late Frank Ellison and John Allen are among the best layouts ever completed, and all of these were "free-lance" systems based very much on prototype practice but with fictitious names like the Virginia & Ohio, Delta Lines, and Gorre & Daphetid.

A TIME CAPSULE TRIP

There is a surprising amount of published information on the prototype Colorado Midland, considering that it's last whistle blew in 1923. Morris Cafke's book, *Colorado Midland* (Rocky Mt. RR Club, 1965) is the best source but it is long out of print and, in fact, a collectors item you'll have to find in a large public library. There are several other books that have a considerable amount of information on the Midland included in one or more chapters: *Basalt: Colorado Midland Town* (Pruett Press, Inc., Boulder, CO); *Roaring Fork Valley* (Sundance Ltd., Denver, CO); and *Rio Grande, Mainline of the Rockies* (Howell-North Books, Berkeley, CA).

The two tiers of the lifetime layout condense the prototype's 18.4-mile Aspen branch line into just about 61 feet (a scale mile in HO) and the Basalt to Leadville portion of the main line from the prototype's 55.6 miles into just 152 feet (2.5 scale miles in HO) without losing much of the action and excitement of the prototype. Here's the map of the Colorado Midland's system (Fig. 20-1) and a close-up of a portion of the railroad; so follow the thick black line on the plans of the prototype and the model, and we'll take a rattling ride from Aspen to Leadville . . . .

It's August of 1906 and the frosts have already hit some of the quaking aspen trees at Aspen's 7,950-foot elevation above the dis-

tant Pacific. We descend to Basalt (6,614-feet elevation) where the trees are still green and then we climb once again to Sellar's 9,619-foot altitude where the leaves have changed to that glorious yellow which marks autumn in the Colorado Rockies. Grab a coat because the snow has fallen twice this season at Ivanhoe's lofty 10,944-foot elevation.

Our train is the Aspen mixed but the samplers have no ore ready for shipment today so there's just the ten-wheeler locomotive and our open platform wooden baggage coach in the one-car train. The engineer barely has time to get the train rolling when he has to slow for the curve that sweeps past the wye (where the Aspen engines are turned) and cattle pens. The tracks sweep through a small cut and, ahead, the world seems to drop away beneath us as the train rattles and clanks over the steel trestle that spans Maroon Creek (Fig. 20-3). The exhaust gets louder as it echoes from the walls of a deep, curved cut and the train slows to pick up a lone sheepherder at Snowmass. Ahead, there's another deep cut that all but hides our train (it does, in HO); and beyond that the Roaring Fork Valley opens up as we thunder along beside the river and over a Howe truss bridge to drift passed the turntable and ice house on the outskirts of Basalt. Our one-car train stops and then backs our combine down the edge of Basalt's aptly named Railroad Avenue to the station.

There's just time to grab a sandwich at the railroad's hotel before we hear the whistle that announces the arrival of Train Number 4, our four-car express transport to Leadville. There's shiny dark green varnish and gold trim on the outside of those wooden cars and plush velvet inside with a hearty fire in the coal stoves to keep us warm. The rails climb a bit steeper as we head west beside the Frying Pan Creek. There are plenty of light beige spots beside the rails to mark where the engineer has had to drop some sand from the locomotive's sand dome onto the rails for traction up the hill.

That's the Peach Blow quarry off to the right with a tiny narrow gauge tram railway to bring the cut stones over the Frying Pan Creek to the loading dock. The train is slowing now for the station at Ruedi. The hardworking consolidation is unusual power for a passenger train but all eight drivers are

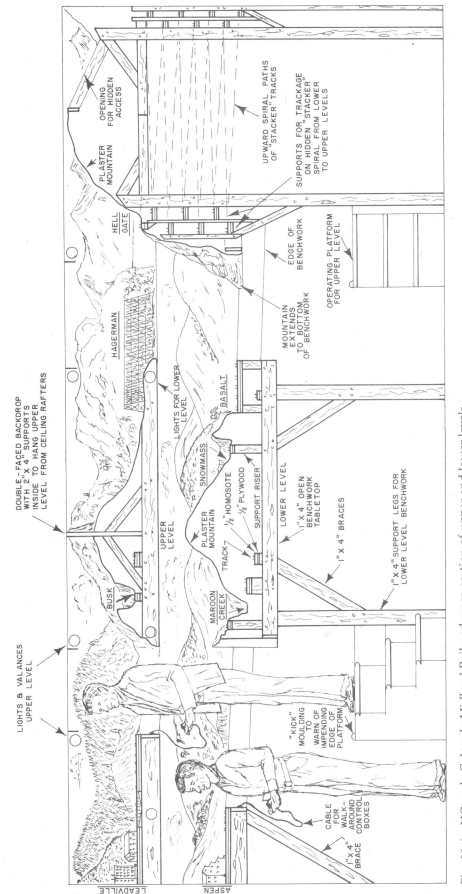

Fig. 20-6 HO scale Colorado Midland Railroad cross-section of upper and lower levels at AA on track plans.

needed to surmount the grades up this valley. All that steam has exhausted most of the water supply in the tender but there's a water tank here to replenish the supply. The lime kilns, plaster manufacturing plant, and cattle pens keep the freight train crews busy at Ruedi.

The clatter of the wheels on the rail joints and the warmth of that pot-bellied stove must have lulled both of us to sleep because that's the Sellar station out the left window. We dozed right through the station stops at Thomasville and Norrie. Most trains require water again by the time they reach Sellar and there's a water tank as well as a sand house to refill the locomotive's tank and sand dome. The grade gets just a bit steeper from here to Ivanhoe and there's a wye to turn the helper engines. Our train pauses just long enough to allow the crew time to pick up the dining car so we can lunch before we reach Leadville.

The air is getting colder now; some of the windows are beginning to cloud as we climb ever higher. Look out the right window as we leave Mallon tunnel just ahead; that's one of the most spectacular views in the Rockies. The way that wind is whistling it's no wonder they call this cliff Hell Gate! Lake Ivanhoe is just around the next curve. During the winter, they cut ice here for shipment all the way to Colorado Springs and Basalt. The snow gets deep, too; deep enough to hide the tracks inside those snowsheds. They're working inside the nearly 2-mile long Busk-Ivanhoe tunnel today so our train is going to take the high route up to the older Hagerman tunnel. Usually, the helper engines are cut off the train here on the turntable inside that round shed, but we'll need ours to make it over the old "high line." The route from Ivanhoe up to the 11,530-foot elevation of the west portal to Hagerman tunnel is a series of

Fig. 20-7   The Leadville roundhouse is almost hidden by the steam from number 53, so you know it's cold. The upper photo was taken from the coaling trestle; the lower from just in front of the roundhouse, circa 1895. (*Photo courtesy of Colorado State Historical Society.*)

ess curves and snowsheds. There's a station built right into the snowshed on the east end of the tunnel but we barely slow down below our 5-mile-an-hour pace. That cut to the right was blasted from the rock before the engineers realized there was an easier way around this part of the mountain; we'll see the other end of it down by Roger's Spur. You can see the Hagerman snowsheds above us to the left and the tracks we'll be on in a moment off to the right from the trestle the train is rumbling across now. Rogers Spur is that deep cut to the left but our train doesn't stop there either. Five-miles-an-hour seems like a bit too much over the trestle that's ahead. It's one of the longest wooden trestles in the country. Those work cars off to the right must belong to the crew that's working on the Busk-Ivanhoe tunnel; it's east portal is inside that snowshed by the water tower. Finish your meal. We have to be back in our Pullman car before the train stops at Arkansas Junction.

That locomotive behind the station brought another Pullman from Leadville with passengers bound for Colorado Springs. They'll take our car and one of the baggage cars back up to Leadville but the rest of Number 4, and that Pullman from Leadville, will swing to the right and head for Colorado Springs. Leadville isn't quite the city it was a few years ago because many of the mines have played-out; but the Rio Grande still runs standard gauge trains here and the Colorado & Southern (Burlington) has both narrow and standard-gauge tracks. The tracks that lead beyond the station eventually connect with the main line at Snowden but they aren't used much since the Midland bought the line between Snowden and Arkansas Junction. We're here so we might as well take a look inside that gorgeous shingled station; the yard master might give us a pass to tour through the roundhouse. It was quite a trip; three trains, a helper locomotive to get us over the pass, and enough changes in scenery to satisfy any mountain man. It was real . . . wasn't it?

We'll have to take a step back to the reality of an HO scale world. That train headed for Colorado Springs would disappear into a tunnel to be stored on one of the three hidden holding tracks at Snowden below Hagerman Tunnel. Later, it would travel around and through Ivanhoe into a tunnel at the end of

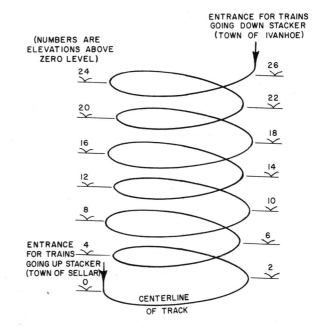

Fig. 20-8 Spiral "stacker" (isometric view of trains' path up or down between levels of the two-tier layout).

the snowshed on the Ivanhoe wye to travel in an enclosed (with a hinge-down access door) shelf over the doorway to the layout room to appear at Leadville station.

We'll use a bit of modeler's license and claim that it arrived there over the old track from Snowden and that it is now headed west as train Number 5. All through freight and passenger trains take this same route west; the connecting trains from Leadville to Arkansas Junction (like the one that picked up our Pullman) bring passenger and freight cars for connections only with the eastbound through trains. The snowsheds at Ivanhoe hide all but a few inches of that "sneak" return loop path around the room from Arkansas Junction to Leadville's station.

THE SPIRAL STACKER'S SECRETS

It takes an engineering "trick" to raise the tracks from the lower tier of the lifetime layout to the upper tier. For years, hidden spirals of trackage have been used by model railroaders in Europe to capture in miniature the soaring tracks of some of the railroads through the Alps, but it's a relatively unknown concept in America. The basic principle is simple enough: average-length trains can only climb about 3 inches for every 100 inches of track; so several hundred inches of track are twisted into overlapping loops.

A circle, or loop, of HO scale track with a 24-inch radius includes about 12½ feet of track; enough length so the track can climb 4 inches every time it makes a complete loop and still only have a nominal 2.7 percent grade (2.7 inches rise per each 100 inches of track). The friction of the wheels on the curved track, however, adds almost 50 percent to the effort required to surmount a grade that is on a curve; and this one is *all* curve. That 4-inch clearance isn't really enough to allow you to reach over the tops of the cars to re-rail them; why not make every other loop a 28-inch radius so there's 8 inches of clearance between the alternating 24-inch and 28-inch radius loops? If we add the bit of straight track that's necessary to swing in and out of the 24 and 28-inch loops, the average length of track works out to a very practical 16 feet of track for each loop. That 16-foot distance and a 4-inch change in elevation for each loop work out to be only a 2 percent grade and, even with compensation for the fact that the grade is all curved track, the effective grade is only about 3.3 percent. That's the basics; now the idea must be adapted so you can actually construct a spiral stacker for HO scale trackwork.

The three track plans in Fig. 20-9 show how the track would look at the lower level (near Sellar), at any of the intermediate levels, and at the top level (near Hell Gate). The two tiers on the lifetime layout are separated by about 24 inches so there must be enough intermediate loops in the spiral to raise the trains that high. With 4 inches per loop, it takes six fulls loops (circles) or a total of 90 feet of track to make the grade. Another half-loop brings the trains around so they can disappear near the wall and reappear near the table edge. The actual trackage isn't going to be visible, so you could spike the rails right to the Homosote roadbed if you have the patience—most of us would use flexible track or Tru-Scale's roadbed to save some time and effort. There is, incidentally, room on any level loop for a switch on either the front or the rear edge of the stacker; so you could branch-off from the spiral, on some other type of layout, for tracks midway along the mountainside.

The only really complicated part of the spiral stacker is the framework to support those tracks. The two views in Figs. 20-10 and 20-11 show the type of benchwork I would suggest. Three pairs of the type of braces shown in the side view will be needed, spaced equally apart as shown in the top view. The solid lines in the top view correspond to the pair of supports shown in the side view; the dotted lines are the locations of two more pairs of identical frames. Notice that the benchwork is braced from the top so the inside of the stacker is completely open for access to the tracks. It's not indicated on the drawings, but some type of one-inch high fence should be applied so that there's no chance that any derailed train could fall to the floor.

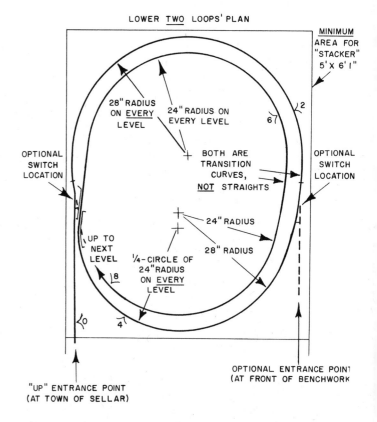

LOWER TWO LOOPS' PLAN

MINIMUM AREA FOR "STACKER" 5' X 6' 1"

28" RADIUS ON EVERY LEVEL

24" RADIUS ON EVERY LEVEL

BOTH ARE TRANSITION CURVES, NOT STRAIGHTS

OPTIONAL SWITCH LOCATION

OPTIONAL SWITCH LOCATION

24" RADIUS

28" RADIUS

UP TO NEXT LEVEL

¼-CIRCLE OF 24" RADIUS ON EVERY LEVEL

OPTIONAL ENTRANCE POINT (AT FRONT OF BENCHWORK)

"UP" ENTRANCE POINT (AT TOWN OF SELLAR)

(NOTE: SELLAR IS 53" FROM FLOOR SO "O" IS 53" ON LIFETIME-LAYOUT PLAN)

There should also be some type of train-detection devise (your dealer should have several, including Campbell's "Signal Monitor") that will light an indicator bulb on the control panel to show that there is a train in there somewhere. You may even want to install a "detector" light on each level so you know the train is making it all the way to the top. The hills beside Sellar hide the portion of the stacker between the two levels, and the cliffs at Hell Gate cover the outside edges on the lifetime layout plan. If the though of hiding the stacker with scenery bothers you, however, there is no reason why it couldn't be hidden behind a wall in a 5' x 6' (the width and length of the "stacker") "closet" with mountain scenery and tunnel portals leading into the wall so the trains literally disappear into tunnels. The mountain method shown on the lifetime layout plan allows about 5 feet of additional visible track on the lower and upper levels that would be hidden if the stacker unit were placed inside its own closet.

A second train can be waiting just out of sight at the top of the stacker so you can operate it while your train winds its way to the top (or bottom). If you use helper engines like the Colorado Midland (and hundreds of other full-size railroads did), you can use the "waiting" time to return the helper locomotive back to the base of the hill (from Ivanhoe back to Leadville or from Sellar back to Basalt).

Fig. 20-9 Spiral stacker track plans at entrance, middle, and exit levels.

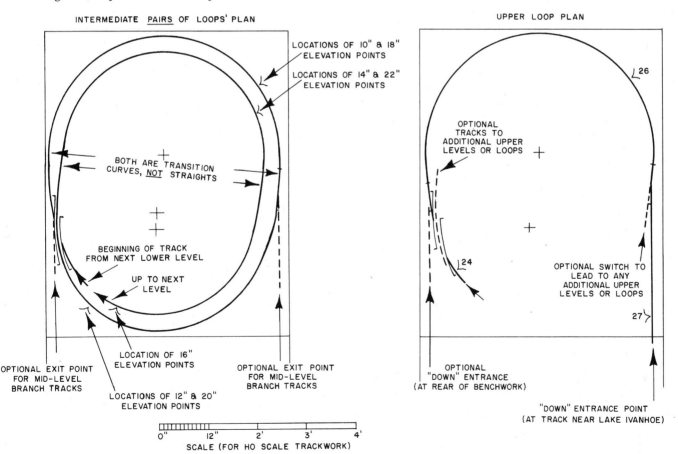

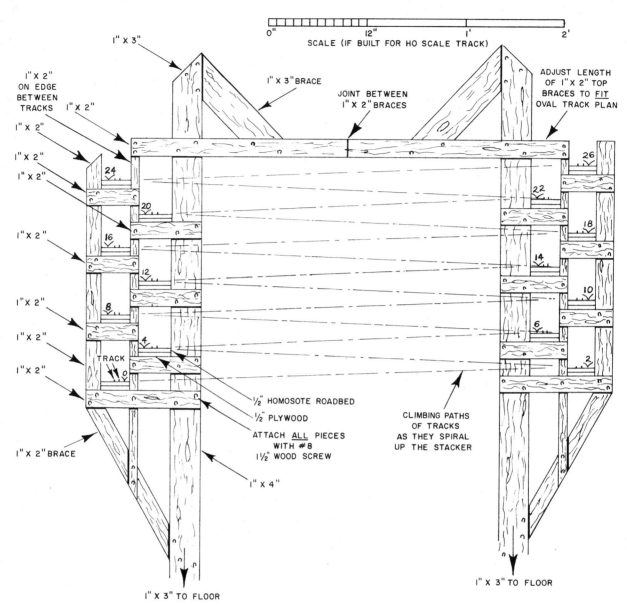

Fig. 20-10   Wood supports (side view) for spiral stacker; three of these right and left pairs are required for stacker benchwork.

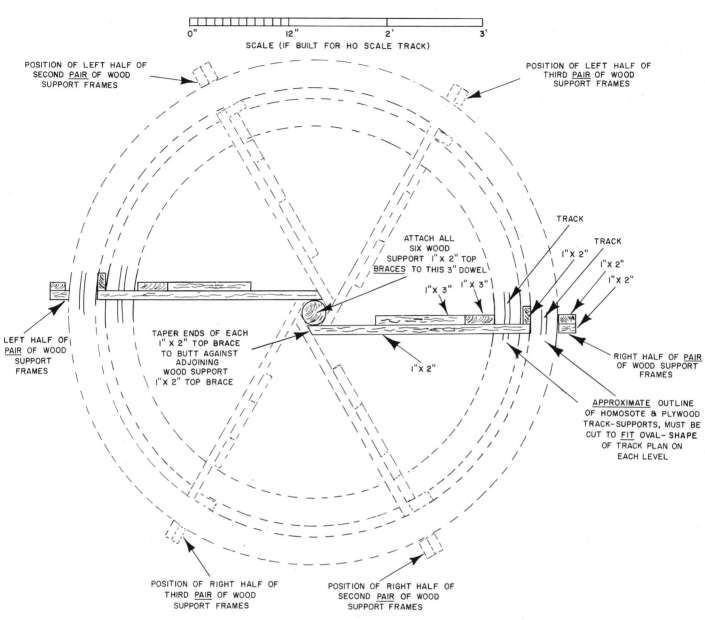

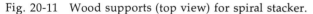

SCALE (IF BUILT FOR HO SCALE TRACK)

0"   12"   2'   3'

POSITION OF LEFT HALF OF
SECOND PAIR OF WOOD
SUPPORT FRAMES

POSITION OF LEFT HALF OF
THIRD PAIR OF WOOD
SUPPORT FRAMES

TRACK

TRACK

1" X 2"

1" X 2"

1" X 2"

ATTACH ALL
SIX WOOD
SUPPORT 1" X 2" TOP
BRACES TO THIS 3" DOWEL

1" X 3"   1" X 3"

LEFT HALF OF
PAIR OF WOOD
SUPPORT
FRAMES

TAPER ENDS OF EACH
1" X 2" TOP BRACE
TO BUTT AGAINST
ADJOINING
WOOD SUPPORT
1" X 2" TOP BRACE

1" X 2"

RIGHT HALF OF PAIR
OF WOOD SUPPORT
FRAMES

APPROXIMATE OUTLINE
OF HOMOSOTE & PLYWOOD
TRACK-SUPPORTS, MUST BE
CUT TO FIT OVAL-SHAPE
OF TRACK PLAN ON
EACH LEVEL

POSITION OF RIGHT HALF OF
THIRD PAIR OF WOOD
SUPPORT FRAMES

POSITION OF RIGHT HALF OF
SECOND PAIR OF WOOD
SUPPORT FRAMES

Fig. 20-11 Wood supports (top view) for spiral stacker.

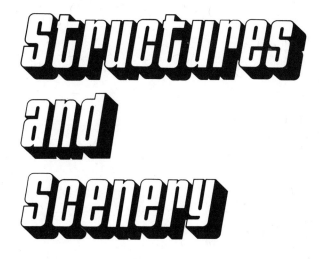

Structures and Scenery

Somehow, there never is enough room for all the model railroad you'd like to have. Every square inch of your layout space can, however, be put to work to enhance both the realism and the operation possibilities of your railroad. That effective space utilization begins with a track plan so you can determine how much track will fit in the space you have available. Since the track plan must be a scaled-down drawing of your space for proper positioning of curves and switches, you can take advantage of the same pieces of paper to pre-plan where to place structures.

The various model manufacturers' catalogs generally state the overall size of their structure kits so you can use those dimensions as a rough guide to how much space a station or engine house or whatever may occupy on your layout. The *NMRA Data-Pack* book (available to members of the National Model Railroad Association) includes dozens of drawings of typical railroad, industrial, and town structures that can also help with your plan. If you're modeling a portion of a real railroad, you may be able to find out (from books about that railroad or actual measurements) how large the various structures should be. Armed with those space dimensions, it's a simple task to determine how many and what types of buildings can be fitted to your layout.

Model railroad buildings, like locomotives and rolling stock, are available as simple plastic ready-built form, plastic kits, and detailed craftsman kits. There is a wide selection of parts (window, door, and other detail castings) with sheets of wood, plastic, and cardboard whose surfaces are detailed to duplicate scale-size bricks, stones, wood sidings, shingles, corrugated metal, and other "typical" structure surfaces. The choice is great enough to provide either a kit or the parts you'll need to duplicate any building you might find in real life.

The plastic building kits usually have the doors, windows, and other details molded into the surfaces of the walls but a few of the more expensive kits have separate window and door pieces. The craftsman kits generally have wood or cardboard walls with realistic surface details and dozens of castings for windows, doors, and other small details. The plastic kits have pre-colored parts, and those with individual doors and such have the

XXI

Structures That Serve

small parts molded in a contrasting color so you might believe that no painting is required. Painting is not *required*, but the plastic is going to look like plastic until it *is* painted and the best time to paint is *before* the kit is assembled. Most plastics have a toy-like gloss, regardless of how much life-like detail may be molded into the surface, and a semi-transparency that immediately identifies the material. Proper painting can make the plastic look like a painted prototype or, with some care, like metal or aged wood. The unpainted pieces in any of the craftsman kits must, of course, be painted as well.

PAINTING TIPS

The detail parts of any kit, whether the simplest plastic model or a complex and expensive craftsman kit, should always be painted before the kit is assembled. Read the instructions so you can familiarize yourself with all the parts and, particularly, with how they fit together. It is often best to complete some of the subassemblies like wall units or bases or roof sections before applying any

179

Fig. 21-1   The walls of this Timberline brand grain elevator were brushed with light touches of grey to simulate weathered wood.

paint so you don't have to worry about removing paint from the various joints that must be glued together. Most of the plastic kits, for example, have instructions that suggest you assemble all the doors and windows in the walls before gluing the walls to one another. In most such kits, though, it is better to assemble the walls and paint them *before* adding doors and windows. The doors and windows can be painted as separate pieces by sticking the backsides of each part to a piece of masking tape and spraying the entire lot. If you find that the areas where the doors and windows join the walls are painted, then the normal liquid plastic cement will not hold. The joining surfaces can be scraped clean but it's far easier to attach such parts with either white glue or, better, with one of the instant-drying cyanoacrylate cements like Eastman 910 or Aron Alpha. The clear plastic windows are best left out until the model is completely painted and, if you wish, weathered or aged.

Structures face the same elements, on prototype railroads, that the locomotives and rolling stock do; and the weathering techniques used on model cars and locomotives are equally effective in improving the realism of any building. Use the same brands of flat (nongloss or matte) finish paints on your structures that you use on your cars and locomotives. Most structures have different colors than a typical freight car or locomotive but the appropriate shades are included in both the Floquil and Scale-Coat lines of model railroad and craft paints.

The matte-finish paint is the first step in weathering since it simulates the sun and wind-bleaching and oxidizing effects. The dust and soot or exhaust smoke that rain and

Fig. 21-2   An artist's airbrush can create the very fine splatter effects of rain splashing the "earth" onto the walls.

Fig. 21-3   Structures can be worked into the "soil" easier if the building "site" is removed from the tabletop.

Fig. 21-4   This Campbell brand craftsman coal yard kit has some details such as bolt-heads and door knobs, but you can improve it's realism.

Fig. 21-5   The prototype for the Campbell coal yard shows the signs of age and weather that can be applied to any model kit.

dew wash down the sides of cars and locomotives appears on buildings too. No two buildings, any more than two freight cars, will have the same degree of weathering in real life, so your weathering effects should vary on model structures. Some structures won't show any weathering at all if they have been freshly painted, while others will look like they haven't seen a paint or scrub brush in decades.

Buildings are generally a bit cleaner than freight cars, but they definitely are "dirty" and weather-beaten to some extent. Take a long look at the buildings near any railroad and make some mental and photographic notes about where the effects of age and the weather appear. The portion of the building nearest the ground will be splattered and shaded with the colors of the surrounding soil. Rain washes streaks of dirt and dust down the roof and dribbles and runs stains from the corners of windows. Brick or stone buildings accumulate smudges in their mortar that turn the seams black. A weathered wooden building may show signs of previous paint colors or the grey of weathered wood. You can achieve some astonishingly realistic results by spraying a wash of about nine parts thinner to one part paint over an entire group of buildings with the paint color matched to the color of the ground in that area. The dust that blows through full-size towns has this same tendency to "shade" the entire area the color of the earth.

A GOOD FOUNDATION

The most realistic model building will look like a toy if it isn't placed *in* the ground. Full-size buildings seldom have the seam around their foundations that is so common around miniature structures. The best way of avoiding that gap around the foundation is to bring the entire building site to the workbench so the building can be assembled right on the ground. If you use Homosote for a roadbed beneath the track, you can easily extend it to include the sites for any nearby structures. Scraps of Homosote can be used for the areas beneath and immediately around buildings that may rest on the sides of hills. If the building is to be placed right beside the tracks (as

an industry or water tower or station might be), then you might want to include the track as part of the building site. The Homosote can be cut with a heavy-duty razor knife so it's not at all difficult to remove a piece that's an inch or so longer and wider than the base of the building. If you pre-planned most of the building sites, the Homosote can be cut before you lay any tracks over the cuts; and the track's rails can be joined near such seams to make it easy to remove that chunk of "land" when you're ready to build.

The various earth-texturing and weed-growing methods can be used on the ground around each structure with artist's Matte Medium to hold the ground to the Homosote. The building itself can be positioned firmly with bits of wood around the *inside* edges of the walls so it can be removed to add lights or interior details later.

BUILDING PERSONALITY

With the exceptions of a few tract or development housing projects, there are seldom two buildings exactly alike in the real world; yet one sees identical structures and colors on dozens of model railroads. There are duplicates of most freight cars (that's one reason why the railroads number them) but you just don't see that type of duplicity in buildings. There are three ways you can personalize your structures: (1) with different paint and details from those suggested by the kit; (2) by combining parts and pieces from several kits (cross-kitting, converting, or customizing); or (3) by scratch-building your own structures from the various wall and roof materials and window and detail castings.

Very few of the model kits are copies of any actual prototype but you could find a similar prototype to obtain ideas for detail changes or different color schemes. Some of the craftsman kits are matched to prototypes; most of the kits in the Timberline, Suncoast, Alexander, and Historical Scale Models lines are precise duplicates of some prototype. Campbell's "Quick Coal" yard (Fig. 21-4) is one example of an HO scale kit with a prototype. The extra braces and electrical wires and weeds on the real structure (on the Colorado & Southern Railroad in

Fig. 21-6   Modify every structure on your layout, in some way, so each appears in only one place in your "world" of models.

184

Cheyenne, Wyoming) can be added to produce a model with breath-taking realism (Fig. 21-5).

The long wall pieces from two of AHM's HO scale plastic kit for the "Gruesome Casket Company" were combined with some detail parts to produce the electrical powerplant in Fig. 21-6. Notice how the rear is set *into* the earth while the front edge is raised on a foundation shaped from molding plaster. The walls and roof are stained and streaked with washes of dark grey and brown to provide a mild weathering touch.

BRINGING LIFE TO THE LAYOUT

The only way to avoid the ghost town feeling of many model railroads is to add some life in the form of people, animals, and vehicles. There are hundreds of figures available in HO scale, and a fair choice in N and O scale, at prices ranging from pennies for people and animals you must paint yourself to a dollar or so for hand-painted masterpieces. Some of the structure kits include small details like boxes and barrels (and sometimes even people) and those same small items are available as separate castings from several firms. There really isn't any way you can have too many of these small details; the "litter" of barrels and boxes and tools and junk is one of the hallmarks of the best-detailed dioramas and layouts in the world.

Some small details, including people, can be glued to the layout with rubber cement. The rubber cement will hold the object in

Fig. 21-7 Jordan brand HO scale automobile kits add some implied action to this collection of Historical Scale Models buildings.

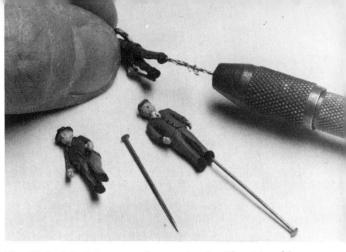

place but leave the mounting flexible enough so you can remove the detail and rub away most traces of the rubber cement. People can be made to stand upright without those toy-like bases by simply drilling a number 70 hole through their leg to accept a common straight pin. Cut off the head of the pin and drill a hole in the layout (or on the station platform or sidewalk or wherever) and press one end of the pin into the figure and the other end into the hole. Smaller-diameter piano wire can be used for N scale figures with a smaller-size wire and hole.

Fig. 21-8   Miniature people can stand without toy-like bases if one leg is drilled, with a matching hole in the layout, to accept a pin.

The scenes that one usually remembers most vividly about either a real or model railroad often center around a train or locomotive passing over a bridge. The bridges, it seems, serve as accent marks to punctuate the railroad's right-of-way and they literally place the train on a pedestal. No wonder, then, that bridge scenes are so well defined in our memories and no wonder, either, that bridges are some of the most desirable prototypes to capture on a miniature railroad system.

In fact, bridges are popular enough with modelers that the various manufacturers offer a wide array of ready-built and kit models. There are excellent brass bridges available from the some of the same firms that import brass locomotives and rolling stock, a few ready-built short spans in plastic, some superbly detailed plastic kits, and dozens of craftsman kits for almost every type of bridge imaginable. The various sizes of stripwood and the Plastruct plastic sheets, channels, I-beams, and the like can be used to scratch-build your own bridges. The *NMRA Data-Pack* book provides the basic data on the various types of bridges and their construction details for those who would rather build their own.

The real railroads seldom designed a bridge or assembled it the way most modelers do; the prototype built the most appropriate type of bridge for whatever they were spanning. Fast-flowing rivers and extremely deep gorges and highways or other railroad tracks were often bridged with a long span like a steel or wood trestle or a steel or concrete arch bridge. The shorter spans often had steel girder bridges; short truss bridges; or concrete, brick, or stone arch bridges. The valleys that were too deep or long to fill with dirt were spanned with steel or wooden trestles or with a series of arch bridges. Culverts of corrugated iron pipe, stone, or concrete often spanned the smallest streams. All these types of bridges are available as HO scale kits or ready-builts and most are also offered in N or O scales.

You can select your bridge style and type the same way real railroads did, but it's difficult to build the valley that bridge would span *before* the bridge is built. It is possible to cut away the tablework beside the tracks to make a valley after the track is laid; but it is

XXII

Bridges

far, far easier to position any bridges while the layout is still in the planning stages. When you plan for those bridges, remember to allow enough room on both ends of the bridge for the fill or embankment that almost invariably leads to the ends of the bridge. The roadbed should be trimmed so it's just a bit wider than the ties where a fill or embankment occurs; and in most cases, you'll want to remove the roadbed completely from beneath the tracks so you can lay the rails and ties right on the bridge like the prototypes. Some full-size bridges do have decks that are ballasted much like the rest of the railroad, but these decks are much thinner than your roadbed and plywood support. If you must leave the roadbed and plywood support beneath it in place, your only bridge choice is a brick, stone or concrete arch or culvert with a design that sweeps the top of the arch just high enough to avoid the roadbed.

There is really no such thing as a "standard" bridge. A few full-size railroads do prefer one type over another but, somehow, they nearly always seem to have at least one example of every type of bridge. The bridge design and types should vary on your model railroad

Fig. 22-1   This scratch-built steel arch bridge graces the HO scale Salt Creek Society of Model Engineers layout near Chicago.

Fig. 22-2   1″ x 4″ wood risers support the roadbed behind the bridge abutments, with the roadbed removed to make way for the bridge spans.

Fig. 22-3   The center spans in this set of bridges carry the tracks over an access aisle with a steel pipe to guard the bridges.

Fig. 22-4   The wooden blocks are only temporary supports for this trestle on the Slim Gauge Guild's layout—the scenery will be built-up to "bury" the bottom edge of the trestle.

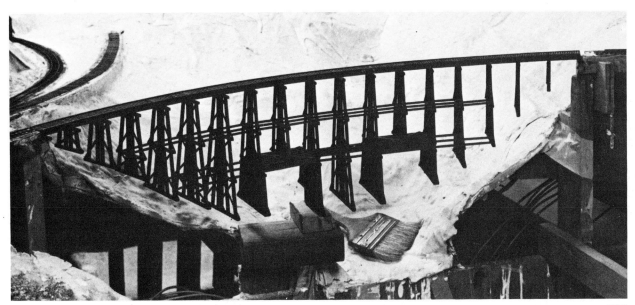

Fig. 22-5 The molded plaster rocks were placed around the feet of this trestle on the Slim Gauge Guild's layout while the plaster was still wet so the plaster could support the bridge.

190

also to give more of a true-to-prototype effect. When you pre-plan those bridge locations, try to vary the length and placement of the bridges so you can use a variety of types. Plan some locations, to match what the prototype does, where two or more different types of bridges are used to span a single area.

The most common combinations are wooden trestles (or arch bridges) on one or both ends of a long span with a wood or steel truss bridge or two over the longest area to be spanned (like the river itself or a pair of tracks). The longer bridge spans can serve a double-purpose, on some model railroads, in providing a bridge over a duck-under gap in the benchwork that allows access to an operating pit or access aisle inside the layout. These steel trusses (Fig. 22-3) are used for that purpose on the HO scale Des Plaines Valley Model Railroad Club layout near Chicago. The pipe that appears on real railroad bridges to carry electrical lines or natural gas lines over the bridged area is duplicated on this model. This super detail, however, serves another function here; it really is steel and it protects the relatively fragile bridges from being accidentally bumped when someone ducks under them to reach the operating area.

The wooden trestle is, perhaps, the most picturesque of all the prototype bridge styles and it is one of many vanishing breeds. The real railroads cannot afford the constant maintenance that wooden bridges require nor can they risk the fire danger of such spans. Most wooden trestles are replaced by simply dumping dirt over the sides until the valley is filled. A short concrete culvert will often bridge the stream or road in one of these filled-in valleys. The trestle is the most difficult of all model railroad bridges to install. Every bridge (including a trestle) must have an abutment at each end to hold back the earth fill and to support the heavily loaded ends of the bridge. It's not particularly difficult to work the plaster "earth" in and around such abutments. Every one of a wooden trestle's many upright "bents" must be placed so it appears to be resting on that plaster "earth." At least every other bent of the trestle should actually be supported by either hidden supports or by the scenery itself. A few modelers really do build the scenery beneath the trestle first so they can cut and fit each of the trestle bents to fill the area between the "earth" and the tie-support beams.

The best method, perhaps, is a combination of bridge-first and trestle-first ideas. The Slim Gauge Guild uses the concept for some of their HOn3 bridges like the one shown here. The first step is to trace the exact track outlines on the Homosote roadbed that crosses what will later be the valley. The ends of the track-supporting plywood and Homosote roadbed are then supported by risers placed ½ inch behind where you will want the bridge abutments to rest. The Homosote over the valley is then cut at each end of the future bridge and removed to be used as template for laying the track that will later be on the bridge. The scenery that forms the valley is then laid in place (paper towels dipped in Hydrocal brand plaster are strong enough, with two or three layers, to support the trestle). The trestle bents can then be measured to see how long each one must be to reach the plaster surface.

If you intend to add additional layers of surface detail such as rocks, the bents should be short enough to allow for the extra thickness of plaster. This short trestle in Fig. 22-5 with a straining beam wooden deck truss in the center is another of the Slim Gauge Guild's many bridges. The rocks (cast in plaster with latex molds taken from real rocks) were added to the basic scenery contours to enclose a portion of the bottom of each of the trestle's bents. There are several different trestle kits available or you can assemble your own from scale-size lumber.

The turntables that are used to turn locomotives and cars or to reach the stalls of a round house are bridges too. There were some turn-of-the-century turntables that were wooden frames with guy wires (called "gallows frame" turntables for the appearance of the guy wire supports). These gallows frame turntables don't necessarily require a turntable pit like the more modern steel turntables but the tracks leading from the gallows frame turntable must be about ½ inch (for HO scale) above the table to allow room for the scale timber supports beneath the ties on the turntable bridge itself. The location of the pits for the more modern turntables should be planned well in advance so they can be cut through the Homosote roadbed and through the plywood. ConCor, SS Ltd., Model Masterpieces, and Gieger are a few brands of turntable kits that you should examine before cutting the pit so that you can match the pit diameter to that required by the kit you choose.

If you have the impression that most model railroad scenery depicts mountainous terrain, you are correct. There is nothing particularly easy about making a mountain; and, in fact, it is really far easier to model gently rolling hills and even easier to model level ground. Frankly, I would be the last person to try to sell you on the idea of duplicating farmland or deserts or pastures, because the mountains are my favorite places. My love of the mountains doesn't begin to explain why so many modelers decide that such steep slopes should be served by their miniature railroads.

The prototype railroads that served the mountains, or those that had to pass through mountain ranges to reach either coast, are often the ones that model railroaders prefer; especially since that list would include all but a few of the railroads in the Midwest, the deep South, and the lines that ran in and out of Texas. A model of any prototype that was photographed or seen running through the mountains looks most realistic in its natural environment.

There are additional advantages to the modeler, however, that are even more important than any efforts to match a prototype's geographic locale. Tunnels and other hidden tracks are one way that a model railroader can imply that his railroad comes and goes from some point miles away from the actual layout room. Tunnels are excellent places to hide the too-sharp curves of virtually any model railroad and they provide places where trains can be hidden from view while other trains resume the "action." The mountains don't necessarily have to be pierced by tunnels; trains can disappear most realistically by diving into a deep cut or by curving around to the back side of the mountain. The narrow gauge railroads were a popular choice of early builders of full-size systems because their sharp curves would allow them to run around, rather than through, the mountains. The Colorado Midland standard gauge line in Colorado's Rocky Mountains managed to make it through the range with less than twenty tunnels because most of the track wandered back and forth across the valleys and around the worst mountain barriers.

Mountains provide yet another advantage to the modeler; they allow him to enlarge his layout space vertically with little sacrifice of available layout space. The spaces that might

XXIII

Man-Made Mountains

be occupied by towns or cities in horizontal directions are taken up by slopes of the mountains. If the mountains are high enough to reach eye level, there is no need for a painted backdrop to provide a difficult-to-capture horizon (as there is with a flatland railroad). The backdrop on a model railroad can be plain blue sky painted on an "endless" piece of linoleum so that it curves around the corners of the room.

The industrial areas of a mountain railroad are usually mines perched on stilts on the steep slopes (as they were on the prototype). Much of the industry of a mountain railroad can be implied by running sidings to simple boxcar-door-level loading platforms, ore docks, or ramps high enough to allow dumping into open-top hoppers or gondolas, or simple cable-braced "stiff-leg" derricks to hoist logs and lumber. There is, then, no need to sacrifice on-line switching operations for the fascinating "peddler" freight trains with a mountain railroad.

If you're still not "sold" on mountains for your model railroad, then don't build them; all the scenic techniques described here will work equally as well on a railroad running through farmlands, prairie, desert, or woods. There are even occasional rock out croppings, particularly when the railroad cuts through a hillside, so the rock-casting tips will be useful.

It is possible to buy a ready-built layout with the scenery already in place. Life-Like, Faller, and others offer such ready-made layouts through hobby dealers. These firms, and others, also have sheets of grass and swampland that can be used to create what might be termed "kit-assembled" scenery. The Mountains-in-Minutes brand of do-it-yourself polyfoam scenery (the kit includes liquid polyfoam, molds to make rock castings from the material, and instructions) can be used for those who prefer kits. For most modelers, though, I would recommend going the do-it-yourself route for building the basic outlines of the terrain; commercial rock castings and dirt or grass texturing materials can then be used to finish the scene.

Gypsum-based molding plaster (available from most lumberyards) is your best choice for the surfaces of any scenery or for use over wire door screen (buy used screen if possible, it's good enough and far cheaper, and pick aluminum over steel if you have a choice). By far the best method of creating hills, valleys, and steep mountain slopes is to use inexpensive, industrial-grade, brown paper towels soaked in plaster. Search through the Yellow Pages to find a building materials dealer who has (or will order) the Hydrocal gypsum plaster. Hydrocal dries to a much harder and stronger finish than molding plaster. Two or three layers of paper towels soaked in Hydrocal are strong enough to be self-supporting after the plaster sets. The Hydrocal is as hard as alabaster (it *is* alabaster) after it sets; it's so hard that it won't take dies or paints and you can barely gouge it with a knife. It is possible to work a reasonably realistic texture into the Hydrocal surface by rubbing over it with your hands during the time it is setting; the half-set portions roll off and serve like sand to roughen the surface. Any detail work, like rocks, plowed fields, hand-carved rock strata, or erosion gullies in dirt cuts, is best done in a regular molding plaster coated over the final layer of Hydrocal-soaked paper towels. Use the paper towel and Hydrocal to achieve the basic shapes of the hills and valleys; then wet it and

apply the surface details with molding plaster.

The only place that Hydrocal might need some support is along the backdrop side of the layout. A few wooden sticks, attached to the benchwork with screws, are enough to give the "mountain" something to hold onto. The painted linoleum sky backdrop should be protected with plastic garment bags (the type that dry cleaners use to protect your freshly cleaned clothes). The basic shapes of the hills, valleys, and mountains can be formed with crumpled-up newspapers. Strips of masking tape can be strung from the few hill-supports to the lower levels to reduce the quantity of newspapers. Just wad the newspaper into loose balls and pile it here and there to get the lumps and depressions of a mountainside. Shops that sell products for hair care often have empty spray bottles with adjustable nozzles; fill one of these spray bottles and use a water mist to dampen the wadded newspapers so they'll stay in place. If the crumpled paper confuses you, the mountainside can be covered with a single layer of moistened paper towels so the contours will be more apparent. You'll find it far easier to shape and

Fig. 23-1 The backside of this mountain-to-be is another mountain but the same contour could be cut in thin plywood.

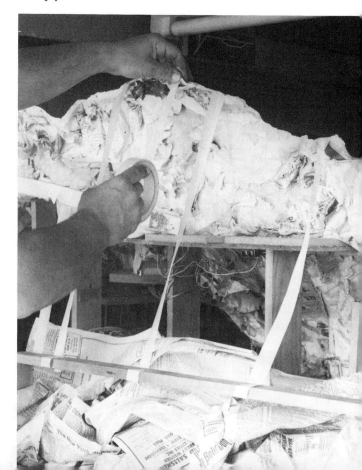

Fig. 23-2 Wadded newspapers over a masking tape grid form the basic contours of the mountain—wet the papers slightly with a spray.

Fig. 23-3 Cut brown paper towels in half to make them easier to handle when they're dipped in the wet plaster mix.

mold and change the scenery contours with this wadded newspaper method than with wire screening, and that first layer of paper towels will give you a preview of what the terrain will look like so you can alter it to suit your tastes. A word of warning—be very careful to keep the wadded paper contours well back from the edge of the track (and, later, the Hydrocal and paper towels) so you don't have trouble later with cars and locomotives hitting the scenery that rises above track level.

The industrial-grade paper towels will be easier to handle if you cut them in half. Use some heavy-duty shears to slice through a pile of a dozen or so paper towels. Mix the Hydrocal in glass pans or bowls to ease the task of cleaning-up later on. Always add the plaster to the water to minimize any problems with lumps. Pour one cup of water into a glass pan and slowly mix-in 2 cups of Hydrocal. That 2-cup portion may be a bit too much or too little, but you'll be able to tell if you mix thoroughly while you add the Hydrocal. The Hydrocal and water should be about the consistency of thick cream. Dip one

paper towel into the pan until it is completely submerged in the Hydrocal and then apply that strip to the newspaper mountains.

Continue to work, one strip at a time, until the plaster is virtually all soaked from the pan. You'll have to work quickly because the Hydrocal will begin to set up (harden) in just minutes. If you find that there isn't enough time, add some of the "retarder" that is supplied with the Hydrocal or about 1/2 teaspoon of hydrous citric acid to each 6 pints of Hydrocal. Clean the glass pan in a bucket of water before the plaster has set completely (it's easier then) and mix another batch of Hydrocal and water. You'll find that the work goes quickly; the mountain in the photos in this section was completed (with about ten batches of Hydrocal) in about an hour. The trackwork and any tunnel portals or bridge abutments (or bridges) should be protected with more plastic dry cleaner's bags and masking tape. Shield the tops of tunnel portals with a double layer of paper towels as well and be sure to leave enough room for 1/2 inch or more of molding plaster rock on the

195

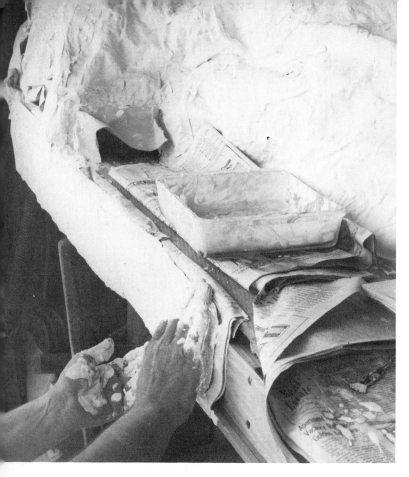

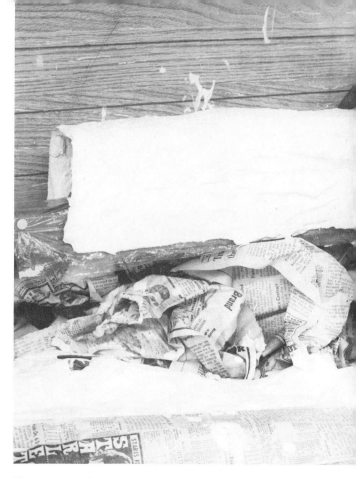

Fig. 23-4   Dip paper towels in the wet plaster and then spread them over the newspaper contours. Overlap each seam between the towels.

Fig. 23-6   Mold a tube of wetted paper towels to match the minimum tunnel clearances and drape plaster-soaked paper towels over the tube to make a "stone" interior liner for a short tunnel.

Fig. 23-5   Dry paper towels and small plastic bags protected this pair of tunnel portals from the plaster. Masking tape hides the tracks.

sides and tops of the portals and along the sides of any cuts through the mountain. You can line the interior of any short tunnel with a few layers of Hydrocal formed over a tightly packed wad of wet newspapers. If you can't reach all the way to the center from both ends, the tunnel lining should be removable so you can reach any derailed trains or to allow minor track maintenance.

ROCK-MOLDING TECHNIQUES

You don't have to be an artist to create scenery that looks like Mother Nature's work, but you need to know some techniques. There are a few modelers who can carve the molding plaster top coat on Hydrocal mountains to look just like real rocks. I would suggest you arm yourself with some photos of the kind of rock you want to carve, a sharp knife, and a stiff wire brush so you can try your own skills at rock carving. You'll find, though, that it's very difficult to make anything but real rock look like real rock—most of the rocks in the photos here are (almost) real rock.

The rocks on most of the layouts in this book were made by pouring molding plaster into latex rubber molds. The latex rubber molds derived their shapes and textures from real rocks and that's why the process is called "rock casting" (bet you thought it was a lesson in rock throwing). Most craft supply stores sell liquid latex for use in making molds for ceramic figurines, or you can order it by mail from Precision Scale Products, Box 74, Far Hills Branch, OH 45419. Find a rock with cracks, crevices, texture, and of the size you want (chunks of coal are good candidates for rock molds) and brush-on the "mold release" that is usually furnished with the liquid latex. Brush on at least two coats of the liquid latex (follow the instructions on the container) and then cover the area with a layer or two of gauze to give the mold some tear-resistance. Brush-on a final coat of liquid latex and let the mold dry. Carefully peel-back the mold from the rock and you're ready to cast.

Mountains-in-Minutes and others sell

Fig. 23-8 Make your own latex molds over real rocks and press the plaster-filled mold against the Hydrocal and paper towel slopes for a rock cliff.

Fig. 23-7 The "rock" is liquid polyfoam that was poured into this latex rubber mold and allowed to expand and set. The mold and the polyfoam are Mountains-in-Minutes products.

Fig. 23-9 Crumpled aluminum foil can serve as a rock mold when filled with pre-colored plaster and pressed in place on a plaster and Hydrocal mountainside.

"rocks" you can use for the mold, the liquid latex, and even the ready-made molds in some cases. The rock and the mold in Fig. 23-7 are included in a Mountains-in-Minutes kit. The rock was made from their liquid polyfoam (it's porous inside but there's a smooth skin), following the kit instructions. When painted and dye-colored, you cannot tell it's not a real rock. You can use the polyfoam rock (or a plaster one) as an individual piece or the rocks can be molded right into the scenery surfaces.

If you're using plaster, the mold should be filled with a plaster mix that's just a bit thicker than heavy cream. Slap the plaster-filled mold against the side of the mountain and hold it there for the few minutes it takes for the molding plaster to set; you'll be able to actually feel it harden through the flexible mold. Gently peel the mold away as soon as you feel the plaster set and mix some more plaster to repeat the process. Again, the work goes quickly; the mountainside in Fig. 23-8 was completed in about 2 hours. Each additional rock should overlap the next and the mold can be turned

Fig. 23-10 Brush or pour Rit clothes dye over the bare plaster rocks to darken the crevices and seams. Most of these rocks were textured with aluminum foil molds.

Fig. 23-11 The majority of this rock on the Slim Gauge Guild's layout is real rock that was hammered into rubble and glued in place at the foot of the latex-molded cliffs.

or distorted slightly so the pattern doesn't repeat itself. For variety, try this same rock-casting technique with a piece of slightly crumpled aluminum foil for the mold.

Most real rocks are surprisingly light in color; it's the myriad of cracks and shadows that often make them seem so dark. There are several methods for achieving a realistic rock color, and I would recommend that you try them all to find out which one works best for you. The plaster can be colored when you mix it by adding a teaspoon (or less) of the powdered colors that are used to pre-color concrete for driveways and floors. The building materials stores should have the dry cement colors in shades like burnt sienna, raw umber, iron oxide, goldenrod (ochre), raw sienna, chocolate brown, and black. These colors are surprisingly strong so try a little the first time.

These same colors can be used to pre-color the Hydrocal contours so there's less to paint and finish, and you can avoid any tell-tale signs of white plaster from accidental chips or missed spots. If you used molding plaster for the rocks (Blue Diamond brand "Green Stripe," 20-minute set is the best I've found,) you can stain them with regular Rit or Tintex household dyes in black or cocoa brown. Apply the dye with a basting syringe or just dribble it on with a teaspoon. The darker dye colors will naturally find their way into the crevices of the rocks to produce natural shading effects. A few areas can be shaded by brushing the dye over portions of the rocks with a paintbrush. The excess colored plaster can be placed in a paper bag and hammered to provide matching stones and rubble that can be glued at the base of any rock cliffs and on ledges. The rubble itself should be dyed to match the rocks it crumbled from on the higher reaches of the mountain.

Plaster mountains will always look like plaster mountains no matter what color they might be. The rock-casting methods described in the last chapter will certainly help to hide the plaster look, but you'll have to go a few steps further if you expect your scenery to look like Mother Nature did it. First, I'd suggest that the Hydrocal hard-shell surface be colored and textured with some pre-colored molding plaster. This coating can be applied when enough plaster has been added to the water to get something about the consistency of cream; just smear the molding plaster over the re-wetted Hydrocal hills with your fingers. Continue to rub the plaster, however, until it begins to harden and keep on rubbing so the partially dried plaster particles will roughen the surface to hide any trace of fingerprints or smooth plaster. Some gently sloping areas can be rubbed in random patterns but any steep slopes should be rubbed up and down in the direction of the slope to simulate the effects of mild erosion. When all the plaster-covered terrain (except for the areas covered with rock castings) has been covered with this roughened coat of pre-colored plaster, then you're ready for the final texturing effects.

A number of otherwise realistic model scenes have been ruined because the modeler made everything to exact scale except the dirt. The problem is particularly evident in N scale where a pebble (or a piece of track ballast) the size of a pinhead becomes as big as a bowling ball in 1/160 scale. Similar oversize "dirt clods" are common on HO and O scale layouts as well.

There's nothing at all wrong with using real dirt (unless it has magnetic particles—check it first with a magnet). The tricky part is getting the dirt to stick without adding fluid that will make it ball-up into those overscale dirt clods. Hardware stores sell a variety of kitchen strainers that can be used to sift the dirt to "heavy" dust, and there is a selection of finer mesh brass screens used for plumbing filters so you can literally reduce the dirt to dust. The same Matte Medium that is recommended for bonding ballast can be used to apply dirt or any other texturing material. The Matte Medium must be brushed on, however, for use as a binder for real dirt and allowed to become almost dry so it is just passed the "wet" stage but still sticky. The dirt

XXIV

Scenic Surface Textures

can then be sifted onto the area through a strainer and patted gently with a fingertip to push it down into the Matte Medium coat. Vacuum away any excess after about an hour. You can effectively simulate dirt roads, even through a solid patch of dirt, by just rubbing over the surface lightly with a "Bright Boy" abrasive eraser (hobby shops sell them for use in cleaning the oxide coating from the track's rails).

One of the easiest and most successful methods of simulating dirt and "new" growths of grass and weeds is what *Model Railroader* magazine calls "zip texturing." Zip texturing is nothing more complicated than plain molding plaster mixed with enough dry powdered coloring to get the desired shade of dirt or grass. Spray the spot that is to be zip-textured with water and a drop or two or Ivory liquid as a wetting agent. Sprinkle the mixture of dry color and molding plaster over the wetted area with a strainer, but keep the strainer moving from side to side (do *not* tap it to keep the plaster pouring) so the plaster doesn't build up into tiny piles in spots. A second mist (as close to a fog as you can get with a spray bottle and a little practice) can be

Fig. 24-1 Apply a coat of pre-colored molding plaster over the bare Hydrocal and paper towel contours. Rock castings can be added next to texture the surface and to frame the tunnel portals. Work has just started on this hill.

Fig. 24-2 Glue finely sifted dirt to the plaster surfaces and, when dry, rub a Bright Boy abrasive block over any areas that should look like roads.

used to "set" the plaster dust; but be careful, that second coat might very well create those overscale dirt clods. Try a second coat and, if you don't like the effect, then re-wet the area and sprinkle some more plaster and dry color. Vacuum away any excess material so it won't blow around the layout.

Green dry color and molding plaster can be used to simulate fresh grass as a second zip-texturing coat after the dirt is in place (or, if you're getting dirt clods with the water, as a first coat over the roughened pre-colored plaster).

The same cement colors that are used for coloring the Hydrocal or molding plaster rocks and mountains can be used for the dry plaster zip-texturing mix, or you can substitute the weaker (and more expensive) artist's dry powdered colors. If you're having problems finding what you need locally, Terra-Tex, P.O. Box 809, Willits, CA 95490 has a complete line of dry colors, pre-mixed zip-texturing colors, and other types of texturing products.

GROWING GRASS

Grass and tall weeds are extremely difficult to simulate on a model railroad but there are some effective solutions. I've all ready mentioned the zip-texturing method for "new" grass and weed sprouts. The second method is called "flocking." Flocking isn't anything new; it's been used to simulate fur and hair on ceramic kewpie dolls and the like for years. What is unusual is the method for applying the flocking strands so that each one "stands" up like grass. The secret is a simple squeeze bottle with a perforated cover over the mouth. The flocking is poured into the bottle and the bottle squeezed to "sneeze" a puff of flocking. The squeezing action rubs the flocking particles together to give them an electrostatic charge and that's what makes them stand up. The flocking can be applied to a coating of Matte Medium or plain white glue. Brush the glue or Matte Medium over the area where you want to have grass; "sneeze" on the flocking; let the glue dry overnight; and vacuum away the excess. Hobby dealers can order the bottle (and the flocking) from Boyd Models.

Pre-flocked sheets of a special flexible

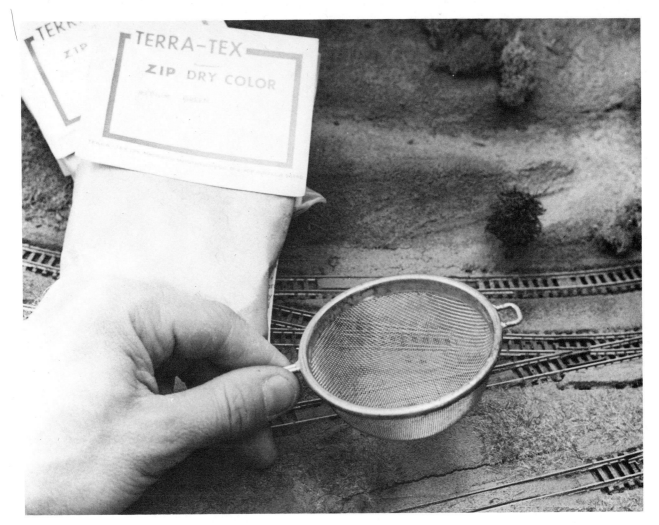

Fig. 24-3 Molding plaster and powdered colors are often better "dirt" than dirt itself. Sprinkle the mix over pre-wetted surfaces; the water will grip the dried plaster without disturbing the dust effect on the surface.

Fig. 24-4 The Boyd "Electro-Static Grass Dispenser" is the best tool for applying flocking materials to ensure that the individual flocking fibers will stand up like grass.

203

Fig. 24-5 Flocking will adhere to glue applied even to steep slopes like this one on the Slim Gauge Guild's HOn3 layout.

paper are imported from Europe and sold under brand names like Kibri and Faller. These sheets are excellent for simulating large areas of grass or weeds because the flocking is a bit more upright and thicker than you can apply it yourself. Similar sheets are available with dark blue/brown clear plastic portions to simulate swamps and marshes. The flocking paper is best applied in random-shaped

Fig. 24-6 Kibri brand flocked paper can be glued in irregular "weed patches" with the edges blended beneath real dirt or zip texturing.

patches (see Fig. 24-6). White glue will hold the grass patch in place, and the glue should be extended a bit beyond the patch so zip-texturing dirt can be applied to blend the area into the rest of the scenery. The material is excellent for simulating weed-covered sidings and branch lines. Rails can be spiked right over the flocked paper for the best effect; or strips of the paper can be glued between the rails and on each side to bury all, but the rails, in weeds.

Grass is a difficult bit of nature to capture in miniature because of it's texture and because grass is really not the bright green you may think it is; it's more of an olive with a lot more biege/yellow tones than you imagine. All the colors you use on your layout, particularly natural colors like the weathering tones on cars, locomotives, and structures, and any type of nature-effects, should be selected and applied under the identical light that you will use on your layout. Incandescent lighting is more difficult to install than fluorescent lighting because there are more individual bulbs and more wires needed to avoid multiple shadow effects. However, the incandescent lighting produces a far more "natural" effect with a warm glow like summer sunlight. Flourescent lighting gives a shadow-free lighting but the effect is often a depressing feeling that the weather is overcast and gloomy. Compare the effects of both on a weathered locomotive or car and determine which one you prefer before you select any of the colors for your scenery; and when you do pick the colors and apply them, be sure to do so under the exact lighting conditions that will appear on the railroad. Obviously, from these thoughts alone, you should install whatever lighting you plan for your railroad before any of the scenery work is even begun.

XXV

Rivers, Streams, and Lakes

The ultimate "water" for a model railroad is not real water at all but plastic or, to be more specific, clear epoxy casting resin. Model railroaders have tried just about anything shiny to represent water—from rippled glass to water glass to water itself—but nothing does quite the job that clear casting resin does. You should be able to buy casting resin at any hobby or craft shop in even the smallest towns and, if not, try boat shops that sell repair kits for fiberglass boats (the epoxy resin is what binds and smooths the fiberglass). There is very little shrinkage factor so you can buy as much as you feel the "capacity" of your lakes or rivers should be.

I would strongly suggest that you build a mini-diorama: use a saucer-size trough of the same plaster and powder color (or whatever) that you will use for the scenery around and especially on the bottom of the "stream." The clear casting resin has a slightly different darkening effect on different plasters, paints, and dyes; and the minidiorama will give you a chance to find out what happens before you ruin any finished scenery on the layout. You

Fig. 25-1   There is no better "water" than clear (epoxy) casting resin. Buy some hardener at a craft shop to ensure that the final surface will not be tacky.

Fig. 25-2   Use the special dyes for resin to color the clear resin while it is being mixed with the catalyst—just one or two drops of blue will do for the deepest lakes.

may find that the bottoms of any rivers, streams, or lakes might have to be pre-painted a shade darker than the surrounding "dry" land to simulate the effects of mud; or the areas that are to be "wet" may have to be lightened a shade if the resin turns the pre-colored plaster too dark.

The casting resin "water" areas require some careful preparation, in addition to checking out the effects of the resin on colors. Unroughened Hydrocal seems to be so smooth that the resin pulls away from it when it sets to produce an effect like cracked ice. The resin seems to work best over slightly roughened molding plaster that has been pre-colored with powdered colors. Do not, under any circumstances put zip-texturing or flocking on the bottom of any stream beds. If you paint the colors on your scenery (with acrylics or oils or whatever), try that paint on

Fig. 25-3   These churning rapids were created by picking and raking the resin during the few minutes when it was changing from the liquid to the solid state.

the mini-diorama test sample to see what the resin's effects might be.

The "water" area must be completely rigid so there should be at least four layers of Hydrocal-soaked paper towels for even a small stream bed and thicker layers, with wooden benchwork supports from below, for anything as large as a lake. The casting resin can be poured in enough layers to fill a lake 6 inches deep, but I do *not* recommend it; a thickness of ½ to 1 inch is about the safe maximum without taking chances of the resin cracking. The resin has much the same reflective effect as water so you might want to make shallow streams a bit deeper; but really deep water can best be simulated by using a bit of blue dye in the first layer or two of the resin.

Finally, the lake or stream must be completely sealed. The resin flows like water until it cures, and it will find its way through the smallest crack or pinhole to "drain" the lake before it has time to set. If a stream or lake ends at the edge of the table, then you must build a water-tight dam to hold the resin while it is still fluid. The dam can be removed once the resin has set. Air conditioner duct tape (a silver-colored cloth tape) seals quite well; but whatever tape or wood you use for the dam, it should be sealed at the edges with Silastic bath tub caulking (don't get it on the scenery, however). The Silastic can be peeled away later. Have ready any details that you may want to "submerge" so they can be inserted in the still-fluid resin. Flocking or hemp rope fibers dyed green or biege make

Fig. 25-4   Heat, applied with a spot lamp while the resin is setting-up into a hardened state, will ripple the surface—the more heat, the more ripples, but don't burn the resin.

Fig. 25-5   The white and blue dye that formed these patterns was brushed through the resin *after* the resin was in the riverbed but before it had hardened.

excellent weeds, but they'll have to be inserted into the fluid resin one bunch at a time during the few moments when the resin is gummy just before it hardens.

The various casting resins have mixing instructions on the side of the can. You may want to buy some "retarder" and some blue and brown dye for the resin to use for some special effects. Mix the resin and the catalyst in a small cup (with just a drop of dye if it is to be a deep water area) and pour this first layer into the stream so it can harden. You'll want to mix enough resin, once you've practiced and have become familiar with it, to fill about ½-inch or less of the stream or lake at each pouring; the next pouring will add another

fraction of an inch to the water level. The final pouring is the one that should be used for placing weeds at the water's edge and for special effects such as rapids.

When the casting resin sets to the point where it is just gummy, you can prod into it with an icepick to produce the effects of rapids bubbling over the rocks and streams; keep prodding and scratching in the direction of the current flow until you see that the resin is chunking off in gelatin-like hunks; then stop and let the surface smooth a bit while the resin completes its setting time. You can experiment with the "retarder" (sometimes called a hardener) to produce steeply sloped rapids and small waterfalls.

Slow-flowing streams, rivers, and lakes have ripples in the surface; these can be simulated by holding a spotlight a few inches from the surface during that critical gummy-to-firm stage of the resin's setting cycle. You can see the surface ripple and you'll also see some steam and vapors rising from the surface; the vapors are fine as long as you don't get the hot bulb so close to the surface of the resin that it burns. The heat speeds the setting time, and the rapidly contracting surface is what creates those realistic ripples.

If you live in a humid climate, or if the ratio of catalyst-to-resin wasn't quite right, the surface of the resin may remain tacky for years. Craft shops sell a clear fluid that can be sprayed (or, better, brushed onto the water to give a smooth finish). You'll find that the meniscus of the resin will creep up the banks (and up the faces of abutments or pilings in the water) a bit more than you would like. There's nothing you can do about that problem except to paint the very edge of the water with a flat-finish paint (that matches the rest of the area) to cover the meniscus. Any submerged items like rocks or logs should be placed in the bottom of the stream or river before the resin is poured. Large ships (like a tug boat or ore freighter in a dock-side scene) can be positioned on top of that first layer so there is a bit of water beneath them. Small row boats can be positioned just before the final layer is added. Current-like white ripples can be added to the edges of that first layer by brushing the dye on the surface of the resin just before it sets. Remind yourself to dust the surface of the "water" from time to time and, occasionally, to clean it with a mild solution of soap so that it will retain it's "wet" shine over the years.

Virtually all the earth that isn't covered by water or rocks is covered by some type of vegetation, and so some should appear on your scale model replica. It might seem a shame to cover all that carefully roughened and colored plaster and zip-textured "earth", but those "earth" undercoatings will be visible enough through the trees and weeds and bushes. There are at least a dozen different "growths" suitable for simulating leaves, blades of grass, and even pine needles. The basic ground cover techniques, green zip-texturing and flocking, have been described in a previous chapter, so we'll pickup from that point with some of the techniques for larger plants.

The scenery on the portion of the layout you are about to "plant" should be completed to the point where all rocks are in place and colored and all the water has been poured. These projects can damage delicate trees and such so it's best to have them finished first. However, there is no particular reason why all the scenery on your layout need be completed at any one time; a few square yards is enough to start the "growing season." The balance of the layout can be in any semi-finished state from empty benchwork to partially completed plaster mountains.

You'll find the hobby far more fun if you switch back and forth from benchwork or trackwork to kit-building to plaster work to scenery—in any order and for as many evenings or as many months as you like. The guys and gals who seem to enjoy the hobby most have their layouts in these various stages of construction, ranging from planning to finished scenery and vegetation.

Most of the materials that are used for weeds and small bushes can also be used for trees. I'll describe them here, and you can spot them in the photos where they have been used for trees as well. The most common particle-size ground covers for model railroaders are these (clockwise from top right in Fig. 26-1): cotton flocking; common hemp rope (dyed and cut to ¼ to ½-inch lengths); bark chips (sold as "earth" under the Kibri, Life-Like, and other labels); fine hemp-like fibers (sold as "Weed-Pak" by Terra-Tex); and ground foam rubber in a variety of colors (sold in sizes ranging from salt crystals to these larger chunks by Architectural Scale

XXVI

Trees, Weeds, and Bushes

Models, Inc., 361 Brannan St., San Francisco, CA 94107).

All the materials in Fig. 26-2 are natural mosses of one type or another (clockwise, from top right): Norwegian lichen moss (the most popular tree and shrub material for model railroads, available from a dozen different suppliers with various spellings of the name lichen); a European fern used in the Preiser-brand pine tree kits; asparagus fern

Fig. 26-1 Here are some of the most common and effective "ground cover" materials.

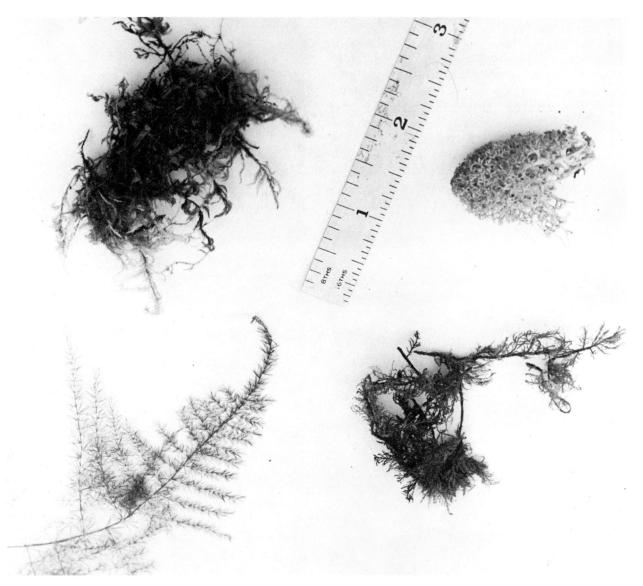

Fig. 26-2 Ferns, lichens, and moss are used for weeds, bushes, or trees.

(grow your own for a dollar in any shady spot, available from a nursery); and florist or nursery fern (used for potting indoor plants).

The Prieser-brand fern and the florist's ferns seem to last almost indefinitely without any special treatment but the asparagus fern and untreated lichen moss will fade and dry to a crumbling, brittle texture if not preserved with some solution. The lichen sold in packages through hobby dealers is already treated but fairly expensive. Untreated lichen can be ordered in bales and treated and dyed and you'll save almost 90 percent of the cost of pre-packaged and treated lichen. The lichen can be treated and preserved for years with a

solution of one part glycerin, one part acetone, and two parts alcohol. Leave the lichen in the solution overnight and then spread it on a newspaper to dry before dying it with various shades of Rit or Tintex clothes dye. The dye can be added to the preserving solution and then sprayed onto any old pieces of lichen that may have lost their color and softness. The asparagus fern seems to resist any preserving solutions because of its oily nature; but a simple spray with thinned Floquil paint seems to keep it fresh for years.

The ground-cover materials like bark chips, flocking, and the finely ground Architectural Models' foam can be applied to a coating of artists' Matte Medium through a strainer or merely vibrated from the edges of a teaspoon. I haven't mentioned the "popular" dyed sawdust as a suitable ground cover (or to simulate tree foliage) because the stuff always looks like just what it is regardless of what the color may be; these other ground cover materials are not readily identifiable (not even the ground foam) so they seem to have a far more realistic effect. The larger ground cover materials and the various ferns can be dipped directly in a shallow capful of Matte Medium

and then placed where desired on the scenery.

Follow some basic common sense when placing such weeds and bushes; vegetation collects in crevices more than it does on exposed slopes, and only a rare bit of bush will grow through the cracks of giant boulders. Pick only the finely detailed tips of the lichen moss and save the bigger "trunks" for ground cover beneath heavily wooded areas.

There are hundreds of weeds small enough for use on a model railroad, but most of them

Fig. 26-3   Vary the variety of vegetation but keep most of it at the crevices.

Fig. 26-4   Goldenrod dyed green with painted-on white trunks simulate aspens.

are indigenous only to certain parts of the country. You can find the ones that grow near you; look for lichen-like tips and also for weeds with a myriad of branches that can be used (like florist's baby's-breath sprigs) for the trunks and limbs of trees. The aspen trees in Fig. 26-4 are effective N scale models; they are made by dying the tips of goldenrod weed green with light grey trunks. They're then inserted in holes in the scenery, and the base of the tree trunk is covered with a bit of loose grass to hide the edges of the holes.

Model railroad shops offer literally hun-

dreds of different trees and shrubs in a variety of ready-built and kit styles and shades. In Fig. 26-5, the "autumn" tree on the left is made by Campbell with ground foam for the "leaves." The other three trees are ConCor brand items with realistic plastic trunks: a small scrub oak with lichen for leaves, a poplar and a maple tree, both with ground foam leaves.

By far the most realistic deciduous tree I have ever seen can be assembled by a method I discovered in the Whistle Stop Hobby Shop in Pasadena, CA (no, they do not *sell* these

Fig. 26-5   A sample of the dozens of different ready-made trees available to modelers.

Fig. 26-6   Tuck the aluminum wool into the thick branches to simulate twigs.

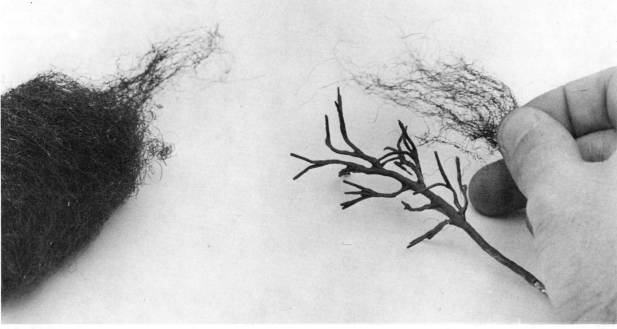

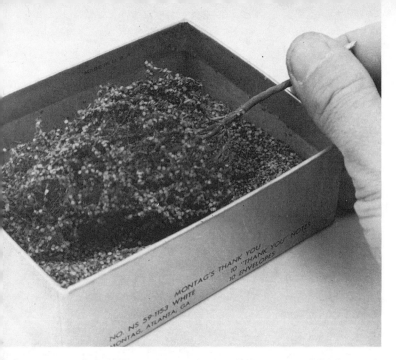

Fig. 26-7 Roll the paint-wetted tree in the check cancellation "leaves."

Fig. 26-8 The check cancellations adhere to the "wool" like individual leaves.

216

Fig. 26-9   Pine trees, both real and model, appear in a variety of shapes.

trees). The basic tree structure utilizes whatever you can find for a trunk and limbs; the tree in Fig. 26-6 is one of the rather expensive metal tree trunks available from Architectural Scale Models. The tiny branches are formed from an aluminum version of steel wool that Architectural Scale Models also sells. Do *not* try to substitute steel wool for this material; the fibers find their way to the tracks and are picked-up by the locomotive's motor magnets and cause short circuits and burned-out motors. The aluminum wool is tucked-in among the branches; you can glue it if you want to.

The leaves are made from the tiny holes that banks punch from your check when they cancel it. At least one bank in your town should have a check-cancellation machine and they'll be happy to give you the holes—it's just litter to them. Dye the check cancellations in a solution of Rit olive green dye and alcohol (water won't work). The coated paper on most checks gives one side of each leaf a light green shade and the uncoated side a darker green shade just like a real leaf. Spray the tree with thinned brown paint and dip it, while still wet, in a boxful of the leaves.

Drill a few trunk-size holes in a board so you can set the trees upright while the paint dries; then insert them in similar-sized holes drilled in the plaster scenery. If you want to add a further detail, dip a few twigs in brown-colored plaster and fan them out around the base of the tree as exposed "roots."

PINE TREES

The various pine tree kits sold by Campbell, Preiser, and others are extremely realistic miniatures if you take some care in assembling them (see Fig. 26-9—a Campbell on the left, Preiser on the right.) Some of the ready-built trees (like ConCor's in Fig. 26-9 center) can be almost as realistic if their too-even taper is roughed-up a bit. These

Fig. 26-10 Drill the pine trunk with a pin to provide a random array of holes for the asparagus fern branches.

Fig. 26-11   Pine trees generally grow, like other trees, in groups.

"bottle-brush" types of trees can be twisted and distorted a bit and huge clumps of the bristles cut away with scissors to better simulate the growth on a typical pine tree. The dime store variety of pine trees that are so popular around the Christmas season can be used for an inexpensive pine forest. Bend and trim the bristles from these bottle-brush trees; dip them in a proper shade of green paint and then in some dark green flocking. The flocking for this texturing method is the wooly, short-cut type available at craft stores.

The Campbell tree kits include a wooden trunk with pre-drilled holes. You can make similar trees, with asparagus fern for the limbs and needles, by tapering down a length of balsa wood and then drilling dozens of 1/64-inch holes at random along the trunk. The sprigs of asparagus fern (see Fig. 26-10) can then be cemented in each of the holes. It is a time-consuming process but the results are well worth the effort, particularly for trees that will be placed near the foreground of the layout.

This "stand" of pine trees (in Fig. 26-11) is just one of the scenic highlights on the Slim Gauge Guild's HOn3 layout. The tree on the left is a handmade pine with asparagus fern limbs, and the leaner trees are trimmed and flocked dime-store Christmas trees. The clutter of rocks and weeds on the ground makes the scene even more true-to-life.

Glossary of Terms

AAR: The full-size railroad's trade group, the Association of American Railroads, that establishes their standards for equipment and saftety.

Articulated: A steam locomotive with two separate sets of drivers, rods, and cylinders beneath a single boiler. Usually one set of drivers, rods, and cylinders is pivoted so it can swing from side-to-side around curves while the boiler remains rigidly attached to the rear set of drivers, rods, and cylinders.

Bad order: The term the real railroads use to describe a malfunctioning part.

Big Hook: The wrecking crane.

Block: A section of track that is electrically isolated from the adjoining sections for multiple train operation or to prevent short circuits.

Bolster: The portion of a railroad freight or passenger car that runs across the underbody of the car to connect the trucks' pivot points to the body of the car. Sometimes used to describe all the cross members, including the ends, of a car's underframe.

Branch: A portion of a real railroad that branches-off from the main line to reach a town or industry or to connect with another railroad.

Caboose: The rolling office and living quarters for the crew of a freight train. Usually identifiable by a small box with windows on the roof (called a cupola) or one on each side (called bay windows) so the crew can see the length of the train from inside. Sometimes called crummy, bobber, or way car.

Catenary: Overhead trolley wires, usually used by prototype interrubans (electric-powered locomotives and self-propelled cars) with diamond-shaped current pick up devices on the roofs called pantographs.

Coaling Station: Any building where coal for steam locomotives is stored and shoveled or dumped through chutes into the locomotives' tenders. When the storage bins are elevated and the coal hoisted by conveyor belts or buckets, the structure is usually called a coaling tower. When the elevated storage bins are reached by a trestle so the coal can be dumped from the cars or shoveled right into the storage bins, the structure is usually called a coaling trestle

Crossing: When two tracks cross each other as in the center of a one-level figure-eight style model railroad.

Crossover: The pair of switches that allows trains to travel from one parallel track to the adjacent one on double-track systems.

Cut: When the railroad has to dig or blast through a hill or mountain to maintain a level roadbed. Also, a few cars coupled together.

D.P.D.T.: An electrical slide or toggle-type switch that is used for reversing the flow of current to the tracks by wiring across the back of the switch. Some types have an "off" position midway in their throw and these "Center-off D.P.D.T." switches are often used for wiring model railroads to allow two-train and two-throttle operation.

Draft gear: The box under the ends of a prototype car or locomotive (and on most models) where the coupler is spring-mounted to center it and to help absorb shocks and bumps.

Fill: When the prototype railroad has to haul dirt to fill-in a valley to bring the roadbed level up to that of the nearest trackage.

Flange: The portion any railroad wheel that guides that wheel down the rails. The flange extends around the circumference of each railroad wheel as its largest diameter.

Gap: A break in the rails to electrically isolate some portion of the track from another to prevent short circuits or to allow for multiple train operation on the same stretch of track.

Gauge: The spacing of the rails as measured from the inside of one rail head to the next. The "standard gauge" for most American railroads is 4 feet 8½ inches; the distance that was also once the standard center-to-center spacing for wagon wheels.

Grade: The angled rise or fall of the track so it can pass over another track or so it can follow the rising or falling contour of the land.

Grab iron: The steel hand rails on the sides, ends, and roofs of rolling stock.

Head-end cars: The cars that are normally coupled to the front of a passenger train, including express refrigerator, express, baggage, and mail cars.

Helper: The locomotive that is added to a train to supply extra power that may be needed to surmount a steep grade.

Hostler: Men who service and sometimes move locomotives from one servicing facility to another to prepare the locomotive for the engineer.

Hotbox: A bearing that has become overheated from lack of lubrication.

Interchange: A section of track or several tracks where one railroad connects with another so trains or individual cars can move from one railroad to the next.

Interlocking: A system of mechanical or electrical controls so only one train at a time can move through a junction of two or more tracks like a crossing or yard throat.

Interurban: Prototype railroads and railroad cars that were self-propelled with electrical power pick-up from an overhead wire, catenary, or from a third rail suspended alongside the track. The cars ran from city-to-city as well as inside the city limits and hence the name. (See also trolley and traction.)

Journal: The end of a railroad car or locomotive axle that actually serves or rides-in the bearing that supports the load.

Kingpin: The pivot point for a freight or passenger car truck where it connects to the bolster.

Kitbash: To combine parts from two or more kits to produce a model different from both. Sometimes called cross-kitting, customizing, or converting.

LCL: Less than carload lot; freight shipments that are too small to require an entire car.

Main line: The most heavily trafficked routes of the railroad.

Maintenance-of-way: The rolling stock or structures that are directly associated with maintaining the railroad or with repairing and righting wrecked trains.

Narrow gauge: Railroads that were built with their rails spaced closer than the 4-feet 8½-inch standard gauge. Two-foot and three-foot spacings between the rail heads were the most common in this country, particularly in the 1880-1900 period.

Piggyback: The modern railroads' special flat car service to transport highway trailers. Sometimes called TOFC.

Points: The portions of a switch that move to change the track's route from the mainline to a siding. The point where the rails actually cross is called the "frog" part of the switch.

Prototype: The term used to describe the full-size version that any model is supposed to duplicate.

Pullman: The passenger cars that were owned and operated by the Pullman company, usually sleeping cars, diners, or parlor cars. Sometimes used to describe any sleeping car.

Rail joiner: The pieces of metal that join two lengths of rail together. They slide onto the ends of the rail on a model railroad; they are bolted to the rails on the prototype.

Reefer: The insulated cars, cooled by either ice in bunkers fed through hatches on the roof or, in modern times, by mechanical refrigeration units.

Right of way: The property and the track owned by the railroad.

Rip track: The yard tracks where bad order cars or locomotives are stored or serviced and repaired.

S.P.S.T.: An electrical switch, called a single-pole, single throw switch that performs the simple function of turning the power in that wire on or off.

Snowshed: The protective buildings that cover the track, usually in mountain areas, so deep snow and drifts won't cover the tracks themselves.

Spot: The switching maneuver whereby a freight or passenger car is moved to the desired position on the track, usually beside some industry's loading platform.

Superelevation: Banking the tracks in a curve so the trains can travel at some designated speed with a minimum of load on the outer wheels and rails and with a minimum of sway.

Switch: Usually used to refer to the portion of the railroad track that allows the trains to change routes, but also used for electrical switches on model railroads like D.P.D.T. or S.P.S.T. switches. Track switches are sometimes called turnouts to avoid this confusion.

Switch machine: The electrical solenoid-type devices that move the track switch from one route to another to allow remote-controlled operation of trains over diverging trackage.

Talgo: Model railroad trucks with the couplers mounted to them so the couplers swivel with the trucks to allow operation of longer cars on tighter radius curves. Talgo trucks can, however, cause derailments when pushing or backing a long train.

Tangent: Straight sections of trackage.

Tank engine: A steam locomotive without a tender where the coal or fuel oil is carried in a bunker behind the cab and the water in a tank over the top of the boiler. Often used for switching on the prototype and on model railroads.

Tender: The car just behind most steam locomotives that carried the water and coal, wood or fuel oil.

Throat: The point where the yard trackage begins to diverge into the multiple tracks for storage and switching.

Timetable: A schedule, usually printed, to tell railroad employees and customers when trains are scheduled to be at certain stations or points on the railroad.

Traction: The term used to describe all prototype locomotives and self-powered cars like trolleys and interurbans that operated by electrical power.

Transistor throttle: An electrical speed control for model railroad layouts that is used in place of the more common wire-bound rheostat to provide infinitely better and smoother slow speed and starting control for locomotives.

Transition curve: A length of track where any curve joins a tangent with gradually diminishing radius to ease the sudden transition of straight-to-curve for smoother operation and to help prevent derailments of extra-length cars that are caused by coupler bind in such areas of trackage. Also called an easement.

Turnout: Where two diverging tracks join; also called a switch.

Trolley: Self-propelled, electric-powered cars that ran almost exclusively in city streets as opposed to the interurbans that ran through the country between cities and towns.

Truck: The sprung frame and four (or more) wheels under each end of most railroad freight and passenger cars.

Turntable: A rotating steel or wooden bridge to turn locomotives or cars and/or to position them to align with the tracks in the engine house or round house.

Vestibule: The enclosed area, usually in both ends of a passenger car, where patrons enter the car from the station platform and where they walk to move from one car to the next.

Wye: A track switch where both diverging routes curve away in opposite directions from the single straight track. Also, the triangular-shaped track (in plan view) where trains can be reversed.

Index

Special note on addresses for manufacturers and products: All firms that specialize in direct consumer sales are listed with their addresses—all others must be contacted through your dealer or one of the mail order model railroad supply shops that advertise in *Model Railroader* or *Railroad Model Craftsman magazines.*